LexisNexis
Questions and Answers

Evidence for Common Law States

LexisNexis
Questions and Answers

Evidence for
Common Law States

David Field

BA (Hons), LLB (Nottingham, UK)
Associate Professor of Law,
Bond University
Former legal practitioner in Queensland and NSW

LexisNexis Butterworths
Australia
2011

LexisNexis

AUSTRALIA	LexisNexis Butterworths
	475–495 Victoria Avenue, Chatswood NSW 2067
	On the internet at: www.lexisnexis.com.au
ARGENTINA	LexisNexis Argentina, BUENOS AIRES
AUSTRIA	LexisNexis Verlag ARD Orac GmbH & Co KG, VIENNA
BRAZIL	LexisNexis Latin America, SAO PAULO
CANADA	LexisNexis Canada, Markham, ONTARIO
CHILE	LexisNexis Chile, SANTIAGO
CHINA	LexisNexis China, BEIJING, SHANGHAI
CZECH REPUBLIC	Nakladatelství Orac sro, PRAGUE
FRANCE	LexisNexis SA, PARIS
GERMANY	LexisNexis Germany, FRANKFURT
HONG KONG	LexisNexis Hong Kong, HONG KONG
HUNGARY	HVG-Orac, BUDAPEST
INDIA	LexisNexis, NEW DELHI
ITALY	Dott A Giuffrè Editore SpA, MILAN
JAPAN	LexisNexis Japan KK, TOKYO
KOREA	LexisNexis, SEOUL
MALAYSIA	LexisNexis Malaysia Sdn Bhd, PETALING JAYA, SELANGOR
NEW ZEALAND	LexisNexis, WELLINGTON
POLAND	Wydawnictwo Prawnicze LexisNexis, WARSAW
SINGAPORE	LexisNexis, SINGAPORE
SOUTH AFRICA	LexisNexis Butterworths, DURBAN
SWITZERLAND	Staempfli Verlag AG, BERNE
TAIWAN	LexisNexis, TAIWAN
UNITED KINGDOM	LexisNexis UK, LONDON, EDINBURGH
USA	LexisNexis Group, New York, NEW YORK
	LexisNexis, Miamisburg, OHIO

National Library of Australia Cataloguing-in-Publication entry:

Author:	Field, David, 1945-.
Title:	Evidence for Common Law States.
Edition:	1st edition.
ISBN:	9780409329674 (pbk).
	9780409329681 (ebook).
Series:	LexisNexis Questions and Answers.
Notes:	Includes index.
Subjects:	Evidence (Law) — Australia.
Dewey Number:	347.9406.

© 2011 Reed International Books Australia Pty Limited trading as LexisNexis.

Inquiries should be addressed to the publishers.

Typeset in Sabon and Optima.

Printed in China.

Visit LexisNexis Butterworths at www.lexisnexis.com.au

Contents

Preface

The Law of Evidence presents students with many challenges. Not only must new technical terms (some of them in Latin!) be learned, but they must also be *applied*. 'Evidence' is a fluid, everyday application of legal principles, and those teaching it do their best to impart the full flavour of this reality. Unlike other legal subjects, which may be learned and applied in compartments, problem questions in Evidence can come glued together like congealing french fries, or entangled with each other like a carelessly-handled garden hose.

All of these factors make Evidence a 'problem based learning' paradise if you are teaching it, and a bottomless pit of nameless writhing horrors if you are the student. If you are lucky enough to be a member of a well-organised and regularly attended tutorial group, you will receive a limited opportunity to test your skill in applying the principles you have learned in hypothetical practical scenarios. You may even be one of those zealous students who goes in search of a previous examination paper, and 'gives it a go' in the privacy of their own bewilderment.

There is, after all, no better experience than experience, and there never seem to be enough of those refreshingly new 'problem questions' against which you can pit your wits. Even more rarely do they come supplied with answers. If you are a 'distance learning' or 'online' student, you may not even have the dubious benefit of those tutorials from which you emerge even more confused than when you went in. This book is for *all* of you, regardless of the 'mode' of your learning.

In the pages which follow, each chapter, or 'lecture', of a typical Evidence book or course has been converted into a small collection of hypothetical problem scenarios. Immediately after each scenario is a suggested 'answer plan', followed by a suggested 'answer', followed by the observations of an experienced examiner regarding the scenario you have just answered and the common errors that students commit when *attempting* to answer them.

In the earlier chapters (which are assumed to correspond with the early weeks of your course of study) you may choose to read the suggested answer plan *before* you attempt your own answer. However, as you gain more experience — and therefore more confidence — in answering, it is hoped (and strongly advised) that you also create your own answer plans, in order to replicate, so far as possible, the situation in which you will find yourself on that ultimate Valhalla — 'exam day'.

In the 'Answer Plan' section of each chapter, I have given full case references for the authorities that I have cited. *These will almost certainly not be required in any exam,* and it will be observed that they are not, as a general policy, reproduced in the final 'answers' themselves; they are included earlier than that in order that the student may pursue their own more detailed reading of those cases, should that be necessary.

The final component of each chapter is a section headed 'Joining up the Dots', in which various elements of *what you are supposed to have already absorbed* are blended with elements of the new topics covered in the chapter, to give you some idea in advance of how sadistic examiners can be in devising questions in this subject area.

The final chapter consists of complete examination questions which have actually been sat by my students in the past. They survived, and so can you — if you have prepared properly. This book will help you to prepare.

David Field

Bond University
May 2011

Table of Cases

References are to paragraphs

Table of Cases

Table of Statutes

References are to paragraphs

Chapter 1

Relevance

Key Issues

1-1 Relevance is the most fundamental principle of Evidence law, because no item of evidence will be deemed to be 'admissible' unless it is 'relevant' to an issue in the case.

'Relevance' at common law means the extent to which a 'tendered' fact tends to prove or disprove the existence of some *other* fact which the court has to decide upon (a 'fact in issue'). Substantive law will normally identify the 'facts in issue', since they are the facts which the parties must prove in order to win their case (for example, the 'elements' which the prosecution has to establish in a criminal case in order to obtain a conviction, or the facts which a plaintiff in a civil action must establish in order to obtain judgment in their favour). As a trial develops, other facts may become 'facts in issue', such as the defence put forward by an accused.

'Relevance' is therefore the degree of connection between the tendered fact and a fact in issue, and its assessment calls for a highly subjective decision based on the 'logical probity' of the tendered fact to the fact in issue (that is, the strength of the relationship between them).

However, it is not necessarily enough in law for the tendered fact to have 'bare' relevance; it must also possess what is termed 'sufficient' relevance before it may be considered worthy enough to take up the court's time. Contrast *R v Buchanan* [1966] VR 9 and *R v Horvath* [1972] VR 533.

Before tackling these questions, please check that you are familiar with the following:

✓ the meaning of 'relevance';

✓ the concept of 'sufficient relevance';

✓ the subjective nature of the decision that must be made before an item of evidence will be 'relevant' enough to justify its admission.

Question 1

> Kevin is charged with causing the death of a motorcyclist, Mick, after the light van which Kevin was driving collided head-on with Mick's motorcyle on a tight bend. There were no other witnesses to the accident other than Kevin himself, who claims that Mick's motorcycle was travelling on the wrong side of the centre white line in the road when the two vehicles collided, and that he, Kevin, was unable to avoid the collision. The prosecution's case — based largely on relevant skid marks from Kevin's vehicle — is that Kevin was travelling too fast for the road conditions, and would have been able to avoid the collision had he been driving slower.
>
> Consider the relevance of the following two additional items of evidence. Crown counsel wishes to call a witness, George, who will claim that he was forced from his cycle three kilometres, and two minutes, from the scene of the accident, by a light van answering the description of Kevin's. Defence counsel seeks leave to lead the evidence of Margaret, a local resident, to the effect that a motorcylist roared past her house and made a rude gesture at her as she was standing at her front gate, before disappearing round a bend in the road. Immediately afterwards she heard a crash, raced down the road, and found the same motorcyclist lying dead in the roadway several yards to the other side of the road from that on which he had been travelling.
>
> **Time allowed: 20 mins**

Answer Plan

If information is not considered relevant, it is inadmissible. 'Relevance' describes the degree of connection between the tendered information and the existence or non-existence of a fact in issue. The question asks for an examination of relevance at common law; central to this is the distinction between logical and 'sufficient' relevance. Therefore, the following matters should be addressed in the answer:

(a) the concept of 'sufficient relevance';

(b) the precise purpose for which each of these items of evidence is being tendered; put another way, 'What does each tend to *prove*?';

(c) the application of these principles to the facts of the question. Illustrate by reference to *Horvath* [1972] VR 533 and *Buchanan* [1966] VR 9.

Answer

(a) The concept of 'sufficient relevance'

1-2   At common law, no item of information will be deemed to be 'admissible' unless it is first 'relevant' to one of the 'facts in issue' that the court has to determine. The test of 'relevance' is therefore the logical connection between the information that is tendered and one or more of those facts in issue. The party who wishes to have the information admitted is required to persuade the court that it is 'relevant' according to that test.

(b) The precise purpose for which each of these items of evidence is being tendered

1-3 Put another way, there must be some connection between an inference that can be drawn from the information tendered and a fact in issue. One therefore approaches questions of this kind by first asking what it is that the tendered information tends to suggest, and then asking whether or not that suggestion may have a logical bearing on a factual issue that the court has to resolve.

The main 'fact in issue' for the prosecution is the allegation that Kevin was driving too fast immediately before the moment of impact to be in a position to avoid it, *regardless of whether or not Mick was by that stage on the wrong side of the road*. Given the absence of any direct eyewitness evidence regarding the speed at which Kevin was travelling at the time of the impact (which might well be deemed inadmissible as 'opinion' evidence anyway — see Chapter 8), George's information regarding Kevin's driving shortly *before* the impact may be of assistance, if 'sufficiently relevant'.

(c) The application of these principles to the facts of the question illustrated by reference to Horvath and Buchan

1-4 However, comparing the two Victorian cases of *Horvath* and *Buchanan*, it can be seen that before information of this type will be deemed 'relevant', it must have a logical connection with what it is being used to prove. Does the fact that George was forced from his cycle two minutes and 3 kilometres earlier tend to suggest that Kevin was driving too fast at the time of the impact? It is tempting to answer 'yes', but the facts we are given are incomplete.

Precisely *how* did Kevin force George off his cycle? Was excessive speed involved? Did Kevin cut a corner, or drive on the incorrect side of the road? Without further information we cannot argue (as the prosecution no doubt will) that there is a 'continuum' between Kevin's driving earlier and at the time of impact such as justified the admission of the evidence in *Buchanan*, but led to its rejection in *Horvath*.

Nor can we 'do the maths' and suggest that covering three kilometres in two minutes (an average speed of 90 kilometres per hour) suggests that Kevin must have been travelling at an excessive speed when he encountered Mick. For one thing, such a calculation is merely an average, and does not eliminate the possibility that Kevin had slowed down for the bend. Also it means nothing unless George's timing of the incident involving him and the timing of the impact involving Mick were in some way synchronised. Even if George and Mick were wearing watches that stopped on impact, can we prove that they were calibrated with each other beforehand?

1-5 Finally, what evidence is there that the van that forced George off the road was the van being driven by Kevin when he collided with Mick? We need further information from George, such as whether or not the van had any distinctive marks like a trade name painted on the side.

Nor does Margaret's information fare any better as 'sufficiently relevant' to be admitted as evidence. While it may assist Kevin's case to have Mick depicted as an antisocial 'hoon', it has no relevance to Mick's skills as a motorcyclist, and will only distract the jury into a prejudiced view of the deceased. One might argue that by focusing his attention on his rude gesture to Margaret, Mick took his eye off the road at the critical moment, but does that in any way detract from the allegation that Kevin was driving too fast to prevent a collision? This is true even of the suggestion that Mick may have been on the wrong side of the road before the accident because he finished up there after it. There is nothing in this aspect of Margaret's evidence that will add to the evidence of the emergency personnel who attended the accident. In addition, Mick may only have finished up on the wrong side of the white line because he was hurled there by Kevin's van.

Neither of these items of information can logically assist the court in the decision it has to make. They are both likely to be deemed 'irrelevant', and rejected as evidence.

Examiner's Comments

1-6 The question required an examination of logical relevance. Most important in such an answer is an unbiased assessment of *precisely what the tendered information suggests*. Are there any gaps in the chain of logic from 'facts tendered' to 'conclusion sought'? Good answers would cite previous case law in this area by way of example, and indicate what extra facts might be necessary to come to a conclusion.

Keep in Mind

- Not understanding clearly what the question asks.
- Not confining the answer to the substance of the question. For example, students should avoid too detailed an analysis of concepts that they have learned by rote, at the expense of applying the basic principles to the facts.
- Drawing 'obvious' conclusions that betray a fundamental inability to be rigidly logical. For example, the temptation to depict Mick as a 'rough bikie type' displays a reliance on prejudice that juries must be prevented from utilising. It is wise to be aware of what a jury *might* conclude, but even wiser to avoid thinking like them. The trial judge will wish to avoid a jury being distracted by prejudice of this sort, when the bare facts do not justify it. Likewise, there is the trap of attempting to argue Kevin's likely speed from facts which just did not warrant such a conclusion.
- Omitting to link the law with the facts of the question.

Question 2

Karen is suing 'Wind Beneath Your Wings' Pty Ltd for damages arising from the death of her husband, Bill, when the light aircraft which he had bought from the defendants crashed in a remote location on their outback stock-farm. The scientific evidence is that the plane was doomed once the starboard wing broke free from the fuselage during the flight. Karen alleges that the plane was poorly constructed, while the defendant's case is that Bill was an inexperienced pilot who attempted to bank the plane too tightly during the stock muster in which he was engaged. This placed undue stress on the wing brace, and caused the wing to break off.

The defendants wish to adduce evidence of the facts: (a) that they had built and sold over a dozen planes of exactly the same type during the past three years, without any recorded accident of this type; (b) that the very plane that Bill crashed in had been used by the firm's own chief test pilot in an aerobatic display only three weeks before Bill bought it; and (c) that five years previously, Bill had been rejected by a commercial flying school because of his poor eyesight.

Are any of these facts likely to be deemed relevant enough to be admitted as evidence in the case?

Time allowed: 15 mins

Answer Plan

This question requires the same response from the student as Question 1, and the answer plan for that question should be studied before answering this one. What mistakes did you make when answering Question 1? How do you intend to avoid making the same mistakes this time? You have five minutes less in which to answer this question than you did for Question 1. This is because you are supposed to have learned something from that first question. Time is at a premium, and your answer should be concise but comprehensive. Do not be 'freaked out' by the time factor into leaving important material out of your answer.

Answer

1-7 At common law, no item of information will be deemed to be 'admissible' unless it is first 'relevant' to one of the 'facts in issue' that the court has to determine. The test of 'relevance' is therefore the logical connection between the information that is tendered and one or more of those facts in issue. The party who wishes to have the information admitted is required to persuade the court that it is 'relevant' according to that test.

All the information that is being tendered in this question comes from the defendants, who will be seeking to persuade the court that the accident was due entirely to Bill's lack of piloting skills, and had nothing to do with the defective construction of the plane. The question for the trial judge is whether each item of information is 'sufficiently relevant' to that.

The lack of previous accidents

1-8 The mere fact that the defendants have built aircraft in the past whose wings have not fallen off does not in any way eliminate the possibility that this particular plane was a 'lemon'. Even if built by the same craftsperson, with the same materials, using the same construction template, it is possible that something went wrong in the construction process that was not picked up during the plane's 'proving flights'. The lack of other accidents is a distraction with no logical bearing on whether or not the plane in question was airworthy, and will be rejected as 'insufficiently relevant' to justify its admission in evidence.

The use of the plane for aerobatics

1-9 The true relevance of this information cannot be assessed without further information on the type of aerobatics concerned. If they were such that stress would be likely to be placed on the junction between wing and fuselage, then whose cause does this information serve? One view of it might be that the plane was clearly capable of sustaining that sort of fuselage stress, and therefore was well built. But, at the same time, how can it then be said that Bill's tight banking maneouvre (and, by implication, his negligent flying of the plane) was the cause of the accident? Clearly, the logical implications of some information can sometimes assist both parties. Or neither. Also, since it is evenly balanced on the 'fact in issue' of the cause of the crash, it may well be deemed 'insufficiently relevant' to it, and therefore inadmissible.

Bill's eyesight

1-10 It is difficult to see what possible relevance this might have to the case for the defendants, who are not pleading that the accident was in any way caused by Bill's poor eyesight. Even then, it would have to be assumed that his eyesight had not been corrected in the five years following his rejection by the flying school. One would also need more information regarding the eyesight standards required by the school, and if they differed in any way from those required for industrial flying on one's own property.

 ## Examiner's Comments

1-11 This question again required consideration of logical relevance. General information concerning these notions was included in the answer to Question 1, and is assumed to be noted in this answer. What was important here was the detailed and unbiased application of logic to the facts of the question. This should have been learned in Question 1, and should therefore have been more of a routine 'reinforcement' exercise in Question 2.

Keep in Mind

- The question asked only if the information was relevant. Answers that dealt with which party was likely to win their case were a waste of valuable time and paper.
- Not applying the principles of 'relevance' rigidly to the facts.
- Not articulating the reasoning process when determining whether the evidence is logically relevant.

 Question 3

Jack is charged with raping Jenny after meeting her at a truck-stop ('The Jolly Jumbuck') just north of Alice Springs where he had allegedly stopped for an evening meal while driving his firm's truck overnight to Darwin. Jenny was hitching north, and accepted the offer of a lift. The rape allegedly occurred at approximately 1.20 am in a lay-by a few miles north of Possums Creek, a one-hour drive north of where The Jolly Jumbuck is located. Jenny was later able to recall the name of the firm painted on the side of the truck, although she did not manage to obtain its registration number, and failed to pick Jack out from a photoboard display compiled by the police once Jack had been arrested.

Comment on the relevance of the following additional items of information:

(a) Troy, the Fleet Manager of the company that Jack works for, can produce paperwork which indicates that Jack was the allocated driver on the overnight run to Darwin, and that the only other truck belonging to the firm which would have been on the same highway that night was one driven by Darren, on its way *back* from Darwin.

(b) Troy can also produce the paperwork associated with the use of a fleet credit card at The Jolly Jumbuck shortly after midnight on the night that Jenny was raped.

(c) Jack has maintained all along that he deviated from his designated route on the night in question for reasons that he does not wish to disclose. However, he claims to have stopped in the main street of Ungamindi, over 80 kilometres from Possums Creek, and on a highway well to the west of it, at around 1.30 am on the day of the rape, in order to use the ATM attached to a bank. He has since lost his receipt for that transaction, but the bank records show that his credit card was used at that bank branch at 1.40 am that day. In addition, a security camera took a rather grainy picture of the man using that card at that time, and Jack's wife, Toni, is prepared to testify that the man shown on that picture is Jack.

Time allowed: 20 mins

Answer Plan

Like Questions 1 and 2, this question requires an examination of logical relevance in the context of the facts of the question.

The following issues should be considered in the answer:
(a) 'relevance' at common law;
(b) the application of logic and the principles of 'sufficient' relevance to the facts of the question.

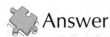 ## Answer

(a) 'Relevance' at common law

1-12 At common law, no item of information will be deemed to be 'admissible' unless it is first 'relevant' to one of the 'facts in issue' that the court has to determine. The test of 'relevance' is therefore the logical connection between the information that is tendered and one or more of those facts in issue. The party who wishes to have the information admitted is required to persuade the court that it is 'relevant' according to that test.

One must therefore ask, first, what it is that the tendered information tends to suggest, and then ask whether or not that suggestion may have a logical bearing on a factual issue that the court has to resolve. In applying those tests, the court will require to be satisfied that the information is 'sufficiently relevant' to justify admissibility.

(b) The application of logic and the principles of 'sufficient' relevance to the facts of the question

1-13 Applying those principles to the facts we are given, the evidence from Troy tends to support the inference that Jack was the driver of the firm's vehicle that was travelling north that night, and who offered Jenny a lift when they met up at The Jolly Jumbuck. By further inference, Jack may be linked, via Jenny's evidence, to the rape.

The use of the fleet credit card proves simply that someone with access to that card was using the facilities at The Jolly Jumbuck at around the time when Jenny was picked up. This, in theory, may have been *any* truck driver who was the authorised user of such a card, or even someone who had simply stolen it, and supplementary questions that may arise from this evidence will be whether or not anyone in the truck stop can link the user of the card with Jenny, or whether or not anyone can remember more than one driver from the same firm in the café at the same time on the night in question. But despite its tendency to raise further issues, this information is sufficiently relevant to justify its admission to support the Crown's case to the extent that a driver from that firm was in the café at around the time when Jenny was picked up. This corroborates at least part of Jenny's allegations.

If the jury is satisfied that the ATM user was Jack, then he clearly cannot have been the person committing a rape 80 kilometres away approximately 10 minutes earlier (NB: How accurate is Jenny's evidence of the precise time when she was raped?). The bank's records tend to suggest that someone using Jack's bank card accessed that particular ATM at that particular time. This will strengthen Jack's alibi for the time of the rape, as would the evidence of Toni regarding the identity of the person using the ATM, if admissible. Unfortunately, case law is against the admission of this form of identification.

In *Smith v R* (2001) 206 CLR 650, the High Court held, in similar circumstances, that police witnesses could not be allowed to identify the accused from security 'stills' taken during a bank robbery, since they would simply be substituting their *opinion* of whether or not that man was the accused, with one which the jury was perfectly capable of forming by making the same comparison with the man in the dock. Therefore, the police evidence was not such as could rationally affect the assessment by the jury of the question of the identity of the person in the photograph. In short, it was insufficiently relevant to justify its admission.

Examiner's Comments

1-14　Like the former questions in this chapter, this question required examination of 'sufficient' relevance with reference to the facts. This was your third attempt at this type of problem, and the only difficulty it posed should have been one of clearly explaining yourself in the time allowed.

As in the previous questions, nothing could be taken on its face value, and the initial issues regarding what the proferred information tended to prove were quite complex, requiring discipline of thought and writing. Good answers would present both sides of the argument, and acknowledge that a certain amount of subjectivity would determine the outcome.

Recognition of the similarity of some of the facts with the case of *Smith v R* would have been a bonus, though assessment would not suffer because of lack of familiarity with this case.

This question was partly inspired by the facts of *Murdoch v R* (2007) 167 A Crim R 329, which you may wish to read.

Keep in Mind

- Omitting to articulate, or confusing, the inferential steps necessary to be taken to establish logical relevance between the information supplied and the facts in issue.
- Being emphatic about the 'right' answer, without considering contrary arguments.
- Becoming distracted by the presence of another possible suspect (Darren), and 'playing detective' in order to show how Darren might

have impersonated Jack, having discovered that Jack was planning to deviate from his route. Jenny only had the truck driver's word that he was travelling north. And once the truck was parked at the truck stop, there was nothing to show that it had in fact been heading south. This sort of thing may be fun, but it does not answer exam questions satisfactorily.

Chapter 2

Burdens and Standards of Proof

Key Issues

2-1 In our adversarial system, the 'finder of fact' (that is, the magistrate, judge or jury) is required to make a final deliberation on the issues of fact that the parties have brought before them. Each of those 'issues' carries with it a *burden of proof*. What this means is that the party who seeks to have that issue decided in their favour must 'adduce' more evidence *in favour* of that issue than the other party adduces *against* it. This process is known as 'discharging the burden of proof' on that issue.

Common law recognises *two distinct burdens in respect of every issue*. The first is the *legal burden* of having that issue decided in their favour. The second is the *evidential burden* of adducing sufficient evidence to justify the finder of fact even considering whether or not the issue should be found in the party's favour.

Each of those burdens must be discharged according to the '*onus/ standard of proof*' which is laid down by law. The identity of the party who bears each of these burdens is determined by substantive law, a process known as '*fixing the incidence of the burden of proof*'.

In practice, in litigation there are two additional burdens which are not always formally acknowledged, but which are equally important. The first of these is the '*ultimate burden*' of *winning the case as a whole*, which consists of 'discharging' the legal burden on all those factual issues that the substantive law demands in order to make out one's case in law. The second is the *tactical burden* of leading evidence on some issue in respect of which the other party has led evidence which is likely to win the day unless evidence is led 'in rebuttal'.

If, after one of the parties has led all their evidence 'in chief' (see Chapter 5), their opponent is of the opinion that, even if the finder of fact believes every word of it, it is not enough in law to win the case for them, then the opponent may make a submission that they have 'no case to answer'. If successful, this submission will result in a finding in favour of the opponent, and the end of the case. If not, the unsuccessful opponent may in most cases then go on to lead 'evidence in chief' of their own.

Before tackling the questions below, please check that you are familiar with the following:

✓   the evidential burden of proof;

✓   the legal burden of proof;

✓   the criminal standard of proof;

✓   the civil standard of proof;

✓   the ultimate burden and the tactical burden;

✓   the 'incidence' of each of these burdens (N.B. the special rules in criminal cases);

✓   no case to answer.

Question 4

> Mark is an unhappily married market gardener who has both his own business and a mistress. He has begged his wife, Linda, more than once for a 'clean' divorce, but she has always insisted that, if they separate, she wishes to retain her majority shareholding in his business, which was founded using her money.
>
> Linda falls ill with an unidentified stomach ailment, and takes to her bed. Mark undertakes to act as her nurse, and to administer the medicine that Dr Burrows, their family physician, has prescribed. Linda's health continues to decline, and finally Dr Burrows is telephoned by a 'frantic' Mark, and races round to the house, where he pronounces Linda dead. A post-mortem examination reveals that she had ingested huge quantities of glysophate, a commercial weed killer, over a period of days, and Mark is charged with Linda's murder.
>
> Assume that all this evidence is revealed to the jury during the Crown's evidence in chief. Mark has instructed his lawyers that he is innocent, and that he believes that Linda committed suicide by gaining access to the weedkiller during one of her regular visits to the market garden, then taking it surreptitiously while alone in her bed.
>
> What options must Mark's counsel now consider?
>
> **Time allowed: 15 mins**

Answer Plan

The question raises the following issues.

(a)   *The incidence of the burdens of proof*

Woolmington v DPP [1935] AC 462 established, probably for all time, that the prosecution bears the ultimate burden of proof of guilt 'beyond reasonable doubt'. The exceptions to that general rule (when the accused bears the legal burden on the issues of insanity, and under statutory provisions that expressly or impliedly transfer the burden to the defence) do not apply in this case.

(b)   The need for the accused to raise a 'reasonable doubt'

This means that, in a case such as this, the accused is only required to produce sufficient evidence to raise a 'reasonable doubt' in the minds of the jury.

(c)   The meaning of 'reasonable doubt'

Discussion of 'beyond reasonable doubt' and warnings against trial judges attempting to explain this standard to the jury.

(d)   Additional considerations

Include references to the 'ultimate burden', and the concept of 'no case to answer'.

(e)   Application

Application of the law to the facts of the question.

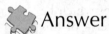 ## Answer

(a)   The incidence of the burdens of proof

(b)   The need for the accused to raise a 'reasonable doubt'

(c)   The meaning of 'reasonable doubt'

2-2   This is a criminal case, and in *Woolmington v DPP*, the English House of Lords laid down the 'golden rule' for common law cases that the Crown must prove the guilt of an accused 'beyond reasonable doubt'. This is the 'ultimate burden' that they bear, and this leaves the accused (here, Mark) with the burden of raising sufficient 'reasonable doubt' to ensure his acquittal because the Crown has failed to discharge this ultimate burden. The trial judge should avoid advising the jury on the meaning of 'reasonable doubt' beyond telling them that if they, as reasonable people, have a doubt about Mark's guilt, then it is, by definition, a 'reasonable' one: *R v Irlam* [2002] QCA 235.

(d)   Additional considerations

2-3   Mark would certainly be well advised to lead some evidence in his own defence. Applying the test in *May v O'Sullivan* (1955) 92 CLR 654, there is more than enough evidence before the court on which the jury 'could', in law (as opposed to 'should', in practice), find Mark guilty. Put in legal terms, he has a 'case to answer', and now bears the 'tactical burden' of doing so, or risking a conviction.

(e) Application

2-4 It is just conceivable that Mark's counsel has achieved enough, in cross-examination, to cause the jury to doubt the reliability of the evidence that the Crown has led, and find Mark 'not guilty'. However, this is a gamble that few experienced advocates would take, and Mark's counsel now has to decide how to bring out the evidence of Linda's suggested suicide. The most obvious witness for this would be Mark himself, but no accused is legally obliged to give evidence on his own behalf, and Mark may not show up well in cross-examination. If he does not testify, the circumstances are not such as to attract a *Weissensteiner* direction from the trial judge.

 ## Examiner's Comments

2-5 This is a question to which the basic answer may be given in a limited number of words, and therefore in a limited time. The answer supplied above neatly incorporated the related concepts of 'legal burden', 'beyond reasonable doubt', 'no case to answer' and 'tactical burden' and applied them to the given facts. There was then time enough to expand the answer into the connected topics of the non-compellability of an accused as a witness in his own defence, and the spectre of a *Weissensteiner* direction if he does not testify on a matter of which he must have some knowledge. These are considered in Chapter 4 of this book, and students seeking a high grade must be prepared to throw in this sort of relevant material *but only if time permits once they have answered the basic question.*

 ## Keep in Mind

- Panicking when confronted with several related concepts mixed into the same question, and failing to take a 'critical path' through them in a logical order.
- Confusing the 'legal' and 'evidential' burdens (which relate to each and every 'issue' in a case) with the 'ultimate burden' of winning the case.
- Failing to recognise the close relationship between the failure of the Crown to discharge their 'ultimate' burden of proof and the 'tactical burden' faced by Mark.
- Failing to refer to the issue of a possible 'no case to answer' submission, simply because the question did not refer to it. It is clearly one of the options open to defence counsel, and this *was* part of the question. Although students are to be encouraged to confine themselves to the issues raised by a question, a 'minimalist' approach to an answer can often result in a 'minimalist' Pass grade, rather than the High Distinction grade to which most students aspire.
- The same considerations apply to the inclusion of references to *Weissensteiner* and the compellability of an accused. If you are certain that you have dealt with every issue that was raised by the

question asked of you, there is no harm (and often 'bonus' marks to be earned) by linking your answer to other areas of the course you have studied, *if relevant*. But do not be 'freaked' into padding your answer with irrelevances simply because you feel that your answer is too short.

* By the same token, *answer the question that was asked — not the one you hoped would be asked.*

 # Question 5

Peter, a self-funded retiree, is suing Martin, an investment consultant, regarding advice that he claims he was given by Martin which resulted in Peter investing $450,000 in Harbour Bottom Trust Pty Ltd, which he lost less than a month later, when the Trust went into liquidation. The alleged advice came during a meeting in a local wine bar, and it is Martin's case that he warned Peter against investing any money in the Trust, which he had heard was experiencing liquidity problems. Peter, by contrast, insists that Martin told him that 'Shares in this trust are at rock bottom at the moment, and can be picked up at less then half their real value because of the liquidity rumours. However, I have it from the inside that a consortium of Middle East investors are about to bail it out as a means of siphoning money out of the government-run oil industry. Buy now and you could make a killing'.

Peter is also armed with documentary evidence that shows that, in return for Peter's investment, Martin was paid a 10% premium on the capital sum that Peter invested, and was also allowed to sell his investment bonds with the Trust back to its directors for the price he originally paid for them.

How is the trial judge likely to approach the issue of the burden of proof in this case?

Time allowed: 10 mins

 # Answer Plan

The question raises one simple issue, namely the appropriate burden of proof to be applied in a civil trial in which allegations of criminal behaviour are raised.

(a) *The Briginshaw test*

* *Briginshaw v Briginshaw* (1938) 60 CLR 336 is High Court authority for the statement that the 'balance of probabilities' test, which governs the ultimate burden in a civil case, is a flexible one. In particular, the more serious the allegations made in the 'pleadings', the more 'persuasive' must the supporting evidence be in order to take the case of the party making those allegations 'over the line'.

(b) Application of the test

- Peter is to all intents and purposes accusing Martin of fraudulent behaviour in his business dealings, and the trial judge will need to be very firmly persuaded of this if Peter is to win his case.

(c) Additional material

- Throw in references to similar cases such as *Helton v Allen* (1940) 63 CLR 691 and *Neat Holdings Pty Ltd v Karajan* (1992) 110 ALR 449.

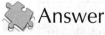 Answer

(a) The Briginshaw test

2-6 This is a civil case, but the plaintiff, Peter, is alleging behaviour on the part of the defendant, Martin, which amounts to fraud. While it remains the case that, as in all civil cases, the successful party need only produce evidence that satisfies the court 'on a balance of probabilities' of its allegations, the High Court in *Briginshaw v Briginshaw* laid down the rule, which has been followed ever since, that when serious, even criminal, allegations are raised in a civil action, the trial judge will require more persuasion than normal to find in favour of those allegations 'on balance'.

(b) Application of the test

(c) Additional material

2-7 The principle was applied in the Queensland case of *Helton v Allen*, when a claimant under a will successfully alleged, during probate proceedings, that the beneficiary had murdered the testator, and in *Neat Holdings v Karajan*, in which it was held that a trial judge should 'not lightly' make a finding of fraudulent behaviour against a party in a civil case. These were both High Court decisions.

Applying this principle to the facts of the case we are given, Peter will have to work harder than the average plaintiff in a civil action to persuade the trial judge, on 'a balance of probabilities', that Martin was committing fraud when he persuaded him to invest in the trust. Professional negligence is one thing, but deliberate fraud is of a different magnitude, and calls for particularly persuasive evidence to make it 'more likely than not'.

 Examiner's Comments

2-8 This is one of those questions for which you can either see the answer immediately, or will spend more than the allotted 10 minutes chewing your pen trying to work out what it is all about. If you 'get it', then it is easily and shortly answered, hence the reduced time limit.

As always, (1) identify and explain the point involved, then (2) apply it to the facts you have been given.

Keep in Mind

- Trying to 'double guess' what the examiner was seeking, and inventing all sorts of spurious issues not actually raised by the question, for which you may be able to supply answers from your own limited exam revision. Experience suggests that gob-smacked students faced with this question would have sought to advise the examiner of the competence and compellability of the parties as witnesses, drifted into a consideration of *Jones v Dunkel* (see Chapter 4) and, almost as a last resort, advised the examiner that Martin would be able to claim the privilege against self-incrimination (again, see Chapter 4). A High Distinction for initiative does not, in this context, translate into even a Pass grade for answering the question. Nor does a long diatribe on Martin's moral bankrupcy, or falling standards in the investment advisory profession.
- Not having the courage of your own convictions when you *do* identify the issue. The examiner is likely to be met outside the exam room by the over-anxious candidate with the question 'Was that question *really* only about the *Briginshaw* rule, or did I miss something else?' Read the question carefully — it asked for your response regarding 'the burden of proof' and nothing else.

Question 6

Janice is suing Twilite Motors for damages arising from the death of her husband Rob at the wheel of a car he had purchased from them only that week. Her pleadings allege that Rob's car left the road because of a defect in the braking system which caused the brakes to lock, and the car to skid off the road at high speed, and she is supported in this by an expert vehicle examiner's report which concludes that the brakes were in a 'seized' state when the vehicle was examined after the accident. Twilite Motors defend with an allegation that Rob's car was forced off the road during a 'road rage' incident involving another (unidentified) motorist. They also tender an expert examiner's report that not only asserts that the brakes could have seized as the result of the car leaving the road, but also refers to serious body damage down the nearside of Rob's car, consistent with it having been side-wiped by an 'undertaking' vehicle. There was nothing at the scene of the accident to account for this side-panel damage.

In finding for the defendants, his Honour Knot J included the following in his written judgment:

> This has been a most difficult case, in which the evidence was fairly evenly balanced. On the one hand, it was urged upon me by counsel for the plaintiff that a vehicle which had, according to the evidence, received a normal pre-sale service check earlier that week, suddenly experienced a brake seizure on a stretch of open road on which there was no sign of any pre-accident application of brakes by the deceased driver. Another possible cause was offered in expert evidence for the defendants for the post-accident state of the vehicle's brakes. The defendants, on the

> other hand, postulate the presence of an unknown aggressor in another vehicle, who forced the deceased's vehicle off the road for reasons regarding which one can only conjecture, but in support of which there was evidence of body damage to the deceased's car for which no other explanation was offered in evidence from either side. Inherently unlikely though this suggestion is, I find it more likely than the theory put forward by the plaintiff, and I find for the defendants.
>
> Advise Janice on the prospects for an appeal.
>
> **Time allowed: 10 mins**

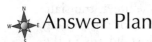# Answer Plan

(a) Burden of proof in an 'unclear' case

The question raises one simple issue, namely the appropriate approach to an assessment of the discharge of the burden of proof in a civil trial in which the evidence is finely balanced, and the trial judge finds the evidence of neither party particularly convincing.

In civil cases, 'He who asserts must prove', and at the end of the day it is for the plaintiff to satisfy the court on 'a balance of probabilities' that their allegations of fact have been proved. The defendant, for their part, must prevent this from happening.

(b) Application of the principle

If, at the end of the day, the evidence is finely balanced, then the plaintiff has lost, and judgment should be entered for the defendants. As the House of Lords ruled in *Rhesa Shipping Co SA v Edmunds* [1985] 1 WLR 948, it is not a case of choosing between two inherently unlikely stories.

(c) Another view of the judgment

Is this what Knott J was doing, or was he simply asserting that the plaintiffs had failed to discharge their ultimate burden of proof?

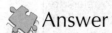# Answer

(a) Burden of proof in an 'unclear' case

(b) Application of the principle

2-9 This is a civil case, and in accordance with the maxim 'He who asserts must prove', it is for Janice to ensure that her factual allegations are proved on 'a balance of probabilities'. While it would be crudely simplistic to describe this as a finding of '51% against 49%', it does convey the reality that the judge must be 'more satisfied than not' that events occurred as alleged by the plaintiff.

This clearly did not occur in this case, but Knott J may have opened the door to a successful appeal by expressing his findings in the way he did. *Rhesa Shipping v Edmunds* was another case in which a judge, faced with two 'improbable' explanations for the sinking of a ship, found R's explanation to be 'less improbable' than that of E. This, said the House of Lords, was a fallacy. The ultimate burden borne by R required it to produce a 'theory of the case' that was more convincing than any *other* theory, and which could bear scrutiny on its own merits. It was not a case simply of producing a better theory than the defendants.

(c)   Another view of the judgment

2-10   The House of Lords in that case overturned the judgment for the plaintiffs, but the present case may be distinguished on the ground that the judgment for the defendants is consistent with a finding that the plaintiff had failed to discharge her ultimate burden. The fact that the judge erroneously went on to imply that the defendants had discharged a burden that they did not possess in the first place does not stand in the way of a finding for the defendants because the plaintiffs failed to discharge a burden that they *did* possess. The judgment may be allowed to stand without any miscarriage of justice, and without any serious inroads being made in the laws of evidence in this area.

Examiner's Comments

2-11   Most examiners would be impressed by a student's ability to *distinguish* between the *Rhesa Shipping* precedent and the facts of the scenario they were given. Another example of the benefits of 'thinking outside the square' — within limits — in exam questions.

Keep in Mind

- As with the previous question, there is a risk of 'over-guessing' what the examiner was looking for. The only possible ground of appeal revealed by the facts was the judge's approach to the issue of the burden of proof, and if you were aware of the principle expounded in the *Rhesa* case, then you would have recognised the scenario for what it was. You must then simply demonstrate the courage of your convictions and stick to that issue.
- There was also the risk that, having recognised the issue, you did not 'look sideways' at the facts, and realise that the judge had come to the correct conclusion on the facts. There were extra marks to be earned for 'distinguishing' the *Rhesa* case. Do not always settle for the first answer that comes into your head.

Joining up the Dots

2-12   The Law of Evidence, unlike many other areas of legal study, cannot be neatly boxed into discrete compartments. Whereas, for example, in Contract Law a problem scenario based on offer and acceptance is likely to involve little else from the syllabus, a problem scenario in Evidence can be compiled from several syllabus topics at once. This reflects real life, in which counsel in court cannot respond to a complex question on admissibility from the trial judge with the explanation 'Sorry, Your Honour, I haven't revised that bit yet'.

In keeping with the importance to students of balancing various elements of Evidence Law in their heads all at once, the final question in this, and the ensuing chapters, will incorporate elements from previous chapters, as well as the current one. Students may, by this means, not only test their understanding of the concepts in the current chapter, but also refresh and reinforce their memory of material which they *believe* that they have already absorbed.

 # Question 7

Alex, Brett, Chas and Don are all charged with various offences arising from a melee in an hotel on the outskirts of Adelaide which they were unwise enough to enter early one Saturday evening sporting the team shirts of their favourite AFL club, which had that afternoon been playing an 'away' game. In the hotel was a group of supporters from the local team, which had just been comprehensively defeated by the visitors, and it was not long before a massive fight developed, resulting in several arrests.

Alex instructs his legal team that the fight started after one of the locals began questioning the sexual orientation of the visiting team's players. In his words, 'I was getting pretty mad at these comments, and then this bloke picked up his beer glass and I thought that he was about to "glass" me in the face, so I took a poke at him'.

What burdens of proof are likely to have to be discharged, and by whom, following these instructions?

Brett tells his somewhat astonished solicitor, 'I had to join in and help Alex. The barman — who was obviously a Klyngon — told me that the bloke who was going for Alex was planning to immobilise him with his zapper, and then beam him up to the planet Krapton'.

If Brett's solicitor acts on his suspicions, how might this affect the forthcoming trial?

On the Monday following the melee, before police had a chance to interview him, Chas travelled to a remote mining location in Western Australia, where he was eventually located driving a gigantic earth-moving machine. It was put to him during his police interview that he had moved away suddenly in order to avoid criminal charges, but he brings his solicitor a bundle of papers to prove that (a) he had been looking for this highly specialised type of job for some time after finishing his trade apprenticeship, and (b) he had finalised the travel arrangements for his new job during the week before the fight, after being offered the job three weeks previously.

Are these papers likely to be required at the trial?

The only evidence against Don comes from one of the witnesses in the hotel, who described one of the principal offenders as 'A little fat baldy-headed git wearing a Demons team jersey'. Although this is an accurate — if uncharitable — description of Don, it also fits several other members of the visiting party. Don denies being involved in the fight, and when he was examined by a police doctor several hours after the incident there was no physical evidence to suggest that he had been.

What tactic is his defence counsel likely to adopt?

Time allowed: 30 mins

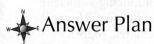 Answer Plan

(a) Alex and Brett

There are four accused, and four separate issues, although the first two are similar in nature and involve 'burden of proof' questions. It may be possible to combine elements of these first two in the one answer, or at least to save time by referring to the first when answering the second.

(b) Chas

It is not made clear by the question why Chas's paperwork might *not* be required, but if the Crown are allowed to suggest that Chas had 'done a runner', then he should be allowed to rebut that. The question probably involves the issue of the 'relevance' of the entire matter.

(c) Don

Likewise, it is not immediately obvious why Don was charged in the first place. There appears to be no evidence against him, and therein lies the clue — it may well involve a plea of 'no case to answer'.

 Answer

(a) Alex and Brett

2-13 This is a criminal case, and, in accordance with the *Woolmington* principle, the Crown must prove the guilt of each of the accused 'beyond reasonable doubt'. This is the 'ultimate burden' that they bear, and it involves the necessity of eliminating any 'reasonable doubt' that may exist in relation to any defence raised by any of the accused.

The normal rule in such cases is that the accused bears the 'evidential burden' of ensuring that there is some evidence before the court from which it could find in favour of any defence raised, but that once this has occurred, the Crown then picks up the 'legal burden' of *disproving* that defence beyond reasonable doubt. Alex appears to have the makings of two possible defences (provocation and self-defence), and it may be possible for his counsel to discharge the evidential burden on each of them by skilful cross-examination of the alleged victim, and without the

— 21 —

need to call Alex as a witness. Whichever way it is done, once there is evidence before the court to suggest either or both of these defences, the Crown must then rebut them beyond reasonable doubt.

Brett is in a different position. His bizarre explanation raises doubts about his sanity which need to be followed up by a professional assessment. If he is indeed insane, and assuming that he is 'fit to plead' in the first place, his formal defence of insanity gives rise to one of those rare situations in which a burden of proof is placed upon an accused, on 'a balance of probabilities'. This is the 'legal burden' that Brett has to discharge, should his defence team opt to go down this road, and Brett also in this instance bears the 'evidential burden' of adducing sufficient evidence of his insanity to warrant leaving the matter to the jury. This will in practice be more than discharged by an expert psychiatric report.

(b) Chas

2-14 The question raised in Chas's case is one of 'relevance'. It is not immediately obvious how his movements *subsequent to* the incident might be relevant, until it is remembered that 'flight' can in certain circumstances be taken as an implied admission of guilt (see Chapter 9). Chas's counsel will no doubt object to the relevance of any Crown evidence regarding his client's travel to Western Australia, but if unsuccessful will then argue that his client is entitled to rebut the suggestion of unpremeditated flight with evidence of his own. If the matter of Chas's subsequent movements is regarded by the trial judge as sufficiently 'relevant' to justify admission, then he must allow the *entire* Pandora's Box to be fully opened, in 'fairness' to Chas.

(c) Don

2-15 The evidence against Don is virtually non-existent, which raises the possibility that, following the close of the Crown's case, his counsel will make a submission of 'no case to answer'. This amounts to a submission that, even taking the Crown's case at its highest, no 'jury properly instructed' *could* in law find Don guilty: *May v O'Sullivan*. If this submission is unsuccessful, Don will still be allowed to lead evidence in his own defence: *Evgeniou v R* (1964) 37 ALJR 508.

Examiner's Comments

2-16 This is another good example of making the correct choice of 'critical plan' through the question. The main alternative — taking it 'chronologically' — would have been of no assistance in this scenario.

Keep in Mind

- Failing to separate out all the issues in advance, and diving into what looks like a long question in the belief that there will not be enough time to write down all that you know. This may well be the case, but writing down all that is *relevant* is not necessarily the same thing, and it is well worth taking a few moments to formulate a 'critical path' through the scenario, if only in one's head. Some scenarios lend themselves to a 'chronological' approach (that is, dealing with events in the order in which they occur), while others, like this one, require each 'client's' case to be followed through in turn.

- Failing to see how time and effort can be saved by referring, in one section of the answer, to material that has already been written in relation to another. Notice how the opening paragraph of the suggested answer lays down the general rule regarding the 'incidence' of the burdens of proof in a criminal case, which it is then possible to apply when examining the position of each individual accused.
- Failing to allocate equal time to each section of the question. Unless the examiner indicates a proportional allocation of marks between sections of the question, your answer must be of equal 'size' (in terms of *relevant* answer) for each part, subject to what was explained above regarding the use of material already written in relation to another part of your answer.
- This scenario was drafted as a full-length examination-type question, but a longer time allocation merely indicates that a more comprehensive answer is required, or that there are several (and perhaps many) separate issues to be dealt with. The allocation of different time periods to different case scenarios of different lengths in all the chapters of this book is deliberate, and is designed to hone your skills in effective time management.
- Examiners are frequently asked, 'How much writing/how many pages are you expecting for each answer?' My flippant response is usually, 'How large is your handwriting?'. My more serious response is, 'As long as it takes to answer the question fully'. This is an equal cop-out, but it does at least confirm that the question should be *fully* answered, and that students vary greatly in how they achieve that. Take this opportunity to train yourself in *effective, economical, but comprehensive* answering of exam questions.

Chapter 3
Shortcuts to Proof

Key Issues

3-1 In certain well-defined circumstances, a party will be entitled to have a fact in issue decided in their favour without the need to lead any evidence in support of that fact. This occurs as the result of the operation of law whenever: (a) the fact may be *presumed*; (b) the fact may be *judicially noted*; (c) the other party is prepared to make an *admission*, or (d) the other party is *estopped* from denying that fact.

Presumptions are many and varied in form, but they have in common that *a fact that has to be proved may be taken to have been proved by the existence of some other fact*. Common examples are the 'presumption of continuance', 'res ipsa loquitur', and the presumption of guilt which arises in the case of a person charged with stealing or dishonestly receiving property after they are found in 'recent possession' of it. Some presumptions are classed as 'presumptions of fact', and are little more than formalised examples of 'circumstantial evidence, which the court may adopt or reject, while others are 'presumptions of law' that *must* be applied unless rebutting evidence is led. These are usually found in statute, as for example in the case of the so-called 'presumption of sanity' (see, for example, Criminal Code (NT) s 43D; Criminal Code (Qld) s 26; Criminal Law Consolidation Act 1935 (SA) s 269D; Criminal Code Act Compilation Act 1913 (WA) s 26).

A fact may be *judicially noted* when it is so 'notorious' (well-known to everyone) as to be beyond any rational dispute (eg, it is dark at night, traffic is heavy in city centres during peak hour, and New Year's Day is 1 January). Such facts may be judicially noted *without* enquiry (as with the examples cited above), or *after* enquiry, when the fact is beyond dispute but not immediately known (eg, the average temperature of the human body, or the capital of Venezuela). In such cases, it is normal practice to look the point up in a respected reference book. Judges in most jurisdictions also have statutory provisions that require them to take judicial notice of a variety of formal matters (eg, Evidence Act (NT) s 36; Evidence Act 1977 (Qld) ss 41–43 and ss 65–66; Evidence Act 1929 (SA) s 35; Evidence Act 1906 (WA) s 72).

Admissions are taken to be acknowledgements of truth that require no further enquiry, on the basis that if someone is prepared to admit to something, then it must be true, and the court need waste no further time considering the possible aternative. In civil cases, they may be made during the 'pleadings', and in criminal cases they will normally be made in open court before the jury (see Criminal Code (NT) s 379; Criminal Code (Qld) s 644; Evidence Act 1929 (SA) s 34; Evidence Act 1906 (WA) s 32). A 'confession' (see Chapter 7) is regarded as an 'informal' admission.

Estoppel is a 'plea in bar' of further action (a procedural device) in relation to some matter that has already been decided in a court of law, and it is designed to prevent unsuccessful litigants from 'having another go'. It thus ensures 'finality of proceedings'. It takes two forms, namely (a) *res judicata* or *'cause of action'* estoppel (which relates to an *entire cause of action*) and (b) 'issue estoppel', which relates to a *single issue* that has previously been litigated between the same parties in the same capacities.

3-2 In **civil cases**, *res judicata* estoppel covers not only matters that *have* been litigated, but those that *might have been dealt with in the previous litigation*, had the parties opted to include it within their pleadings. This has become known as 'Anshun estoppel', after *Port of Melbourne Authority v Anshun Pty Ltd* (1981) 147 CLR 589. 'Issue estoppel' can involve some fine points of distinction regarding whether or not the precise 'issue' being raised in the new case is one which was dealt with previously; see *Jackson v Goldsmith* (1950) 81 CLR 446.

3-3 In **criminal cases**, *res judicata* estoppel is better known as the 'double jeopardy rule', and prevents an accused being tried more than once for a criminal action that has already resulted in a verdict. This is well illustrated by the long and tortuous saga behind the Queensland case of *R v Carroll* (2002) 194 ALR 1. In *Rogers v R* (1994) 181 CLR 251, the High Court held that *issue estoppel* has no place in criminal law when the 'issue' that has previously been litigated between the Crown and the accused is merely an evidential 'building block' in the Crown's case on a new matter that does not require proof of the accused's guilt of the previous matter as one of its 'elements'.

Under the Evidence Act 1977 (Qld) s 79, the fact that a person has been convicted of a criminal offence sets up a presumption, for the purposes of any subsequent civil action, that they committed that offence.

Before tackling the questions below, please check that you are familiar with the following:

✓ the role played by presumptions in proof of facts in issue;

✓ the role played by judicial notice in proof of facts in issue;

✓ the role played by admissions in proof of facts in issue;

✓ the role played by estoppel in proof of facts in issue.

Question 8

Sandra is suing Zooworld Pty Ltd for damages arising from severe injuries she received when she was mauled by a Bengal tiger which bounded through the open front gates of the 'Talk to the Animals' Safari Park while she was standing in the roadway in front of the gates, attempting to contact 'Road Assist' on her mobile phone after her car had broken down at the entrance to the park. The tiger leapt upon her at full speed, and clawed and bit her head and shoulders without any provocation from Sandra.

In its defence, Zooworld argues (a) that since there is no evidence as to how the animal escaped, they cannot be found liable in negligence, and (b) they had never before known one of their tigers to attack a visitor. Are either of these lines of defence likely to succeed?

Time allowed: 15 mins

Answer Plan

(a)   Res ipsa loquitur

There are two questions to be answered here, and equal time should be devoted to each. The first is a suggestion that, in the absence of positive proof of negligence on the part of Zooworld, there can be no factual finding of negligence. But when it is borne in mind that they were the ones responsible for the escape, *however it occurred*, it should be obvious that they are liable for what ensued. This 'obviousness' should ring the bell labelled 'res ipsa loquitur'.

(b)   Judicial notice

Just because a disaster of any given type has never occurred in the past does not mean that it cannot happen in the future. There is an inherent risk involved in keeping animals such as these, which are known to be man-eaters, given half a chance. Therein lies the clue — if 'everyone' knows that Bengal tigers are dangerous, then perhaps the trial judge may be invited to take 'judicial notice' of that fact.

Answer

(a)   Res ipsa loquitur

3-4   The defendants in this case have allowed a dangerous event to occur that was within their exclusive control to prevent. It does not matter preisely *how* the animal escaped; if the management had exercised appropriate care, then 'in the ordinary course of things' the escape would not have happened. If all the evidence amounts to is that the tiger got out through the front gate, then, in the absence of any other explanation as to how this happened, there is a 'factual presumption' of negligence on the part of the defendants through the operation of the doctrine of res ipsa loquitur ('things which speak for themselves'). Such an inference of negligence need not be drawn if there is evidence pointing to some other cause, but the defendants may certainly not sit back and claim that they have no case to answer.

(b) Judicial notice

3-5 The savagery of Bengal tigers is notorious. This particular beast may not have attacked before, but it belongs to a breed that has proved its potential to do so in the past, to the point at which it may be 'judicially noted' that tigers are dangerous animals that must be contained and confined. The point may be established 'after enquiry' by consulting a suitable reference text, should this be required. There is case-law precedent for this type of judicial notice: in *McQuaker v Goddard* [1940] 1 KB 687, the High Court in England consulted appropriate references in answer to the question of whether or not a camel was a domestic animal.

The defendants cannot claim the legal right to do nothing to confine any one of its tigers until it attacks someone. Given that it may be judicially noted that their tigers are dangerous, they have a 'case to answer' if one of them escapes for no reason and injures an innocent person.

 ## Examiner's Comments

3-6 Many students, having 'spotted' *either* res ipsa loquitur *or* judicial notice, will be tempted to apply it to the facts as the entire answer. It is in fact the *interaction* of the two that works in favour of the plaintiff in this case, and it is entirely possible that even a comprehensive answer to only one of these constituent elements will gain the student barely a 'Pass' mark.

 ## Keep in Mind

- Failing to appreciate what the question is all about. In similar questions I have set in the past, students have given me several paragraphs of moral outrage at the suggestion that the defendants in this case can simply sit back and make the plaintiff prove the obvious, without appreciating that it is the very 'obviousness' of the matter that supplies the real answer.
- Failing to link the res ipsa loquitur issue with the judicial notice one. There is no 'thing which speaks for itself' unless and until judicial notice is taken of the fact that tigers are dangerous animals — only then does the failure of the defendants to manage something potentially dangerous which was within their control fall into place. If what escaped had been a tortoise, would the same presumption (of res ipsa loquitur) have applied? Clearly, in that hypothetical scenario, no-one would have been injured and the case would not have arisen. But if what escapes is something as dangerous as a tiger, then common sense has to be allowed to prevail when seeking

the correct legal outcome. Presumptions and judicial notice are both examples of formalised common sense with labels attached to them.

 # Question 9

Merv is charged with an armed robbery on a local convenience store. The person responsible for the robbery made their getaway in a Ford Fandango estate wagon whose registration number was recorded by the store owner, and which turned out to have been a vehicle left for a service at 'Merv's Motors', owned and operated by Merv. The vehicle itself was subsequently found wrapped around a tree in a remote bushland location, but Merv's fingerprints were located all over the interior of the vehicle, most notably on the steering wheel and dashboard.

At his trial, Merv's counsel announces in open court, before the jury, that 'My client is prepared to admit, for the purposes of this trial only, that his fingerprints were identified at various locations in the interior of the vehicle identified as that used in the robbery'.

What evidential implications does this admission have for the conduct of the ensuing trial?

Assume that Merv is found guilty of the armed robbery, and that the insurers of the vehicle wish to sue Merv for the damage caused to the vehicle when it was effectively written off during the crash.

May they make any evidential use of either Merv's admission at the start of the criminal trial, or the finding of guilt at the end of it?

Time allowed: 15 mins

 # Answer Plan

There are, once again, two or possibly three questions to be answered here. They are:

(a) the evidential effect of an admission;
(b) the evidential significance of a conviction in a subsequent civil case.

Assume that each attracts an equal proportion of the available marks for the question, since the examiner did not indicate otherwise. The first part of the question is a 'gift', since the answer seems to be a fairly clear one, but the second question is a 'nightmare' for which there is no obvious answer in most jurisdictions. Be prepared to think 'outside the square' in answering the second part, and arguing from 'first principles' in all jurisdictions except Queensland. Even in that state, the issue of the ongoing evidential effect of the admission appears to have no obvious answer, and original thought is required. This is not something, in my experience, that students happily embrace, but it is a good opportunity to earn big 'Brownie points'.

Answer

(a) The evidential effect of an admission

3-7 Merv's admission, made on the record, serves to relieve the Crown of the need to lead any evidence to prove that the fingerprints inside the vehicle used for the robbery were his. He will presumably have a perfectly rational reason for making this admission, on legal advice, and no doubt he can explain how the fingerprints came to be there (eg, while he was working on the car), and how/when the car itself came to be stolen.

In making the admission on Merv's behalf, his counsel was careful to limit the application of it to the trial in which it was made, but the question then arises whether or not this will be legally effective. None of the statutory provisions (here cite the appropriate one for your jurisdiction) indicates whether or not admissions are evidentially limited to the trial in which they are made, but the assumption at common law has always been that this is the case. However, as emerges in Chapter 7, such admissions operate as an exception to the 'hearsay rule' when recalled by someone who heard them or as documentary exceptions to the same rule when they are contained in official transcripts of court proceedings. This is the use that may be made of Merv's admission in any subsequent civil proceedings involving the car's insurer, although it does not seem to be of much help in proving that he was driving the car when it hit the tree.

(b) The evidential significance of a conviction in a subsequent civil case

3-8 Under Queensland statute, the effect of the Evidence Act 1977 s 79, is that the fact of Merv's conviction for armed robbery sets up a *rebuttable* presumption of law that he committed it, and therefore that he was the driver of the getaway vehicle when it crashed, which he is free to rebut if he has evidence that will do so. Even though a criminal jury appears not to have had a 'reasonable doubt' that he was behind the wheel at the time, he is free to try again before a judge in the civil court to argue successfully that, for example, he was working on the car when he took a lunch break, during which time it was stolen because he left the keys in the ignition. There is also the technical argument that the person who committed the robbery (adjudged by the previous jury to have been Merv) was not necessarily the person at the wheel when it crashed, although the 'presumption of continuance' may provide that link.

None of the other common law jurisdictions possess such a provision, and without it one is forced to fall back on the argument that if a previous jury concluded beyond reasonable doubt that Merv was behind the while of the car when it was used for the robbery, and subsequently crashed, then it would be strange indeed if a subsequent civil court could not reach the same conclusion on a balance of probabilities. This was the unsuccessful argument in the English case of *Hollington v Hewthorn*, the 'common sense' reaction to which led to amending legislation in England which was then copied in Queensland, but apparently nowhere else in the common law jurisdictions of Australia.

 ## Examiner's Comments

3-9 Once again, the examinee was given an opportunity to display their ability to take a basic principle and apply it in the absence of any 'clear law' on the topic. They also had the opportunity to draw from different areas of the syllabus, demonstrating yet again that the Law of Evidence cannot easily be compartmentalised.

 ## Keep in Mind

- Failing to answer part of the question simply because no obvious answer appears to exist. Provided that you are certain that there *is* no answer, and that your lack of knowledge does not arise from your inadequate note-taking or revision, then have the courage to say so, and argue from the other first principles of the subject that seem most relevant. In the answer above, for example, it was possible to suggest an alternative solution in the absence of a statutory presumption, which should result in bonus marks from the examiner for knowing the subject so well, and being able to think 'sideways'.

 ## Question 10

> Several months ago, Redgum Shire Council was awarded $230,000 in damages following lengthy and protracted litigation against their principal insurers, CastIron Guarantees Pty Ltd. The litigation arose from damage to the Redgum Lower Road Bridge, a metal construction that was left dangling perilously over the river when a barge that had broken free upstream during a recent flood crashed into the centre stanchion of the bridge. The legal dispute between the parties had focused on whether or not such an event was covered by 'flood damage' as defined in the policy that the Shire Council had with the insurers, and the court had held that it did, and awarded damages as per the plaintiff's Schedule of Loss that had been compiled by the Shire Engineer, based on repair estimates.
>
> The council has now been advised that, as the result of the failure of the centre stanchion, the remainder of the bridge's structure has become weakened by stress, and that the bridge will need to be completely replaced, at an estimated cost of some $1.3 million. Advise the council on their prospects of successfully suing CastIron Pty Ltd for the shortfall in insurance compensation that they have received.
>
> **Time allowed: 10 mins**

Answer Plan

Light a candle at the shrine of the Patron Saint of Law Students for this one, which is clearly based on the 'Anshun estoppel' principle, and for which there is case precedent in the English case of *Conquer v Boot* [1928] 2 KB 336. But do not be tempted to save time and energy by simply citing these two cases and moving on; you have been allowed 10 minutes, and an answer of that length is required.

There are clearly two elements to the answer:
(a) the Anshun estoppel principle;
(b) the case precedent of *Conquer v Boot*.

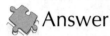

Answer

(a) The Anshun estoppel principle

3-10 It was laid down for Australian common law by the High Court in *Port of Melbourne Authority v Anshun Pty Ltd* that when the parties enter pleadings in a case such as that which Redgum had against CastIron, they must take care to include *all* relevant matters that fall to be litigated between them. If they do not, then anything left out will be taken to have been litigated to finality, and either party seeking to have a 'second bite at the cherry' will be faced with what has become known as an Anshun estoppel argument.

(b) The case precedent of Conquer v Boot

3-11 If Redgum had done their sums more carefully, or waited until satisfied that the full extent of the damage to the bridge was known, they would have been in a position to claim the *full* amount of their loss. One cannot expect to be able to litigate by instalment, and the 'quantum' of the damages award in the previous case is no longer open to litigation. Apart from the *Anshun* authority, there is close factual precedent for this case in the old English case of *Conquer v Boot*, in which a man who had successfully sued a builder for damages in respect of defects in a house he had built was denied the right to litigate a second time when new defects became apparent after judgment had been entered.

There must be 'finality' to litigation, and the estoppel principle is the best procedural device for preventing the re-opening of matters that have proceeded to final judgment.

Examiner's Comments

3-12 While the 'Anshun' aspect of the case is fairly obvious, only students who had fully revised the materials they had been given or directed to would have spotted the factual analogy to *Conquer v Boot*. A straight 'Anshun' answer would probably attract 70% of the overall mark for the question.

Keep in Mind

- Failing to recognise the factual similarity of the given scenario to the precedents. If you cannot 'spot' this as an 'Anshun' case, then you will wallow around looking for the answer in all sorts of unlikely places which will not impress the examiner. In the past, I have received answers from students who solemnly advised me that since Redgum had already received judgment in their favour, it was a simple matter of requesting the court to re-open the judgment and increase the size of the damages awarded. In response, I did my bit to ensure that these students never had the opportunity to put their theory into practice.
- Examiners find it difficult to dream up new case scenarios for one examination after another, and will often fall back on a set of facts drawn closely from an existing case that has been considered in class. *You must ensure that you are in a position to recognise when this has been done.*

Joining up the Dots

Refer to the section of the same name in Chapter 2 for the significance of this part of the chapter.

Question 11

Julie is charged with the murder of her husband Peter, and is claiming self-defence. Earlier in the evening of Peter's death, Julie had received an urgent telephone call from her brother Mark, advising her that he was in a bar in town, where he had just taken part in a disturbing conversation with Peter, who was very drunk, and was accusing Julie of conducting an affair with her tennis coach. Peter told Mark that he was on his way home, and was going to 'beat the daylights out of' Julie with a tyre lever which he had borrowed from his place of employment as a tyre fitter. Julie also told police that a few minutes after her call from Mark, Peter kicked open the front door of the family home, yelling abuse at Julie and accusing her of infidelity. He then began to set about her with a tyre lever which was still lying in the living room when police arrived in response to a neighbour's call. They also found Peter's body, a large quantity of blood, and a long kitchen knife which Julie had armed herself with when warned of Peter's intention in the telephone call from Mark. Peter had been stabbed to death, and Julie told police 'He came at me with that metal bar, so I stabbed him'.

Is the evidence of Mark's call to Julie likely to be of any relevance in the case? If so, why? What role may it play in the discharge of the burdens borne by Julie and the Crown?

Time allowed: 20 mins

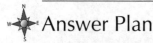

Answer Plan

(a) Setting the background, and explaining the importance of Mark's telephone call to Julie's defence

It is obviously very important to Julie's defence to be able to have some corroboration of her 'story' that Peter had returned home in a violent mood, armed with a tyre lever which will be part of the 'exhibits' in the case, and attacked her so viciously that she was obliged to fight for her life. One of the potential weaknesses in her case will be the fact that she was pre-armed with a knife, but the evidence of the call from her brother Mark will explain why.

(b) Julie's defence in the context of the burdens of proof in the case

This somehow has to be woven into the formal framework of the burdens of proof in the case, and the relevance of the evidence of the call from Mark to Julie has to be justified and explained.

Answer

(a) Setting the background, and explaining the importance of Mark's telephone call to Julie's defence

3-13 The Crown bears the 'ultimate burden' of proving Julie guilty of murder 'beyond reasonable doubt': *Woolmington v DPP*. Julie, for her part, bears the 'evidential burden' of ensuring that there is some evidence before the court that justifies the jury even considering the possibility that she was acting in self-defence when she knifed Peter to death. Once she has done this, the Crown then picks up the 'legal burden' of disproving this version of events beyond reasonable doubt.

It is crucial to Julie's case to prove that Peter came home with serious violence in mind, and that she had to fight for her life. It is also important for her to explain how she came to be pre-armed with the knife. The content of Mark's phone call is highly relevant to both of these issues of fact, but the Crown may challenge its admissibility.

In fact, its admissibility is the very result of its relevance. It is 'sufficiently relevant' to what happened at the time when Peter died (the 'res gestae' — see Chapter 7) that it cannot be excluded if the court is to receive the complete story. Although Mark's revelations about his conversation with Peter do not relate directly to the events at the time of death, they are linked to them by means of the 'presumption of continuance'. This is a common law 'presumption of fact', under which an intention that a person possessed at a given moment in time can be 'presumed' to have still been their intention at a given — and crucial — moment of time later. It partly explains why courts regularly receive evidence of statements made by subsequent murder victims regarding their intention to meet with a certain person who is now accused of being their murderer (as in *Walton v R* (1989) 166 CLR 283); the 'presumption of continuance' allows the court to assume, in the absence of any rebutting evidence, that the victim carried out their intention.

(b) Julie's defence in the context of the burdens of proof in the case

3-14 In this case, what Peter told Mark that he *intended* to do was precisely what Julie is now saying he *did* do, namely go home and beat Julie with a tyre lever. The fact that she was forewarned of the danger she was in explains why she armed herself with a knife. The overall effect of the evidence of Mark's telephone call (which can come from the testimony of either Julie or Mark, but preferably both of them) is to corroborate Julie's version of events. It is almost certainly enough to discharge the evidential burden on the 'issue' of her defence, and, in the absence of any rebutting evidence to cast doubt upon it, the Crown may fail to discharge its legal burden on that defence, and Julie will be acquitted.

 ## Examiner's Comments

3-15 Once again it has proved possible to include reference to other areas of the taught syllabus than the obvious one to which the question refers. Many students would be likely to overlook the process of logic involved in 'presuming' that Peter went on to carry out his declared threat, and the examiner is likely to be favourably impressed by the answers of those who refer to the almost silent use of the 'presumption of continuance'.

Keep in Mind

- Failing to explain precisely *why* the evidence of the phone call is relevant, because it seems 'obvious'. It is common (and understandable, if wrong) for students to write something along the lines of 'Obviously it is important for Julie to be able to prove that the phone call took place', without taking the trouble to define precisely the line of logic that lies behind such a statement. Simply because Peter was unwise enough to announce his intentions in advance does not guarantee that he carried them out, *without the intervention of the presumption of continuance that allows the court to conclude that he did, unless there is evidence to show that he did not*. If, for example, Peter had been pulled over for drunk driving on his way home, searched and found to be in possession of a tyre lever that was confiscated by the police, and then only released from custody when sober, the Crown could reasonably raise the counter-suggestion that Julie knifed him in a rage because he would be losing his driver's licence (and possibly his livelihood), and because she had been obliged to collect him from the police watch-house. But in the absence of such additional information, the court is allowed to draw the natural inference that, left to their own devices, people will carry out their intentions.

- Failing to give sufficient attention to those parts of the question dealing with relevance and burdens of proof because 'This is basic stuff that is boring — I know what it's all about, and so does the examiner, so let's get on with the sexier bits, where I can *really* show off my knowledge'. The question asked for three things, and marks will be allocated for *each* of those three. However brilliantly you answer two-thirds of a question, you cannot hope to exceed 67% of the marks allocated to the question as a whole.

Chapter 4

Competence, Compellability and Privilege

Key Issues

4-1 A person is *competent* to testify as a witness in court if they are *allowed by law to do so*.

A person is *compellable* if they can be *forced by law to do so*.

Even though otherwise compellable, a person may have a *privilege* against *answering certain questions*.

Evidence may either be 'sworn' (ie, given after the swearing of some religious oath appropriate for the witness) or 'unsworn' (without the taking of an oath, but subject to the normal laws of perjury).

All the common law jurisidictions have statutory provisions that govern a witness's competence to testify on oath (under the Oaths Act (NT) s 25A, Evidence Act 1977 (Qld) ss 9A–D, Evidence Act 1929 (SA) s 9, and Evidence Act 1906 (WA) s 106B).

As a general rule at common law, *competence implies compellability*. The vast majority of people, these days, are both *competent and compellable*, and the only exceptions to that general rule exist under statute. On the whole, these statutory provisions are designed to ensure that as many people as possible are both competent and compellable to testify on oath, with only the Evidence Act 1977 (Qld) s 9A, and the Evidence Act 1906 (WA) s 106C, disqualifying a person from testifying if they are not capable of giving 'an intelligible account' of what they saw, heard or otherwise experienced.

Not even the parties to a civil action, or their spouses, are disqualified from testifying, and in most cases they are both competent and compellable (see Evidence Act (NT) s 7, Evidence Act 1977 (Qld) s 7, Evidence Act 1929 (SA) s 16, and Evidence Act 1906 (WA) s 7).

So far as concerns the accused in a criminal case, he/she is made competent but not compellable as a witness for the defence (Evidence Act (NT) s 9, Evidence Act 1977 (Qld) s 8, Evidence Act 1929 (SA) s 18, and Evidence Act 1906 (WA) s 8). The same sections in Queensland and the Northern Territory also make the spouse of an accused person both competent *and* compellable for both the Crown and the defence, with or without the consent of the accused person. In Western Australia (s 9), the spouse is compellable for the defence, but only compellable for the Crown in selected cases, while in South Australia (s 21) the compellability of the spouse for the Crown (as a 'close relative' of the accused) is subject to the grant of an 'exemption' from the need to testify if to do so would cause 'serious harm' to either their relationship with the accused or their physical or mental health.

Particular difficulties arise when an accused person, who is competent to testify on their own behalf, chooses not to do so. There are natural inferences that might be drawn from this, but the jurisdictions vary on whether or not, under statute, adverse comments may be made by either the trial judge or Crown counsel.

In South Australia and Western Australia, only Crown counsel is prohited from making 'any comment', while in the Northern Territory that ban also extends to the trial judge. The Queensland Act contains no restrictions on comments by either.

The High Court has been called upon to rule on the precise circumstances in which it is 'fair' to allow such comment, even if it *is* permitted by statute, in cases such as *Weissensteiner v R* (1993) 178 CLR 217, *Azzopardi v R* (2001) 205 CLR 50, *RPS v R* (2000) 199 CLR 620 and *Dyers v R* (2002) 210 CLR 285. The net effect of all of these rulings is that it is appropriate for adverse comment to be made to the jury when there is an explanation that the accused *could* have given regarding some fact in issue in the case, but which they chose not to give, even to the police. This rule was adapted from the equivalent rule for civil cases known as the 'rule in *Jones v Dunkel*', in which it was held that adverse inferences may be drawn from the failure of a party to that civil action to testify when one might have expected them to do so.

In all the common law jurisdictions, a witness who might otherwise be compellable to answer questions may be relieved of the obligation to do so as the result of the existence of a 'privilege' against having to. These privileges are in relation to (a) self-incrimination, (b) communications between lawyers and clients, and (c) negotiations that were conducted under 'without prejudice' arrangements, in a genuine effort to settle a civil action.

In addition, there is, in all jurisdictions, a 'public interest immunity' claim that may be raised in suitable cases against being required to disclose information which it is in 'the public interest' not to disclose.

Some jurisdictions recognise other claims to privilege. For example, the Evidence Act (NT) s 12, recognises privilege in respect of communications between clergymen and parishioners and between doctors and patients, while as noted above, in South Australia a 'close relative' of a criminal accused may seek exemption from testifying against them in certain circumstances. But at common law, the ones listed above are all that remain of what was once a much longer list that included, among other things, 'marital communications'.

Before tackling the questions below, please check that you are familiar with the following:

✓ the distinction between the 'competence' and 'compellability' of a witness;

✓ the precise statutory rules that apply in your jurisdiction regarding competence and compellability;

✓ the special positions occupied by parties to a civil action and the accused in a criminal trial;

✓ the number and extent of 'privileges' that exist in your jurisdiction.

 # Question 12

Jim is charged with the attempted abduction of his own seven-year-old daughter, Tamsin, from the primary school that she attends. The Crown case against him is that he waited until she was leaving school later than normal because of her extra-curricular clarinet class, crept up behind her, threw a blanket over her head and bundled her into the back of a panel van. At no stage did Tamsin see who had abducted her, except briefly when she was hauled out of the stationary van when Jim had a change of heart, and left her standing at a bus stop. She told police that 'the man looked like Daddy, but he wouldn't do a thing like that to me'. Tamsin rarely sees her father, who is separated from her mother.

The only other witness to the proceedings was nine-year-old Jason, who was also leaving the music class, and who saw the entire incident outside the school, and gave the police a description of the van. He also told the police that he thought that the person who snatched Tamsin was 'Uncle Jim', a friend of his mother's who has been very good to both of them since Jason's father died the previous year. It can be proved that 'Uncle Jim' is the accused. Jason has been diagnosed with 'Attention Deficit Disorder', as the result of which he is rated as below average for his educational year.

What difficulties might the Crown experience in having the evidence of either Tamsin or Jason admitted?

Time allowed: 20 mins

 # Answer Plan

(a) Competence and compellability of a 'child' witness

The difficulty with these two items is that the law varies from one jurisdiction to another, and the detailed answers will vary accordingly, as the result of different statutory provisions. But the general theme is the same in all cases, and involves the competence and compellability of child witnesses.

(b) Issues regarding the quality of the evidence each could give

In Tamsin's case, she is very young, and will almost certainly have to give her evidence 'unsworn'. In the circumstances, she may well find this an emotional challenge, given that she is being asked to testify against her own natural father.

Jason may have the same problem himself, if 'Uncle Jim' has become his new paternal role model. In addition, he may have educational difficulties, and this might affect his ability to give 'an intelligible account' of what he saw.

 Answer

(a) Competence and compellability of a 'child' witness

4-2 Both Tamsin and Jason qualify as 'child' witnesses, whom the law always treats with great care due to the inherent unreliability of their evidence. Under the Evidence Act 1977 (Qld) s 9, there is a statutory presumption that a 'child' is not only competent to testify, but also to do so on oath. However, under s 9A, a party to a case may challenge that competence on the ground that the child is incapable of giving 'an intelligible account of events', whether it is intended that they do so on oath or not. Under s 9C, an expert witness may be asked to give guidance on this point, but it is unlikely that Jason will fail this test, since ADD is not a mental illness, and Jason seems perfectly clear about what he saw. Unless he is diagnosed as delusional, it is likely that he will be allowed to testify. There appear to be no such problems with Tamsin, and the fact that the evidence she has to give will be given unwillingly, and may have repercussions for her relationship with Jim, will not affect her competence and compellability.

(b) Issues regarding the quality of the evidence each could give

4-3 Section 9B contains the tests that the trial judge must apply in order to decide whether either of these children may testify on oath, which in view of their ages is highly unlikely. In order to be allowed to take the oath, they must satisfy the trial judge (normally by means of a question and answer process) that they appreciate that the giving of evidence is a 'serious matter', and that if they do so, then their obligation to tell the truth is 'over and above the ordinary duty to tell the truth'. If they cannot, but are nevertheless competent to testify, they will do so 'unsworn', after the trial judge has explained to them 'the duty of speaking the truth'.

Similarly, under the Evidence Act 1906 (WA) s 106C, there is provision made for a child under 12 to give 'unsworn' evidence if the trial judge is satisfied that they are able to give 'an intelligible account of events'. Alternatively, and preferably, under s 106B, a witness, irrespective of their age, may testify on oath if, in the opinion of the trial judge, they understand that 'the giving of evidence is a serious matter', and that in doing so they have 'an obligation to tell the truth'. As under Queensland law, Tasmin's 'close relationship' with Jim will not affect her compellability to testify under s 7.

Under the Evidence Act (NT), there are no special rules provided for child witnesses, but under the Oaths Act (NT) s 25A, there is a general provision that states that a witness aged under 14 who 'is capable of giving an intelligible account of his experience', but who does not '[comprehend] the nature of an oath', may give their evidence unsworn. There are no provisions that would cover the fact that Tamsin is being asked to testify against her father, or that Jason has educational challenges.

Only the Evidence Act 1929 (SA) deals comprehensively with the issues raised in Tamsin's case. Section 9 provides a presumption that every witness is capable of testifying on oath unless the trial judge forms the opinion that the witness 'does not have sufficient understanding of the obligation to be truthful entailed in giving sworn evidence', in which case they may give their evidence unsworn provided that the judge is satisfied that the witness knows the difference between the truth and a lie, and tells the witness that 'it is important to tell the truth'. The witness must then 'indicate that he or she will tell the truth'.

Any reluctance on Tamsin's part to testify against her father can be accommodated under s 21, which provides that whereas a 'close relative' (which would include Tamsin but not Jason) is as a general rule 'competent and compellable' for both sides in a criminal case, and remains both when testifying for the defence, if they are called for the Crown and it appears to the trial judge (following an application to that effect by the prospective witness) that if they were to testify there would be a 'substantial risk' of 'serious harm' to either the relationship in question, or of a 'material, emotional or psychological nature' to that witness, then the trial judge may exempt the witness from giving that evidence. When the prospective witness is 'a young child or is mentally impaired', the trial judge must consider this exemption even if no formal application is made.

However, before doing so the trial judge must take into account the 'nature and gravity' of the offence, and 'the importance to the proceedings of the evidence' in question. Although Tamsin was the victim in this case, and ordinarily the evidence of a victim is the main plank in a Crown case, there is also the available evidence of Jason, who saw who was taken away (no doubt kicking and screaming) and who it was who took her. Given what appears to be Tamsin's reluctance to face the fact that it was her father who did it, it might give rise to less complication during the trial to restrict the evidence of the actual abduction to that of Jason. A compromise arrangement might be to allow Tamsin to testify that she was taken against her will, but not to ask her who she thinks was responsible.

Examiner's Comments

4-4 This is a good example of a question that looks to be simple to answer, and to require only a minimum amount of time, but in fact turns out to be more onerous than anticipated. Students would be expected to work their way systematically through the issues of competence and compellability, before examing the specific difficulties that each of the witnesses presents.

Keep in Mind

- Failing to appreciate the problem of Tamsin being reluctant to believe that Jim would so such a thing to her. There are only statutory provisions to deal with it in South Australia, but it requires a mention even in the other jurisdictions.
- Being 'spooked' into believing that Jason's ADD would affect his capacity to give 'intelligible' evidence. This was an unfortunate choice of words by the drafters who employed it, since it implies something to do with coherence or 'flow' of narration, rather than genuine mental affliction, poor recall etc., which is what it is really aimed at.
- Attempting to answer the question without being aware of the relevant statutory provisions for your jurisdiction.

Question 13

Tom is on trial for a burglary at the new home of his ex-wife Linda, during which nothing was taken, but the interior of the house was seriously 'trashed'. The only evidence against Tom consists of his fingerprints on the outside of the flyscreen on the loungeroom window, which had been removed in order to gain access to the house while Linda was away on holiday. When Tom was asked by the police to explain the presence of those prints on the flyscreen, he replied 'I was spying on her through the window to see if she had a new boyfriend, because if she has then I want my maintenance payments reduced. But I don't want my girlfriend to know, in case she gets the wrong idea'.

Tom gives strict instructions to his legal team that there is to be no reference to what he told the police when the matter comes to court, because his girlfriend will be present. He is advised that this will not help his defence, but he is adamant. In an attempt to save something from this dilemma, his counsel asks the first police witness, 'Did my client in fact offer an explanation as to why his fingerprints were on the flyscreen?', to which the officer replies, 'Yes he did, sir, but we discounted that possibility'. At this point, Tom sends urgent instructions to his counsel not to pursue this line of questioning.

In summing up to the jury, the trial judge advises them that:

'You might have expected the accused in this case to explain how his fingerprints came to be on the flyscreen of the loungeroom window of the burgled house. After all, they were his fingerprints, and he should know. The Crown says that they were there because he was the one who burgled the house, and in the absence of any alternative suggestion from the accused himself, you may find that explanation easier to accept.'

Tom was convicted, and now seeks your advice on the prospects of an appeal.

Time allowed: 10 mins

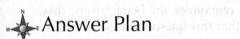

Answer Plan

(a) Background law on 'Weissensteiner directions'

Again, a 'gift' question to those who are good at 'issue spotting'. We are given a scenario in which an accused who could give an explanation for some fact of which he is aware fails to do so. This situation was dealt with in *Weissensteiner v R* (1993) 178 CLR 217, and the answer should explain in full what the High Court laid down in that case.

(b) Specific application in given scenario

There is the additional complication that Tom has not, unlike Weissensteiner himself, remained totally silent on the matter, but did offer an explanation to the police. But that explanation was not made known to the jury, who do not have the benefit of any alternative 'case theory' than the one offered by the Crown. Despite this, there is some case authority to suggest that in these circumstances a '*Weissensteiner* direction' should not be given to the jury.

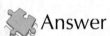 Answer

(a) Background law on 'Weissensteiner directions'

4-5 This scenario is reminiscent of *Weissensteiner v R*, in which the High Court held that, when an accused who is in a position to give an explanation regarding some fact in issue within his knowledge fails to do so, it is permissible for the trial judge to direct the jury that, in the absence of any explanation from the accused, they may find it easier to accept the Crown's explanation. The trial judge's direction in the present case seems to have been in accordance with what the High Court laid down, and cannot be criticised on that score. An accused who maintains his right to silence in the face of a credible Crown case against him is taking a risk of not discharging the 'tactical burden' that has been imposed on him.

(b) Specific application in the given scenario

4-6 However, since that case, there has been a gradual process of cutting back on the circumstances in which it is appropriate to give a

Weissensteiner direction. In *R v Ryan* [2002] QCA 92, the Queensland Court of Appeal held that it was not appropriate to give one when, as in this case, the accused had given an explanation to the police, *even though this had not been brought to the attention of the jury*. This does not of course assist the jury, but it would seem that the trial judge should not have said what he did to them, and that this was a miscarriage of justice that should result in a successful appeal.

Examiner's Comments

4-7 Students would have received only 50% of the marks for remembering *Weissensteiner*, and the remainder for being aware that there are limits to its application, and that this question involved one of them.

Keep in Mind

- Failing to spot the relevance of *Weissensteiner* to the facts of the case. Whenever you are given a scenario in which an accused fails to give evidence regarding facts of which he must be aware, this is likely to raise the *Weissensteiner* issue. Students in the past who have failed to spot it have wallowed around instead dealing with factual issues regarding the likely impact on an accused's credibility of not testifying, or have wandered into the areas of 'the right to silence' or 'the privilege against self-incrimination'.
- Failing to be aware of the 'climbdown' from the full rigour of *Weissensteiner* which has occurred in recent years.
- Not linking *Weissensteiner* with the right to silence and the tactical burden.

Question 14

> Gerard is a solicitor who acts for Michael, a local roofing contractor, in a civil action that Michael is defending against Pablo, an artist, for whom he installed a large domed roof over the private art gallery attached to Pablo's house. Due to alleged negligence on Michael's part, the roof blew off during a storm, and several valuable paintings were destroyed. Pablo's total claim against Michael amounts to over a million dollars, and Michael advised Gerard that he had no reasonable defence to offer. Michael then asked Gerard if it would be possible to transfer all his assets into his wife's name in order to avoid having to pay any judgment sum that might be awarded, to which Gerard replied, 'That would be both unlawful and unethical, and I can't advise you on that'.
>
> Michael subsequently lost the case brought by Pablo, who was awarded damages. Michael then petitioned for personal bankruptcy, claiming that he had no assets with which to meet the judgment. Pablo is listed as a major creditor in Michael's bankruptcy, and Gerard is subpoenad to

the bankruptcy hearing, at which he declines to answer two questions put to him. The first is whether or not Michael asked Gerard's advice regarding ways of avoiding a judgment debt, and the second is whether, at their last meeting, Michael appeared to be as affluent as usual, with a gold watch, several rings and expensively tailored clothing. Gerard declines to answer either question, on the ground that such information is 'privileged'.

Is he correct?

Time allowed: 10 mins

Answer Plan

If you did not spot that this question is about the extent of lawyer–client privilege, then you have no business taking the Evidence exam in the first place. Once again there are two separate questions, but they both may be preceded with an explanation of the background law before the specific issues raised are dealt with.

Answer

The nature of legal professional privilege

4-8　The common law recognises what is known as 'legal professional privilege', which is the right to decline to answer any question relating to communications between a legal practitioner and their client which had to do with either the giving of legal advice or preparation for litigation. The reason for the continued existence of this privilege is to promote candour between the client and the legal adviser, and the privilege is that of the client, who may 'waive' it if they wish.

Limitations to the application of the privilege

4-9　However, there are limits to the questions that may be evaded by means of this privilege, and two of these limits are demonstrated by the facts of the scenario. The first limitation is that no-one may hide behind legal professional privilege in order to frustrate the processes of law (*R v Bell, Ex parte Lees* (1980) 146 CLR 141), and Gerard is both legally and ethically bound to advise the court that Michael *did* enquire about transferring property into his wife's name.

The second is that a lawyer may not claim privilege (even on behalf of the client whose privilege it is) against disclosing matters that they observed for themselves, as opposed to information they were given by the client. Therefore, in this case, Gerard must advise the court of any observations he made of Michael which suggested that, at a time shortly before the civil action, Michael appeared to be financially comfortable.

Examiner's Comments

4-10 In a question as simple as this, the examiner expects little short of perfection in the answer. Not only must the precise nature of the privilege be well explained, but its limitations must be appreciated and applied accurately.

Keep in Mind

- Not relating the law to the questions asked. It is not unheard of for students, in their enthusiasm to write down all they can remember on a topic that they have revised and which has actually appeared on the examination paper, to forget to apply that law to the specific fact scenario(s) they have been given.
- Wasting time writing the same 'background' for each specific answer, when that background is common to both.

Question 15

> Roger is suing the state government in respect of injuries he received whilst serving a sentence of imprisonment. These injuries were incurred when he was attacked without provocation by a fellow inmate who had escaped from the psychiatric wing of the prison by means of a catering corridor between the psychiatric wing and the kitchen in B Block, in which Roger had been working when he was attacked.
>
> It is Roger's contention that the prison authorities were negligent in allowing a direct connection to exist between the two separate portions of the prison, and failing to maintain a permanent guard in the corridor in question. His solicitor brings an application ahead of the trial for the 'disclosure' by the defendant (ie, the state government) of the detailed plans of the prison, and for a copy of a report on the incident which was compiled three days after the event by the prison Security Officer at the request of the government solicitor who has the conduct and carriage of the matter. This application is opposed by the defendant on the ground that both items of information are 'privileged'.
>
> What legal arguments may be mounted both for and against the application?
>
> **Time allowed: 20 mins**

Answer Plan

Although the question refers to 'privilege', and this area of law was once known as 'Crown privilege', its current contemporary title is 'public interest immunity'. The bulk of the answer must be taken up in explaining precisely what this is, and the arguments for and against its application in the scenario we are given. But don't forget the second question, which concerns not so much public interest immunity as legal professional privilege.

The facts of this scenario are drawn from *State of Victoria v Brazel* [2008] VSCA 37, although you wouldn't necessarily be expected to know that in the exam.

 ## Answer

Nature and application of 'public interest immunity'

4-11 Although the defendant's counsel in this case referred to 'privilege', they are really referring, so far as concerns the release of the prison plans, to 'public interest immunity', under which exemption may be sought from the need to disclose certain evidence if it is held not to be in 'the public interest' to disclose it. Such claims are traditionally reserved for 'matters of State security', or matters relating to state or federal government, but in recent years there has been a tendency for the categories of public interest immunity to extend into quasi-government areas such as hospital, police and community records.

The defence argument in the present case will presumably be based on the claim that to make 'public' the details of the internal layout of a prison would constitute a risk to the security of the prison itself, and the activities conducted within it. They may add to that the fact that Roger should already have had a good working knowledge of the layout of the unit, having been an inmate there for some years, and can no doubt give direct evidence himself of the layout of the area in which he was attacked, so that nothing new would be learned from disclosing the prison plans, which is a frequently successful argument against disclosing public documents (see *Sankey v Whitlam* (1978) 142 CLR 1).

The counter-argument may well be that the relevant area of the prison is now much changed from that which existed when the incident occurred, and that the information is therefore basically historical, and its disclosure would pose no risk to current prison security.

There is always a balancing act to be performed in cases such as this, and it is essentially one between the 'powerful public interest' in the maintenance of a secure prison system (which the disclosure of the requested information might arguably harm), and a 'strong public interest' in ensuring the safety of both prisoners and prison staff, and ensuring that wrongful acts are properly redressed.

On that final point, it should be argued on Roger's behalf that it is the very *absence* of adequate prison security which is the basis of his claim, and that to allow the defendant to hide behind the smokescreen of public interest immunity would not only deny individual justice to Roger, but might leave other prisoners at risk from similar incidents.

It may also be argued by the defendant that, in the circumstances, Roger's demand for the plans of the entire prison is somewhat excessive, since all he would seem to need in order to support his claim is a plan of the immediate area in which he was attacked, which, as already pointed out, is something that he could probably testify to himself anyway.

Legal professional privilege

4-12　So far as concerns the report that was sent to the government solicitor, it may be asserted that the contents of this are covered by 'legal professional privilege', since it was a document created for the purposes of litigation, or at a time when litigation was in contemplation.

It was held by the High Court in *Waterford v Commonwealth* (1987) 71 ALR 673 that this privilege covers communications between 'in-house' government lawyers and their departmental clients, and the obvious analogy here is with *State of New South Wales v Jackson* [2007] NSWCA 279, in which the completion of a report following a school accident which had the dual purpose of preventing future accidents was nevertheless deemed to have been created for the 'dominant' purpose of preparing for anticipated legal proceedings. Since the case of *Esso v Federal Commissioner of Taxation* (1999) 201 CLR 49, it has only been necessary for the document in question to be supplied for the 'dominant' purpose of preparing for anticipated litigation, and not the *sole* purpose. Even if the report had some additional function (eg, to improve prison security), it will therefore still be covered by legal professional privilege.

Examiner's Comments

4-13　The examiner will be looking for a detailed analysis of how two fairly well-known principles apply in practice, and the ability of the student to argue *both* sides of a case. They will also be alert to the legal professional privilege point being overlooked or downplayed, and will expect some case precedents to be employed in backing up arguments.

Keep in Mind

- Not appreciating that the appropriate privilege in respect of the report is 'legal professional privilege', and noting the factual analogy to the *Jackson* case. Also failing to clarify that government lawyers may also claim the privilege.
- Spending too long on the arguments and counter-arguments at the expense of statements of principle, and dreaming up all sorts of additional scenarios beginning with 'If Roger ...', or 'If the facts were amended to include the fact that ...' in order to create the illusion of a lengthy answer. There is enough material there for a 20 minute answer, if you have the law at your fingertips.

Joining up the Dots

Refer to the section of the same name in Chapter 2 for the significance of this part of the chapter.

Question 16

Margaret is suing dive company 'Fathom It' for the death of her husband Philip during a diving lesson when he should have been under the careful and continuous supervision of the dive instructor, Fred Fish. In fact, it appears that Philip was allowed to resurface too quickly, and as a result he got 'the bends', and was unable to be resuscitated once back on the dive boat because there was no decompression chamber available.

When called to the witness box, Fred Fish refuses to answer any questions relating to why Philip was allowed to resurface so quickly, claiming that 'I need to keep my dive instructor's certificate'.

May he do so?

No-one is called to give evidence on behalf of Fathom It, and at the end of the trial Margaret's counsel submits to the trial judge that 'There was a clear case of negligence here, which neither the dive company nor any of its employees gave evidence to rebut. My client has clearly discharged the burden of proof that she bore, simply because there has been no evidence to rebut the clear inference that the defendant in this case was negligent'.

Is he correct?

Time allowed: 20 mins

Answer Plan

Although the question is framed to suggest that there are two issues here, in fact there are three. The first one is clearly the extent of the 'privilege against self-incrimination'. The second, regarding the discharge of the burden of proof, not only involves the application of the 'rule in *Jones v Dunkel*', but also the possibility of Margaret's case proceeding on the basis of the presumption known as res ipsa loquitur.

Allow only 6–7 minutes for the privilege question, and devote the remaining 13 minutes to untangling the remaining 'compound' issue.

Answer

The privilege against self-incrimination

4-14   Fred is in effect claiming the 'privilege against self-incrimination', which in its original form allowed a witness to claim a privilege against answering any question, the truthful answer to which might reasonably be expected to expose them to a criminal charge or a civil penalty. But more recently it has been extended to cover loss of professional registration (*Rogerson v Law Society (NT)* (1991) 1 NTLR 100), and possibly even just one's livelihood, at least in public office: *Police Service Board v Morris* (1985) 156 CLR 397. It does not affect the claim of privilege that it is not made during a criminal trial, and, by analogy with the cases quoted above, the loss of a certificate that is presumably required for one's employment might well be judged to be an appropriate matter to be claiming a privilege in respect of.

The burden of proof issue and the effect of res ipsa loquitur and Jones v Dunkel

4-15 The claim by Margaret's counsel that Fathom It have in effect lost their case because of their failure to call evidence involves two separate, but in this case linked, areas of law. The first is the operation of the so-called presumption 'res ipsa loquitur' ('things which speak for themselves'), which states that when someone is responsible for the management of an operation of some sort, and an accident occurs that should not have occurred, then, in the absence of any rebutting evidence, the court is entitled to presume that the accident resulted from mismanagement on the part of the manager. Applied to the facts of the present case, Philip should not have been allowed to resurface so quickly, and there should have been appropriate equipment available to resuscitate him when he did. Both factors would have contributed to his death, and it is for the defendants to explain away their apparent failure to take reasonable care of him by leading 'rebutting' evidence to show otherwise.

Their failure to call any evidence at all makes matters worse for them, and invokes the so-called 'rule in *Jones v Dunkel*' ((1959) 101 CLR 298), under which the failure of one party to lead evidence on a fact in issue makes it easier to accept the interpretation of those facts suggested by the other party. That case involved the failure of one of two parties to a road collision (the other being dead) to lead any evidence to explain how a truck came to collide with another truck. The absence of the truck driver from the witness box, said the High Court, made it easier for the trial court to draw the inference of negligence on the part of that truck driver in the absence of any other evidence. The principle laid down in that case has since been applied in some criminal cases, following the leading High Court ruling in *Weissensteiner v R*.

 ## Examiner's Comments

4-16 The examiner will be assessing the extent to which the examinee can think laterally, and demonstrate how different aspects of the law link together to provide a practical solution. Part-answers are likely to be sternly assessed.

 ## Keep in Mind

- Not appreciating the connection between res ipsa loquitur and the rule in *Jones v Dunkel*, which in this scenario work together like the blades of a pair of scissors. The presumption sets up the need for the defendant to adduce rebutting evidence, while their failure to do so makes it easier for the trial judge to draw the adverse inference that arises from it. Had the defendant led *any evidence at all*

(for example, that Philip had struggled with Fred and fought him off in his panic to regain the surface), then the case would have been more evenly balanced. As it was, the defendant effectively discharged the plaintiff's burden of proof by their silence.

- Not connecting Fred's refusal to testify with the extended application of the privilege against self-incrimination that applies to loss of livelihood through professional registration.
- Inadequate allocation of time between parts of the question.

Chapter 5

The Course of a Trial

⊙ Key Issues

5-1 Under the common law 'adversarial' trial system, the evidence which the court will eventually rely on in order to reach a verdict will come from witnesses called by each 'side'. This is true both for criminal trials and civil actions, and with only a few exceptions the *course* which that trial will take will be the same for both types of case.

Traditionally, the party who bears the 'ultimate burden' in the case (ie, the burden of proving their facts to a greater degree than the facts from the other side) will make an 'opening address' to the court, outlining the 'case' that they will be setting out to prove. They will then call their witnesses in whatever order seems most appropriate. *Each witness* will then go through a three-part process of:

Examination in chief: questions will be asked of them by *the counsel calling them*.

Cross-examination: questions will be asked of them by *counsel for the other side*.

Re-examination: their 'own' counsel has the *option* to ask them further questions.

Once all the witnesses for that party have been through this process, the roles are reversed, and counsel for the *other side* makes an opening address, then calls their witnesses, each of whom will go through the same process as above, but with the respective roles of counsel reversed. This means that the counsel who examined their own witnesses in chief will now be cross-examining the other side's witnesses, and vice versa.

Many issues covered by the Law of Evidence arise during the course of this seemingly simple process. It is an area of study in which students sometimes fail to see the wood for the trees, and set out below is a list of those issues, categorised according to the stage in each witness's progress through their testimony at which they most commonly arise.

This is not intended as a substitute for your textbook or a good set of lecture notes; it is merely a simplified synopsis of 'what goes where'. You should learn the detailed application of the law of your own jurisdiction from your textbook or university materials. The questions that follow assume that you have done so.

Examination in chief involves issues of:

(a) 'leading' questions;
(b) previous consistent statements;
(c) 'hostile' witnesses.

Cross-examination involves issues of:

(a) 'improper' questions;
(b) previous inconsistent statements;
(c) the rule in *Browne v Dunn*;
(d) the 'finality' rule.

Re-examination involves:

(a) all the same issues as in examination in chief;
(b) limitation of questions to 'matters arising' in cross-examination.

Before tackling the questions below, please check that you are familiar with the following:

✓ The distinction between examination in chief, cross-examination and re-examination.

✓ The specific issues that can arise during each of these processes.

✓ The detailed amendments to the common law principles that may have been imposed by statute within your jurisdiction.

✓ Under what circumstances may one ask 'leading' questions of a witness during examination in chief?

✓ If a witness is allowed to refresh their memory from a document, is the document then admissible, and, if so, for what purpose?

✓ What are the common law exceptions to the rule that counsel calling a witness may not adduce evidence of a previous consistent statement made by that witness?

✓ What needs to be established before a witness may be declared 'hostile' at common law?

✓ What limitations are placed on the type of question that may be raised in re-examination?

Question 17

> Ned is charged with the attempted armed robbery of a convenience store owned by Bruce, who was behind the counter when Ned came into the otherwise deserted store shortly after midnight, brandishing a screwdriver, and demanding that Bruce open the till and hand over all the cash. Bruce, who was getting tired of being robbed in this fashion, reached behind the counter for an iron bar which he kept there, and which he waved at Ned, who turned tail and fled.

When Bruce begins to give evidence, he first of all explains that he was serving behind the shop counter on the night in question. He is immediately asked by Crown counsel: 'Then I believe that this man here (pointing at Ned) came into the shop brandishing a screwdriver and demanded that you hand over the contents of your till, am I correct?'

Ned's counsel leaps to her feet immediately and objects to the question. Is she correct, and why?

Time allowed: 10 mins

Answer Plan

There is only one fairly obvious issue here, and that is *the 'leading' nature of the question.*

Answer

5-2 At common law, there is a ban on what are called 'leading' questions — that is, questions that either suggest the desired answer, or take for granted some fact that has yet to be proved. The reason for the ban is that each witness is required to advise the court of what they recall from their own memory, and not to answer 'yes' to every question in accordance with a script fed to them by the counsel calling them.

The question asked by Crown counsel was obviously requiring Bruce to both identify Ned and tell the court what happened by the simple process of answering 'yes' to a loaded question that required no exercise of memory by Bruce. Defence counsel was correct in objecting to the question being asked in that form, and Crown counsel will be asked to re-formulate it along the lines of 'Did anyone come into the shop?', followed by 'What, if anything, happened then?' and 'Did you ever see that person again?' if it is desired to get Bruce to advise the court that he identified Ned from a police photoboard, or by some other method.

The first part of Bruce's evidence (ie, the fact that he was serving behind the shop counter shortly after midnight) *could* be put to him in 'leading' form, since it is not denied by the defence (that is, it is not 'contentious') and it is only 'setting the scene' for the disputed evidence that is to follow.

Examiner's Comments

5-3 An examiner would be likely to take a very dim view of the abilities of an examinee who could not spot what was wrong with the question asked by Crown counsel in this example. But it is not enough simply to write, 'This is clearly a leading question, and will be disallowed', and then move on to the next question. The answer needs to be 'contextualised' in the manner suggested above.

Keep in Mind

- As indicated above, giving a 'bare' answer without explaining *why* leading questions are banned, and the type of context in which they may be tolerated.
- Regarding, as a 'leading' question, something that goes to the very heart of the case but that does not assume the desired answer (eg, 'Did you give permission for anyone to remove any money from your shop till?').

Question 18

> Clive is being sued by the insurers of a motor vehicle owned by Charlie that was severely damaged in a collision at a set of traffic lights which it is alleged were at red when Clive drove through them in his car. An important witness for the plaintiff is Diane, who was standing waiting to cross at the traffic lights at the time of the collision, and who told police immediately after the accident that the lights were at red when Clive drove his car through the intersection. Clive is disputing this fact, and is in fact alleging that the lights were green for him when he went through the intersection and that therefore, by inference, they must have been at red for any vehicle coming from Charlie's direction.
>
> Diane is called as a witness for the plaintiff at the trial, many months later, but she then claims to be unable to remember what colour the lights were for Clive's car.
>
> (a) May she 'refresh her memory' from her original police statement?
>
> (b) If she insists that the lights were at green for Clive's car, may she be reminded of her statement to the police and asked which is the correct colour?
>
> (c) May she be declared 'hostile'?
>
> (d) May the plaintiff call another witness who was nearly run down when Clive's car drove through the intersection, and who will confirm that the lights were indeed red for Clive?
>
> (e) May Diane be asked if she has been threatened by anyone regarding her testimony? If she denies it, may it be put to her that three weeks before the trial, she complained to police about a telephone call she had received, threatening to fire-bomb her house if she gave evidence?
>
> **Time allowed: 20 mins**

Answer Plan

There are clearly five separate issues involved here, and, in the absence of any indication of an order of importance, they should be given equal 'weight' in your answer. They are:

(a) Diane's failure to 'come up to proof' on the statement she gave to police, and the possible reason(s) for that;

(b) the possibility that Diane requires to refresh her memory;

(c) the possibility that Diane is deliberately setting out to lie to the court;

(d) any 'bias' that may have crept into her testimony, and the possible reason(s) for that;

(e) the question of whether or not the testimony of another witness may be substituted for Diane's.

Your answer should incorporate reference to any statutory provision that covers any of these points within your jurisdiction. The answer that follows does so directly for Queensland, with reference in brackets to where you will find the equivalent answers for the other common law jurisdictions.

 # Answer

(a) Diane's failure to 'come up to proof' on the statement she gave to police, and the possible reason(s) for that

5-4 The inability or unwillingness of a witness to 'come up to proof' on a previous statement *always* brings into play those provisions of the common law relating to 'refreshment of memory', and those of ss 17–19 of the Evidence Act 1977 (Qld) regarding 'adverse' witnesses (for South Australia, refer to the Evidence Act 1929 (SA) ss 27 and 28; for Western Australia, Evidence Act 1906 (WA) ss 20–22; and for the Northern Territory the Evidence Act (NT) ss 18–20). Diane is a witness for the plaintiff, and she is not 'delivering the goods', which places the ball firmly at the feet of the plaintiff's counsel. She may honestly not remember, or she may have decided to lie for reasons best known to herself. If the latter, then she may be accused of 'bias' arising from pressure from the defendant.

(b) The possibility that Diane requires to refresh her memory

5-5 Before Diane may be allowed to refresh her memory, certain common law tests require to be satisfied. First of all, she has to demonstrate the *need* to refresh memory, which may perhaps be explained by the mere passage of time, but perhaps not. She must then be demonstrated to have made her statement to the police at a time 'reasonably contemporaneously' to the event that it describes (in practice, often not the case, but here we are told that she gave it 'immediately after the accident'), and she must have acknowledged it in some way as her statement (the normal police practice is to get the witness to sign the entry in the police notebook which has just been recorded at the witness's dictation). The essential question will be whether she has any memory left to refresh, or whether or not she will really 'remember', even when faced with her previous statement.

Simply reminding Diane of her previous statement would be a form of asking a 'leading' question, in the sense that she would be 'prompted' into the answer expected of her. Counsel for the plaintiff might just as well ask her, 'The lights were at red, weren't they?'

(c) The possibility that Diane is deliberately setting out to lie to the court

(d) Any 'bias' that may have crept into her testimony, and the possible reason(s) for that

5-6 An 'adverse' witness (or a 'hostile' one, as they are described at common law) is one who is 'unwilling to tell the truth for the advancement of justice' (*R v Hayden and Slattery* [1959] VR 102), and, before that dubious status will be bestowed upon any witness in Queensland, the trial judge requires to be convinced.

There are many factors that can indicate that a witness is hostile, and the mere fact that the witness has given an inconsistent statement in the past is only one factor: *McLellan v Bowyer* (1961) 106 CLR 95. Section 17 of the Evidence Act 1977 (Qld) provides that counsel calling the witness may apply to the judge for leave to ask Diane whether or not she ever given a statement that is inconsistent with the evidence that she is now giving. During the course of this, plaintiff's counsel will be allowed to refer to the fact that she made a statement to the police shortly after the accident, and it may certainly be put to her that she previously complained to police about being threatened, and that this has 'biased' her testimony.

If the trial judge is convinced that Diane is 'adverse', the plaintiff's counsel will be allowed to cross-examine her as if she were a witness called by the defendant. She may then be asked if she has ever made a statement inconsistent with the testimony she has just given, and if she denies that fact, her 'previous inconsistent statement' may then be put to her, and if lodged in evidence as an exhibit for the plaintiff, it becomes evidence of the truth of its contents, per s 101 of the Evidence Act 1977.

(e) The question of whether or not the testimony of another witness may be substituted for Diane's

5-7 An alternative to this process is for the plaintiff's counsel simply to call another witness who can testify that Clive's car did indeed go through the lights at red, in an effort to minimise the damage created by Diane's testimony. In the circumstances, this is likely to be less attractive to counsel, given the risk of leaving Diane's testimony on the record.

Examiner's Comments

5-8 The examiner will be looking intently to ensure that students have dealt with *all* the possibilities that arise in this deceptively lengthy scenario, and have not just opted for the ones that occurred to them immediately. They will also be seeking clear distinctions between each of the alternatives of memory loss, bias, lies and alternative witnesses.

 ## Keep in Mind

- Dealing with only one aspect of the question. It is very easy, under examination conditions, to read a scenario like the one supplied and grasp only one aspect of it, such as the possibility of refreshing Diane's memory, or the fact that she may have been 'got at', without considering alternative approaches. Since this is what counsel would be expected to do in a real-life situation, the ability to 'think through the alternatives' is very much a test of a good student of Evidence.
- Confusing memory loss with bias. When I have set questions like this in the past, students have proved themselves very eager to accuse the witness of perjury without considering the distinct possibility that memory may have faded over time. 'This is hardly something that Diane is likely to have forgotten' would be a typical response, which not only ignores the realities of life, but also leaves the examination question partly unanswered.

 ## Question 19

Neville is charged with indecently dealing with his 13-year-old daughter, Lisa. The offence is alleged to have occurred when Lisa was staying with Neville for the weekend in accordance with a normal arrangement that Neville had with his estranged wife Kelly. Also staying over for the weekend was Lisa's 14-year-old brother Kevin.

Lisa said nothing to Kevin or her mother, either that weekend or during the next few days. However, at school on the Wednesday following the alleged incident, Lisa's teacher, Karen, noticed that she was uncharacteristically withdrawn and anxious-looking, and she asked Lisa what was wrong. Lisa replied, 'My Dad fancies me'. Following normal school procedures for incidents such as this, Karen asked a few more discreet questions, realised that Lisa may have been sexually abused by her father, then reported the matter to the School Principal, who in turn called in the police.

Is evidence of this conversation admissible? If so, at what point in the case would you introduce it into evidence, and which witnesses will speak to it? What 'evidential weight' will it carry?

The defence have obtained a statement from Lisa's brother Kevin, to the effect that on the day after he and Lisa returned from visiting their father, he was searching Lisa's room for a computer game she had borrowed, when he came across a copy of *True Life Experiences* magazine, which was opened at an article headed 'How My Dad Went to Jail for What He Did to Me'. In cross-examination, Lisa denies having seen the magazine before. May Kevin be called to rebut that denial?

Time allowed: 15 mins

Answer Plan

The scenario suggests that this might be a question relating to a possible failure on the part of Lisa to complain early enough after the alleged offence against her by her father, together with the suggestion of her possible 'bias' against him. The best way to answer these questions, and indeed all scenario questions like this, is to (a) identify the legal issue(s) raised, (b) establish the parameters and tests set by the law, and then (c) assess the facts against them.

Employing this approach, there appear to be two separate, but linked, issues here.

(a) the timing and nature of Lisa's first complaint, and its evidential significance;

(b) Lisa's possible bias.

It is also possible to impress the examiner by being able to put the specific questions asked in the context of the 'finality rule', the 'hearsay rule' and the 'rule in *Browne v Dunn*'.

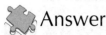

Answer

(a) The timing and nature of Lisa's first complaint, and its evidential significance

5-9 At common law, there is a general ban on counsel who calls a witness (in this case, Crown counsel calling Lisa) seeking to elicit evidence (whether from Lisa or anyone else) to the effect that Lisa has, prior to giving evidence at Neville's trial, given a statement *consistent with* the evidence she is now giving. The reason for this exclusionary rule is that every witness is assumed to be telling the truth in the witness box, and there is therefore nothing to be gained by boosting their credibility by showing that they have always maintained this version of events.

There are exceptions to this rule, one of which arises in the case of a 'fresh complaint' by a sexual offence victim. Not only may such evidence be led, but it is actively sought by the trial court, and juries are still warned by trial judges to be additionally cautious before convicting in cases in which there has been no such 'fresh complaint'.

The only evidential effect of the making of a fresh complaint is to enhance the *credibility as a witness* of the person who made it; at common law, a fresh complaint is *not evidence of the truth of the allegation contained within it*.

There is no hard and fast rule about what is, or is not, 'fresh' in terms of the delay in time between the event and the complaint. The courts are also quite flexible with regard to the person to whom the complaint should have been made. All these factors will vary with the circumstances, as will the attitude of the trial judge as to whether or not the victim has responded reasonably in the circumstances. The modern common law approach to the question of whether or not such a complaint was made 'at the earliest reasonable opportunity' is detailed in *R v M* [2000] QCA 20.

Applying the principles laid down in that case to the facts of our scenario, there is nothing sinister in the fact that Lisa said nothing on the day of the offence; shock, disbelief and embarrassment would be sufficient on their own to explain her silence; but, in addition, to whom was she supposed to complain? Case histories show that mothers are reluctant to believe such things of fathers, and that children in Lisa's position feel that they have somehow betrayed their mothers. As for Lisa's 14-year-old brother Kevin, it is almost a matter of 'judicial notice' how unsympathetic pubescent boys are to the sexual sensitivities of their female siblings, and girls in general.

The way in which the complaint eventually came to be made is all too familiar, and convincing. Lisa herself took no steps at all to voice her complaint, and the fact that it was her changed mood that first attracted the trained eye of a teacher who knew her gives her eventual complaint a greater degree of credibility, unless she is a consummate actress with a degree in child psychology. The opening words she eventually used ('My Dad fancies me') are also typical of the confusion and denial displayed by genuine sexual assault victims of Lisa's age and level of maturity, and one would have been less convinced had Lisa been pre-prepared with a heart-wrenching and graphic description of events, or had she performed like a precocious drama-queen.

Since 2003, all 'fresh complaints' by sexual assault victims under Queensland law may well also qualify as 'preliminary complaints' in terms of s 4A of the Criminal Law (Sexual Offences) Act 1978 (Qld) when they are made *prior to* any formal complaint to a police officer. Lisa's complaints to Karen (both her initial comment *and* any subsequent details) may well qualify under s 4A (for which there is no time limit, although even at common law three days is probably acceptable in the circumstances of this case), and the evidential significance of it coming within s 4A is that it will constitute yet further confirmation of Lisa's consistency (and therefore enhanced credibility) as a witness. There is not even any need for it to be 'fresh' in the chronological sense. But in *R v RH* [2005] 1 Qd R 180 it was confirmed by the Queensland Court of Appeal that 'preliminary' complaints are no more evidence of the truth of the complaint than 'fresh' complaints. (For South Australia, see s 34M of the Evidence Act 1929 (SA); for Western Australia, see s 36BD of the Evidence Act 1906 (WA); and for the Northern Territory, see s 26E of the Evidence Act (NT)).

The question also asks how the evidence is to be led, and by whom. Lisa should be asked, during her evidence in chief, to confirm that she did make a complaint to Karen, and then the latter should be called to confirm both the making of the statement, and its details. Given that under s 4A the statement is being received as evidence simply of the fact that it was made, and not as evidence of its contents, then it does not constitute 'hearsay'.

(b) Lisa's possible bias

5-10 At common law, counsel cross-examining a witness is in theory constrained by something called the 'finality rule' on questions relating to 'collateral' issues; that is, issues that do not form part of the 'facts in issue'. One of these is the issue of a witness's 'credit' (that is, his or her pre-determined character), which must be distinguished from his or her 'credibility', which goes to their 'believability' on the facts they are narrating. The finality rule states that if a witness has been asked a question relating to a collateral issue, then the issue should not be pursued.

However, the finality rule as applied to witness credit admits to several exceptions, one of which relates to any perceived 'bias' on the part of the witness. 'Bias' in this context encompasses more than it normally does, and has been defined as 'a motive for giving false evidence': *R v Umanski*) [1961] VR 242.

Defence counsel took care to ask Lisa in cross-examination whether or not she had seen the magazine before, so as not to fall foul of the 'rule in *Browne v Dunn* (1894) 6 R 67 (HL). He should, ideally, also have put to her that her allegations are all fantasies arising from what she read in the magazine, since this is what will be alleged as part of the defence 'theory of the case'.

The fact that Lisa appears to have been reading a magazine article startlingly similar to the allegations she is now making against her own father suggests at least the possibility of a fantasy on her part, in which she becomes the tragic heroine of a similar scenario. She may even have been seeking 'revenge' against her father for reasons that his defence team will seek from him. Given that her denial involves an issue that may be crucial to her motivation for making the complaint, the defence will be allowed to pursue it by calling Kevin as a witness. There is an obvious parallel here with the facts of *R v Schneider* [1998] QCA 303.

Examiner's Comments

5-11 This is a potentially lengthy question that tests the student's ability to write economically, while at the same time 'covering all the bases', and putting the specific issues into the broader context of the conduct of a criminal trial in which allegations of a sexual nature are raised. Over the years, special rules of evidence have been developed to deal with these, and the examiner will be seeking confirmation that the student is aware of them.

Keep in Mind

- Dealing with only one aspect of the given scenario. The question clearly raises several issues, which the examiner has been merciful enough to 'flag' for you.
- Poor time management between various sections of the question. Clearly, the first part of the answer took longer to explain, and there was a risk that the examinee would leave inadequate time to do justice to the remainder of the question.
- Failure to support the legal statements made with relevant case authority.

Question 20

Hiram is suing an alleged client, Mongo, for management fees in his capacity as Mongo's agent in his dealings with the Western Wombats NRL Club which resulted in Mongo being awarded a $1 million dollar playing contract over the next three years. Mongo claims that there was never any formal contract between himself and Hiram, while Hiram asserts that, over lunch three weeks prior to Mongo's contract with the Western Wombats being finalised, he (Hiram) was appointed verbally as Mongo's exclusive management agent, and that the contract was only finalised after consistent pressure by Hiram on the club.

During the civil action that follows, Hiram's counsel (Hugo) asks him, during his examination in chief, whether there were any other communications between him and Mongo relating to his appointment as Mongo's manager. Hiram replies, 'No, that was it — just what was agreed over lunch'. In cross-examination, Mongo's counsel (Ian) restricts his questions to what was said between the parties during the lunch, and in effect accuses Hiram of inventing the suggestion that he was hired by Mongo only *after* it was announced that Mongo had been contracted by the club.

In re-examination, Hugo asks Hiram, 'Getting back to my earlier question, did you send a fax to the defendant the following day, thanking him for the lunch and assuring him that you would do your utmost in your negotiations with the Wombats?'. Ian leaps to his feet, asserting, 'I object to that question on three grounds, Your Honour!'

What three grounds might those be?

Assuming that this objection is overruled, what use might Hugo make of the fax message, assuming that it is still available as an item of evidence?

When it is Mongo's turn to give evidence, he is asked by Ian, 'Did you have any further communication with the plaintiff in this case, following your lunch with him?' Mongo gets as far as replying, 'Yes — I sent him an email three days later in which —'. He is interrupted as Hugo rises to his feet and objects to both the question and the answer.

What ground might he have for doing so?

Time allowed: 20 mins

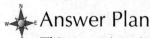

Answer Plan

This scenario arises during the course of a trial, and there are two questions asked that relate to counsel objecting to questions asked by the other side. The first arises during re-examination, and is therefore probably in connection with the asking of a question that does not deal with anything arising from cross-examination. The second is less obvious to spot, until it is recalled that Ian asked no question of Hiram during cross-examination which related to any communication after the lunch. There has therefore probably been a breach of the so-called 'rule in *Browne v Dunn*'.

Hidden in amongst all this is the possibility that Hugo might now be able to 'exhibit' Hiram's fax to Mongo as an exception to the rule against previous consistent statements arising from the allegation that Hiram's assertion that he had been hired by Mongo is a 'recent invention'. It would also seem that the form in which Hugo originally framed his question to Hiram was 'leading'.

There is a need to keep all these issues distinct from each other when answering the question, but to show how they are linked by the course that the trial has taken. The issues may be identified as:

(a) Hugo's question in re-examination;
(b) the potential significance of the fax from Hiram to Mongo;
(c) the format in which the question was asked;
(d) Ian's question regarding Mongo's email.

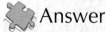

Answer

5-12   There are several inter-related issues raised by the facts of this scenario. They are:

(a)   *Hugo's question in re-examination*

(b)   *The potential significance of the fax from Hiram to Mongo*

(c)   *The format in which the question was asked*

5-13   The rule at common law is that questions asked of one's own witness in re-examination must be related to issues arising in cross-examination. Re-examination may *not* be used in order to ask supplementary questions that one forgot to ask the witness during examination in chief. There was no direct reference during Ian's cross-examination of Hiram to any communication beyond what was said over lunch, only a suggestion that Hiram had 'recently invented' his appointment as Mongo's manager.

However, the rebuttal of an allegation of 'recent invention' by a witness constitutes one of the two main exceptions to the common law rule against the adduction into evidence of a 'previous consistent statement' by that witness. The other is a 'fresh complaint' by a sexual assault victim, but the added advantage of a 'recent invention' allegation under

Queensland law is that, by virtue of s 101 of the Evidence Act 1977 (Qld), it is admissible as evidence of the facts which it contains.

It is therefore permissible for Hugo to ask Hiram, in re-examination, whether or not he sent a fax to Mongo following their lunch, in order to rebut the allegation that Hiram has recently invented the suggestion that Mongo hired him to negotiate with the Wombats. Once Hiram has verified the fax as being a true copy of the one he sent, it may be admitted as a plaintiff exhibit, and as evidence of the fact that, at the time it was sent, Hiram regarded himself as having been hired as Mongo's agent.

One final issue concerns the way in which Hugo framed the question that he asked in re-examination. The rules that govern re-examination are identical to those governing examination in chief, and they include a ban on the asking of 'leading questions'; that is, questions that suggest the desired answer. All that was required of Hiram by the single 'compound' question put by Hugo was that he answer 'yes'. It would have been far preferable for Hugo to have asked a series of questions, as follows:

Q.1 'It was put to you in cross-examination that you only asserted that you had been hired by the defendant to act as his agent after he was recruited by the Wombats. In fact, was there any communication between you and the defendant following your lunch meeting?'

A.1 'Yes, I sent him a fax.'

Q.2 'When did you send this fax?'

A.2 'The day after our lunch.'

Q.3 'Would you take a look at this document, please? Do you recognise it?'

A.3 'Yes, it's a copy of the fax to which I was referring'.

Q.4 'Would you please read it out loud for the benefit of the court record?'

(d) Ian's question regarding Mongo's email

5-14 The so-called 'rule in *Browne v Dunn*' requires that before any evidence is admitted as part of a party's case, the relevant witnesses for the other party must be afforded an opportunity to comment on what is to be alleged. This means, in the context of the scenario we have been given, that before Mongo could be asked whether or not he had sent an email to Hiram (whatever it may have contained), Hiram should have been asked in cross-examination whether or not he had received it. This was not done, and one of the consequences of this breach of the rule (which is a matter of discretion for the trial judge) is that Ian may not be allowed to follow this line of questions 'in chief' with Mongo. A less serious alternative would be to allow Hiram to be recalled to the witness box and asked (by Ian, in renewed cross-examination) whether or not he (Hiram) received any fax from Mongo subsequent to their lunch.

Examiner's Comments

5-15 This is a question designed to test the student's ability to follow the tangled progress of a trial, and allocate issues accordingly. In particular, it tests the student's ability to distinguish one issue from another, and to see the multiple application of several issues arising from one set of facts. Questions of this nature are not to be attempted unless you have a thorough grasp of the dynamics of the adversarial system.

 Keep in Mind

- Failing to appreciate that certain issues only arise in examination in chief, some in cross-examination and some in re-examination. Failing to allocate them correctly.
- Failing to appreciate the potential multiple relevance of certain issues that arise. For example, the fact that Hugo's question to Hiram in re-examination is not just 'leading', but may be appropriate even though it appears to transgress the normal rule limiting re-examination to matters arising in 'cross', because the nature of that 'cross' has opened up the issue of Hiram's alleged 'recent invention'.
- Becoming so 'bogged down' in sorting out the issues that there is insufficient time left to answer the question.
- As always, the temptation to answer only the first point that is recognised, and failing to look deeper into the question.

 Joining up the Dots

Refer to the section of the same name in Chapter 2 for the significance of this part of the chapter.

 Question 21

> Suzy has brought a civil action for damages against Orson in respect of his alleged negligent navigation of a powerboat during a river race which resulted in the death of her husband Bruce. It is alleged that Orson failed to take sufficient care when changing direction, and swerved into Bruce's powerboat, forcing it into the far bank of the river, where it exploded in flames.
>
> Comment on the following evidential issues that arise during the hearing of the action.
>
> (a) Suzy is the first witness in the plaintiff's case, and the first question she is asked by her counsel, Ben, is: 'Did you see the defendant in this case drinking in the bar of the Brahms and Liszt Hotel earlier on the day of the race?'
>
> Counsel for the defendant, Phil, immediately rises to his feet and objects to the question. Is he correct to do so, and how would you

frame the question(s) in order to obtain the same information from the witness?

(b) In cross-examination, Suzy is asked by Phil: 'Is it not the case that both you and your husband had, and in your case still have, a serious alcohol problem?'

Ben leaps to his feet in order to object to the relevance of the question, to which Phil responds, 'It has relevance, Your Honour, both to the issues in this case and to the credibility of this witness when she states, as she has done, that she saw the accident clearly from the far bank of the river'. Is he correct?

(c) The first witness for the defendant is Orson himself, who testifies that he was obliged to swerve his powerboat towards Bruce's boat in order to avoid a race marshal's pontoon that had broken free from its moorings and drifted into the centre of the navigable channel of the river. During cross-examination he admits that no witness will be called from the race organising committee to confirm this point, and, in his closing submissions for the plaintiff, Ben urges the trial judge to discount this portion of Orson's evidence. What case authority might he cite for this submission?

(d) Assume that Orson is eventually found liable in damages to Suzie. May he then raise a separate civil action against the organisers of the race, Swanee River Promotions, for a contribution towards the damages he has been obliged to pay because of their negligence in allowing the pontoon to drift out into the river? Give reasons for your answer.

Time allowed: 30 mins

 Answer Plan

The first issue raised seems obvious enough, namely that of the forbidden 'leading' question. The questions that you are asked to substitute for the one asked should roll in a 'domino effect', so that each one leads naturally to the next.

In part (b), the examiner has had the decency to highlight the issue(s) raised, which is the difference between the 'credit' and the 'credibility' of a witness, and the 'finality rule' that normally applies to the former.

Part (c) is a question arising from the failure of a party to a case to 'back up' the case theory that they are advancing with sworn testimony. It probably therefore involves the 'rule in *Jones v Dunkel*' (see Chapter 4).

Finally, if part (d) looks vaguely familiar, it is because it is based on *Port of Melbourne Authority v Anshun Pty Ltd*, which we dealt with in Chapter 3.

The examiner has not indicated any time or mark allocation to the individual questions, so equal time should be devoted to answering each of them.

Answer

(a) *The question asked of Suzy is both a 'compound' question (ie, it contains several questions at once) and a 'leading' question — that is, one that either suggests the desired answer, or takes for granted a fact that has not yet been established by the evidence*

5-16   Leading questions may not be asked of one's own witness 'in chief', because they result in the evidence of that witness becoming less of a spontaneous recollection of events by them, and more the guided response by them to a script fed to them by counsel.

Ben would have been better advised to ask a series of 'domino' questions, each of which invited either a 'yes or no' answer, and the totality of which elicited the information he was seeking. Thus, he might have asked:

1. 'Is the defendant in this case known to you by sight?' *[yes]*
2. 'Did you see him, on the day of the race, at any time prior to the race?' *[yes]*
3. 'Where did you see him?' *[in the Brahms and Liszt Hotel]*
4. 'What was he doing when you saw him?' *[drinking]*
5. 'Do you recall what precisely he was drinking?' *[it looked to me like whisky or brandy]*
6. 'Do you recall how many such drinks you saw him consume?' *[it could have been four or five]*

Such an approach also eliminates the problem generated by the asking of a 'compound' question, which is that if Suzy in this scenario had simply answered 'yes' to the question as it was originally framed, it would have been uncertain whether she was agreeing that she had seen the defendant, that she had seen him in the hotel, that she had seen him prior to the race, or that she had seen him drinking.

(b) *The mere fact that Suzy and Bruce may have had an alcohol problem is not directly relevant to how Bruce came to be killed, but it may be of 'sufficient' relevance to the facts in issue in this case, depending upon how it is used*

5-17   The fact that Bruce was an alcoholic *may* have relevance to the issue of whether or not he was drunk at the time of the collision, but it would have been more direct and useful simply to ask Suzy how much Bruce had drunk that day. If it is being alleged that Bruce's alcoholism left him with problems that made him a hazard in the water (eg, brain damage, neurological impairment, poor depth of vision etc.), then one would expect this evidence to come from an 'expert' witness who could also confirm the underlying alcoholism. Nevertheless, asking Suzy to confirm this may be simple caution on the part of counsel in not falling foul of the rule in *Browne v Dunn* if he later adduces the evidence of an expert.

Since Suzy is also a witness, another factor enters the equation. There are two ways of regarding the purpose behind establishing the fact that Suzy may have alcohol problems. The first is that it might affect her 'credibility' regarding what she saw of the events leading to the crash, and the second is that it reflects 'discredit upon her as a person'.

The common law recognises a distinction between a person's 'credit' (ie, the reputation they enjoy in society), and their 'credibility', which is their believability as a witness. As a general rule (known as the 'finality rule'), questions relating to mere 'credit' may not be pursued, whereas questions designed to test 'credibility' may. This distinction is recognised and maintained by s 20 of the Evidence Act 1977 (Qld), which forbids a question put to a witness that, if answered truthfully, would not 'materially impair confidence in the reliability of the witness's evidence'. (See also Evidence Act (NT) s 15; Evidence Act 1929 (SA) s 23; Evidence Act 1906 (WA) s 25).

Therefore, if the question is being asked as a precursor to an attack on Suzy's ability to observe the accident clearly, it may be permissible, particularly since the common law also recognises a 'physical or mental incapacity' exception to the general rule against pursuing 'collateral' issues, one of which is regarded as being the 'credit' of a witness: *Toohey v Metropolitan Police Commissioner* [1965] AC 595.

This is relevant even if counsel *concedes* that the question was really only seeking to diminish the 'believability' of Suzy's evidence by lowering her 'credit' as a person in the eyes of the court. The question may have been a precursor to a more direct question relating to Suzy's financial circumstances, giving her a motive to seek financial compensation from the defendant, which in *Natta v Canham* (1991) 32 FCR 282 was held by the High Court to be a valid exception to the 'collateral issue' banning of questions relating ostensibly to 'credit' when in reality they are more about 'credibility'.

(c) *In* Jones v Dunkel, *the High Court established a general rule to the effect that when a party to a civil case fails to testify, so as to provide sworn evidence in support of the theory of the case that he or she is advocating, this may be taken into account when assessing the 'pros and cons' of accepting their theory of the case, as opposed to the other side's*

5-18 Also, at least for civil cases, the *Jones v Dunkel* rule was expanded so as to encompass situations in which a party fails to call a crucial witness who could support his or her theory of the case, as in *West v GIO* (1981) 148 CLR 62 (passengers in a vehicle involved in a road accident). In our scenario, Ben is therefore well within the law in inviting the trial judge to bear in mind the failure of Orson to call any witness from the race organising committee to confirm his evidence that he was forced to take evasive action in order to avoid their pontoon. Against this is (a) the possibility that none of that committee had any first-hand knowledge of those facts, and (b) the fact that they would have a legal interest in conflict with his. Whether or not he should in fact have joined them as Second Defendants is an issue taken up in this next part of this answer.

(d) It is well established by the principle known at common law as 'cause of action estoppel' or 'res judicata' that once an action between A and B on a particular issue has been litigated to finality, the same 'cause of action' may never be re-raised. This is in order to avoid a multiplicity of lawsuits, and to prevent 'bad losers' from re-raising actions they have already lost, in the interests of judicial economy (eg, Conquer v Boot)

5-19 In *Port of Melbourne Authority v Anshun Pty Ltd*, it was held by the High Court that the same principle extended to issues that *might have* been litigated in the previous action, but were not. In that case, it was the division of liability for negligence between a firm of stevedores using a crane, and the plaintiff from whom they had hired it, towards someone injured by its negligent use. This liability had already been fixed at 10% and 90% respectively in a previous civil action by the injured party, and when the PMA attempted to raise a new action to enforce a clause in the hire contract that made the hirers 100% liable for any accidents involving the crane, it was held that they were 'estopped' from doing so, since the contractual indemnity could have been raised during the previous litigation.

Likewise here, it may be argued that Orson could have joined the race organisers as Second Defendants in the action against him by Suzy, and is now estopped from re-raising the matter.

Examiner's Comments

5-20 'Time management' is always a major issue in multi-part examination scenarios of this type, which are very popular in Evidence exams. What seems, up-front, like a simple issue can take longer to properly explain than a more obscure one; compare, for example, the length of the answer to part (a) with that for part (d).

As always, it is not enough simply to 'pin the tail on the donkey' and move on. One-paragraph answers do not necessarily convey to the examiner that the student fully understands what the issue is all about, and usually fail to link the answer with the facts of the question.

Keep in Mind

- As indicated above, failing to allocate sufficient time to answering each part of the question *fully*. Linked to this is the failure to assess in advance roughly how much time each question is likely to take.

- Again, as always, giving only superficial answers that identify the issue involved, but that fail to demonstrate a proper understanding of the issue itself, and how it applies to the facts of the given scenario.
- These 'joining up the dots' questions are always drawn from different chapters of this book, in order to replicate a true exam question, which will be drawn from separate areas of the syllabus. A common error is therefore that of failing to identify the issue in the first place.

Chapter 6

Character, Propensity and Prejudice

Key Issues

6-1 It is important to the integrity of the common law trial system that decisions by a court (and most notably those which are left to a jury) should be based on *facts directly relevant to the issues raised*, and not other factors that are strictly irrelevant to those issues, but that might 'prejudice' the court against one or other of the parties.

The risk of a court reaching a decision based on irrelevant but prejudicial considerations is potentially at its greatest when 'evidence' is admitted of the poor moral character, or previous misdeeds, of one of the parties or key witnesses. While this can in theory taint the outcome of even a civil action, the problem is most acute in a *criminal trial*, when the moral character or previous behaviour in question is that of *the accused* or *the complainant*.

For example, while a jury may consider the fact that the accused charged with, say, armed robbery has a 'prior' conviction for the same offence carries a great deal of 'probity' (on the basis of the flawed logic that 'He has done it before, so he probably did it this time'), they would be drawing that conclusion purely on the basis of prejudice, and without reference to the actual facts of the case. To guard against such 'forbidden reasoning' (*Boardman v DPP* [1975] AC 421), the common law has enacted certain rules that prohibit such evidence being adduced unless it is relevant to the case for some better reason than merely the old adage 'Once a thief, always a thief'.

So far as concerns an *accused*, the common law has always permitted them to lead evidence of their own *good* 'character', which in this context includes their general reputation in the community: *R v Rowton* (1865) 169 ER 1497. It also includes their *previous good behaviour* — for example, as evidenced by their lack of previous convictions. However, so far as concerns their *previous bad behaviour*, such evidence may only be revealed to the court before which they are on trial for a new offence in a limited number of circumstances.

These circumstances may include the fact that *the accused has raised the issue of his/her character* by leading evidence of 'good' character, which the Crown is entitled to rebut with evidence to the contrary.

Alternatively, the accused may have attacked the character of one of the Crown witnesses, or of a co-accused, in which case the Crown or the co-accused may respond 'in kind'. These possibilities are now controlled by statute, although the precise wording of these statutory provisions varies slightly from jurisdiction to jurisdiction (see Evidence Act (NT) s 9; Evidence Act 1977 (Qld) s 15; Evidence Act 1929 (SA) s 18; and Evidence Act 1906 (WA) s 8).

Finally, the evidence of an accused person's previous misdeeds (whether or not they resulted in a conviction), or their 'tendency' to behave in a certain way may be admitted in evidence in support of their likely guilt of the new offence, when the 'prejudicial' effect of doing so is outweighed by the 'probative value' that such evidence possesses (under the Evidence Act 1906 (WA) s 31A), or when the effect of the 'previous behaviour' evidence, taken together with the new evidence in the case, is such as to leave 'no reasonable view consistent with the innocence of the accused' (per *Pfennig v The Queen* (1995) 182 CLR 461).

Controversially, the 'tendency' of an accused person to behave in a certain way extends to their *relationship* with other persons, most notably their victim. At common law, for example, it was held by the High Court in *Wilson v R* (1970) 123 CLR 334 that, on the trial of a man for the murder of his wife, his previous antagonism towards her might be taken into account by the jury when considering whether or not her eventual death was accidental. This has become a statutory rule encompassing *all* previous domestic relationships between an accused and his/her victim under the Evidence Act 1977 (Qld) s 132B.

Even more controversially, 'relationship' evidence is admissible against a person charged with sexual abuse of a child in the form of evidence of *other* sexual acts against that child that are not specified on the indictment, on the ground that it establishes the 'relationship' between the parties at the time of the offence(s) alleged on the indictment. This is usually referred to as 'uncharged act' evidence; see *HML v The Queen* (2008) 235 CLR 334.

Another context in which the 'moral' history of a person can be employed for the wrong reason is that of the complainant in a sex offence trial. If the court is allowed to form a poor opinion of the complainant's sexual morality, it may be more difficult for it to be convinced that the offence with which the accused is charged occurred without that victim's consent. Defence counsel therefore developed the habit of cross-examining sex offence complainants on their sexual history to an embarrassing, and largely irrelevant degree, until prevented by statute (see Sexual Offences (Evidence and Procedure) Act (NT) s 4; Criminal Law (Sexual Offences) Act 1978 (Qld) s 4; Evidence Act 1929 (SA) s 34L; and Evidence Act 1906 (WA) s 36BC).

Before tackling the questions below, please check that you are familiar with the following:

✓ the distinction between 'character', 'propensity', 'relationship', 'probity' and 'prejudice';

✓ the circumstances in which the previous misbehaviour of a criminal accused may be adduced in evidence;

✓ the circumstances in which the sexual history of the complainant in a sexual offence trial may be adduced in evidence.

 # Question 22

> Tom is facing trial on a charge of attempting to rob a bank.
>
> The Crown's case is that at approximately 11 am on the morning of the attempted robbery, Tom walked into the bank branch carrying his motorcycle safety helmet under his arm, and smiled up at the security camera while in the queue to speak to a teller. When he got to the head of the queue, he used his bank card in order that the teller could advise him of the balance of his account, was advised that his account was in fact overdrawn, then handed over a card, on the back of which he had written a demand for $10,000 in cash, with the threat that if he did not receive it, he would activate an explosive device in his pocket. His demand was refused, whereupon he ran from the bank, leaving behind the card on which he had written the demand. The card turned out to be an appointment card for his next meeting with his Probation Officer, which clearly displayed his name and address.
>
> Tom's counsel argues that the Crown should not be allowed to adduce the evidence of the card, because it will reveal to the jury the fact that Tom has a previous conviction that led to a Probation Order. The Crown, for its part, argues that it is an essential link in the chain of evidence identifying Tom as the attempted robber. What decision is the judge likely to arrive at, and what legal precedents are likely to be cited in argument?
>
> Would the legal outcome be different if, instead of the above facts, Tom ran into the bank branch with his face still covered by his tinted motorcycle helmet, bypassed the queue and simply handed the same demand card over to the teller?
>
> **Time allowed: 15 mins**

 # Answer Plan

The general 'target area' of the question is identified by Tom's counsel's submission, and it is the possibility that the revelation of the fact that Tom was on probation at the time of the offence will influence the jury into convicting him out of 'moral prejudice' and without reference to the facts of the case. On the other hand, the Crown is asserting that the appointment card is a key factor in the identification of Tom as the offender, and that 'the interests of justice' must take priority.

The balancing act represented by these two alternative interpretations of the 'logical probity' of the evidence identifies the scenario as one involving 'propensity' evidence, and the tests to be employed in assessing its admissibility.

 ## Answer

6-2 Revealing to the jury the fact that Tom has a previous conviction involves the use of 'bad character' evidence against him. There is a risk that the jury will find him guilty, not because the facts of the new case clearly prove beyond reasonable doubt that the failed robber was Tom, but because 'He's a criminal, and he's more likely than most to have offended *this* time'. This is despite the fact that we don't know what precisely he did *last* time — for all we know, the offence for which he is on probation was drink-driving, or assault.

In particular, the Crown has no basis for arguing that the facts of the new case are so strikingly similar to those of the previous offence that they fall within the category of 'similar fact evidence'. As the House of Lords ruled in *Boardman*, evidence of a person's previous misdeeds is only admissible when its 'probative' value exceeds its 'prejudicial' potential, as it may do in cases that involve 'strikingly similar' facts that constitute the accused's 'modus operandi' or 'signal behaviour'. There are no such facts here, and we fall back on what was handed down as the definitive statement of the law on 'bad character' evidence by the High Court in *Pfennig*.

This is that the evidence should be 'so significant that together with the other evidence there [is] no rational explanation consistent with the innocence of the accused'. In *Pfennig* itself, that 'significance' came from the similarity of the facts of the previous and 'instant' cases, but 'significance' need not be limited to such cases.

In the first factual scenario, there is a very strong case against Tom *without* the evidence of the information on the card that he handed over. He was under surveillance from the security camera, he made no attempt to disguise his face, and he had to reveal his bank card details in order to obtain his account balance. Clearly, the bank's security system already has him identified, so what need do we have of the bonus information on the card?

However, the 'marginal' nature of this evidence from the card may be employed as an argument both *for and against* the admission of the evidence from it. On the one hand, the defence may argue, 'Why does the Crown need this additional evidence, when it has Tom identified already? They are just 'sticking the boot in' by revealing his prior criminal history to the jury'. For the Crown, it may be argued, 'The *ratio* of *Pfennig* is clearly to the effect that it is *precisely* in cases such as this, when the Crown case is so strong, that the addition of the 'bad character' evidence leaves no rational explanation consistent with the accused's innocence. It is, to use a colloquial expression, the final nail in the coffin.'

In all common law jurisdictions other than Western Australia, the Crown will have to demonstrate the admissibility of the card on the basis of the test in *Pfennig*. The person attempting to rob the bank may be identified from the security camera if the bank has any photographic records of its customers. That same identity is confirmed by the bank card. The existence of Tom's name and address on the card left behind by the robber, which confirms that he has offended in some way in the past, is merely the icing on the cake.

Another approach is suggested by the wording of s 31A of the Evidence Act 1906 (WA), which still requires 'probity' to outweigh 'prejudice'. On the one hand, the 'prejudicial effect' of the jury learning that Tom is on probation is not great, particularly not if his 'priors' are for minor matters such as non-payment of motoring fines. If this is the case, then it would be a good idea for the defence to lead evidence of precisely *why* Tom was on probation, rather than leaving the jury to speculate that Tom might be a murderer or a rapist, in which case their 'moral prejudice' against him will be even stronger.

Compared with that relatively minor prejudicial effect, the 'probative value' of the card in proving exactly who it was who attempted to rob the bank is very strong, despite the fact that Tom, as a customer, has already been identified. At least the card is likely to reveal his current address. Put another way, the Crown is not adducing the evidence in order to show that Tom has committed a crime in the past, but to identify the person who handed over the card during the robbery. This, it will argue, is its true significance in the case. The *probative* value of a criminal conveniently leaving his name and address at the scene of the crime far outweighs any *prejudicial* effect on the jury being told that he was on probation at the time. When the jury learn what was on the card, will they not be far more likely to be interested in it as evidence of the identity of the failed robber than as evidence that he was on probation at the time?

On balance, the Crown is likely to be successful in the first scenario.

In the second factual scenario, the evidence from the card takes on a different significance. It is the *only* evidence the Crown has of the identity of the would-be robber, and it will argue that the evidence from the card shows far more than the mere fact that the accused has a propensity or a disposition to commit a crime. Put another way, the Crown is not adducing the evidence in order to show that Tom has committed a crime before, but to identify the person who handed over the card during the robbery. This, they will argue, is its true significance.

The defence argument is the predictable one that, according to what was said in *Pfennig*, bad character evidence is only admissible when, if it is combined with the *other* evidence in the case, it leaves no rational conclusion consistent with innocence. Here, it is the *only* evidence in the case.

It would seem that the Crown argument is even stronger in this second scenario.

Examiner's Comments

6-3 In this scenario, identifying the 'area of law' involved is one thing; explaining how it works in practice is another. The examiner will be seeking (a) a clear explanation of the test to be employed, and (b) an equally clear explanation of how the test works when applied to the facts of *each* scenario. This is not as straightforward as it may seem at first glance.

Keep in Mind

- Failing to identify the legal principles that the scenario involves.
- Failing to argue *both* sides of the case.
- Omitting to answer the second question posed. Particularly if pressed for time, many students overlook caveats in scenario questions.

Question 23

> Matt is on trial for an alleged indecent assault on Sandra, which the Crown allege took the form of his fondling her breasts under her t-shirt while they were both on the beach, watching a surfing carnival. May defence counsel, when cross-examining Sandra, ask her the following questions?
>
> (a) 'Is it not the case that shortly before this alleged assault, you ran up and down the beach, with your t-shirt pulled up to your chin, displaying your naked breasts in a shameless manner and shouting "Never mind the surfers, what about these?"'
>
> (b) 'And did you not also, shortly after my client is alleged to have assaulted you, invite his brother Vincent to fondle your breasts, with the words "See what your big brother just did — your turn next, baby brother"?'
>
> (c) 'Would I be correct in stating that you are a single mother of two children, both of which are illegitimate, and both by different fathers?'
>
> (d) 'You told the jury that you are by nature a very modest young lady. But is it not the case that you frequently pose naked on your Facebook website?'
>
> **Time allowed: 20 mins**

Answer Plan

Clearly, this question has to do with the limits that are imposed on the cross-examination of a sexual offence victim by defence counsel. These limits are defined in general terms in different pieces of legislation in each common law jurisdiction, and the answer given below is the appropriate one for Queensland.

There are four separate questions, which must be given equal attention. This allows little time for each of them.

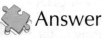
Answer

General

6-4   These questions are clearly based on the provisions of the Criminal Law (Sexual Offences) Act 1978, which are designed to impose strict limits on the questions that may be asked, in cross-examination, of the victim of any alleged sexual offence falling within its provisions. Indecent assault is one of them, and the main concern of Section 4 of the Act is to ensure that while questions may be asked that are relevant and germane to the matter in hand (and in particular, questions that may be necessary for the proper development of the accused's defence), questions may *not* be asked that are designed simply to be embarrassing, intimidating and unnecessarily personal for the victim/witness without any real relevance to the case under enquiry.

Alleged provocative behaviour

6-5   It may be argued that this question falls into the 'permitted' category of s 4(2), in that it has 'substantial relevance to the facts in issue'. The 'provocative' way in which Sandra was alleged to have been behaving shortly before the alleged incident could be said to have operated as an invitation to assault her. Others would argue that this is a sexist attitude, and that merely displaying one's nakedness is not to be construed as an invitation to commit an assault. To an extent, the trial judge will attempt to be guided by what they regard as the current societal attitude towards public nudity, and may well decide *against* allowing the question so as not to be accused of encouraging this sort of attack on topless bathers on local beaches.

Alleged invitation to Vincent

6-6   This question appears, superficially, to have parallels with the case of *Starkey* [1988] 2 Qd R 294, in which an alleged rape victim was shown to have issued an invitation to engage in 'bondage' sex to another man on a previous day, claiming that she and the accused had already done the same the previous evening.

However, is this really the same thing? This invitation to Vincent occurred *after* the alleged assault on Sandra by Matt. What relevance does it have to the possibility that she consented to what Matt did? Is it not equally explicable on the grounds of a sarcastic, shocked outburst by a victim who feels cheapened by what has happened to her? Perhaps that is the question for the jury.

Again, a marginal decision, but probably a permissible question to rebut Sandra's claim of 'modesty', as described in part (d) of the question.

Sandra's children

6-7 This question is completely and utterly irrelevant, and impermissible as the result of s 4(1), which prohibits any evidence being led in cases such as this regarding the complainant's previous sexual history. As indeed it should, since it is not even relevant to the issues arising in the case. It would be utterly in conflict with the spirit of the legislation to allow counsel to insinuate that, since Sandra is a single parent, then she must be morally 'loose'.

Sandra's claim of modesty

6-8 Very relevant and admissible, if Sandra has indeed attempted to set herself up as a lady of modest demeanour. There are obvious parallels here with *Holt* [1983] 2 Qd R 462, and the admission, against a victim who claimed to be of limited sexual experience, of evidence of her prior activities in a brothel.

Similarly here, Sandra's 'shameless' use of her nakedness to attract website 'hits' has become 'proper material for cross-examination as to credit' under s 4(2), since she has given evidence that can be demonstrated to be untrue. But such evidence goes only to *her credit as a witness*, and the mere fact that she has behaved in this way is no more an implied invitation to assault her than her behaviour on the beach was. In particular, it does not make it any more — or less — likely that Matt committed the act alleged against him. Had Sandra not 'set up' her modesty in this way, then her previous internet activities would have been irrelevant.

Her claim of modesty is also inconsistent with her alleged behaviour with Vincent, considered in part (b); put the other way round, her behaviour with Vincent (and for that matter with Matt, prior to the alleged assault) may be admitted *on the issue of her credibility as a witness, but not directly in respect of the issues on trial*.

Examiner's Comments

6-9 Whichever jurisdiction you are in, the appropriate legislation has to be interpreted with discretion and sensitivity. The examiner will be looking for indications that you are able to apply the legislation in that way, and in particular that you can formulate the arguments *for and against* admission of each of the items.

Keep in Mind

- Being distracted from supplying a 'legal' answer by the strength of your views on the use of this type of evidence. When setting this type of question in the past, I have frequently been rewarded with long feminist diatribes on male attitudes towards women in general and sex offences in particular, which obviously earned their earnest authors no marks whatsoever.

- As usual, a failure to allocate time correctly between sections of the question.
- Failing to appreciate the significance of Sandra's assertion of modesty to the potential admissibility of the first two items of evidence. All Evidence scenarios should be answered *as a whole*, since some fact that appears in a later sub-question may well affect the admissibility of an earlier item.

Question 24

Pedro is charged with possession of cannabis, following the discovery of several 'joints' in his jacket pocket when he was searched by police following his arrest during a disturbance outside a nightclub. He instructs his solicitor that he did not have any joints in his jacket prior to his arrest, and that he can only conjecture that they were 'planted' on him by the officer who arrested him. He also tells his solicitor that this was his first encounter with police, and that he is shocked by their behaviour. The police brief in fact reveals that Pedro has a previous conviction for indecent exposure, which was dealt with by way of a letter pleading guilty, following which he was fined $100.

At his trial, his counsel objects to prosecution evidence being led regarding why Pedro was in police custody when the joints were discovered. Is counsel likely to succeed with this objection?

When Pedro gives evidence, he is asked in cross-examination, 'You say that these joints weren't in your pocket prior to your arrest — are you suggesting that the police planted them on you?' Pedro replies, 'All I'm saying is that I didn't have them before I was arrested'.

Pedro is then asked, 'Have you got a bad attitude towards police?', to which he replies, 'I'd never had any dealings with them before, so I hadn't formed any opinion'.

The prosecutor then seeks leave to adduce evidence of Pedro's previous conviction for indecent exposure. What ground(s) may be used to support that application, and, if it is successful, what would be the evidential effect of the previous conviction?

Time allowed: 15 mins

Answer Plan

There appear to be three separate issues arising from this scenario

(a) *The admissibility of the reason why Pedro was arrested*

Strictly speaking, this is 'propensity' evidence that will reveal to the court the fact that Pedro had allegedly been involved in a disturbance. This is potentially prejudicial. However, it may be part of the *res gestae*, and in any case it is better that the court be told precisely why Pedro had been detained, so as to avoid possible speculation that it may have been for something worse.

(b) Pedro's implied attack on police integrity

(c) Pedro's assertion that he had never been in trouble with the law before

Both of these could result in Pedro losing the statutory 'shield' that normally prevents the previous convictions of an accused being revealed to a court in which they are on trial for a new offence. However, it is arguable that Pedro took great care to avoid alleging police misconduct while asserting a legitimate defence. Also, Pedro did not claim to have no previous convictions, simply that he had not been involved with police before; on the other hand, can one be charged with *any* offence without at least being spoken to by a police officer?

The evidential effect of his previous conviction is simply to diminish his credibility as a witness; since his previous offence was not for dishonesty, this may not unduly detract from his credibility.

The answer below incorporates references to the Queensland legislation; students from other jurisdictions should incorporate their own.

 Answer

This question involves three separate issues.

(a) The admissibility of the reason why Pedro was arrested

6-10 In theory, the court may be prejudiced against Pedro by learning that he had been arrested for a disturbance outside a nightclub. As a general rule, the common law disallows such 'propensity' evidence for that reason, but it *may* be admitted when it is impossible to give the court the 'full picture' without disclosing previous bad behaviour on the part of the accused. The prosecution here will argue that Pedro's arrest is part of the *'res gestae'* of the case — that is, the very matters into which the court is enquiring. It has to be explained to the court why the police had a legitimate reason for searching Pedro (ie, that he was in custody), and part of that arguably involves what he was in custody for. It may be better for Pedro for the court to learn the real reason for his apprehension anyway, rather than let them speculate that it might have been for something much worse.

(b) Pedro's implied attack on police integrity

(c) Pedro's assertion that he had never been in trouble with the law before

6-11 In terms of the Evidence Act 1977 (Qld) s 15(2)(c), Pedro may have thrown away the 'shield' supplied to all accused persons from having their previous convictions revealed to the court, by (a) making 'imputations on the character' of a prosecution witness, and/or (b) giving evidence of 'his own good character'.

As to the first, it is generally accepted that the shield will only be lost where the implications in question are spurious, and unnecessary to the proper development of one's defence: *Phillips v R* (1985) 159 CLR 45. The only defence available to Pedro, on the facts we are given, is that he was not in possession of the joints prior to his arrest. He was also at pains to avoid claiming directly that they had been 'planted' on him, although that inference naturally arises from his defence. It will be a moot point for any appeal court should Pedro lose his shield on this ground.

The second ground is more promising for the prosecution. The clear implication of Pedro's assertion that he had no prior dealings with the police is that he has no prior convictions. This is not the case, and the court is entitled to learn that he has. However, this evidence may only be used, at common law anyway, in order to detract from Pedro's *credibility as a witness*, and cannot be used to infer that he is more likely to have been in possession of cannabis, to which a previous conviction for indecent exposure has no logical relevance anyway. Had his previous conviction been for perjury, or some offence of dishonesty, then of course it would have had more serious implications for Pedro's credibility as a witness.

 ## Examiner's Comments

6-12 The issues relating to Pedro's loss of his 'shield' should have been easy enough to spot, but the objection to the evidence regarding the reason for his arrest may have caused some students to nibble their pens for a moment. Only the better candidates would have identified and mentioned the counter-arguments in respect of each item of evidence.

 ## Keep in Mind

- Focusing only on the 'shield' issues, and either accidentally or deliberately overlooking the 'propensity' question, or not identifying it for what it was.
- Failing to argue both 'sides' of the arguments for and against admission in each case.

 ## Question 25

> Mary has brought a civil action against 'Stagecraft Pty Ltd', a firm specialising in staging outdoor concerts, and her former husband Mitch's employers. It is her 'case' that Mitch died as the result of poor equipment and system maintenance by Stagecraft, which led to his being electrocuted while working alone laying out extension power cables in a wet field late at night.
>
> The senior foreman for the defendant company, Alf, is available to give evidence that Mitch had been warned 'almost on a daily basis' against taking short cuts by connecting live cable extensions, contrary to the company's well-known safety policy of only turning the power on once all the connections had been made.
>
> Will Alf be allowed to give this evidence, and if so how may it be used?
>
> **Time allowed: 10 mins**

Answer Plan

It is sometimes overlooked that 'similar fact' or 'propensity' evidence can be both relevant and admissible in *civil* cases. The previous working, or other, habits of a person can become the only evidence available following an incident to which there are now no witnesses, employing the 'presumption of continuance' in an implied way to suggest that what the person in question is known to have done regularly in the past may be assumed, in the absence of evidence to the contrary, to have been what he or she was doing at the time in question. In *Joy v Phillips, Mills and Co Ltd* [1916] 1 KB 849 it was the habit of a stable boy to tease the horses, while in *Eichsteadt v Lahrs* [1960] Qd R 487 it was the habit of a cyclist to walk his cycle down a particular hill.

That is the issue highlighted in this case scenario.

Answer

6-13 'Similar fact' evidence — that is, evidence that a person has in the past exhibited a tendency to behave in a certain way — is admissible in civil cases even more readily than in criminal trials, in which there is always a risk that a court will convict an accused out of prejudice, rather than on the basis of the facts in the case, when they learn of his/her prior record.

In *Joy v Philips, Mills and Co*, for example, evidence was admitted, in a case concerned with the cause of death of a stable boy, of his habit of teasing the horses, while in *Eichsteadt v Lahrs* the court was told that a cyclist who had died in a road accident at the foot of a hill was in the habit of walking his cycle down that particular hill. In cases such as this, implied use is being made of the 'presumption of continuance', under which, in the absence of any rebutting evidence, it will be assumed that a person continued in the habit that he/she is shown to have followed.

In the present case, Mitch had been in the dangerous habit — contrary to instructions — of handling 'live' cables when rolling out extensions. The suggestion that he did so on the occasion now under scrutiny provides a perfect cause of death scenario, given the wet ground. Alf will therefore be allowed to give his evidence, and in the absence of any other explanation it is unlikely that Mary will discharge her burden of proof of showing that Mitch's death was due to some fault on the part of the defendant company.

Examiner's Comments

6-14 A 'gift' question if the student is aware of the application of 'propensity' reasoning to civil cases, but a morass of speculation if not. Students in the past who did not 'get it' have answered questions such as this on the basis of the relevance of the proffered evidence, with or without reference to the 'presumption of continuance', which is of course what 'propensity' evidence is based upon. They were rarely awarded more than half marks for their answers.

Keep in Mind

- Failing to apply 'similar fact' logic to the facts of the case.
- Failing to see the strong factual analogy with the *Joy* case.
- Failing to 'state the obvious' in relation to the 'presumption of continuity'.

Joining up the Dots

Refer to the section of the same name in Chapter 2 for the significance of this part of the chapter.

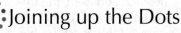

Question 26

Mark is charged with three separate acts of rape, on victims identified only as Miss X, Miss Y and Miss Z. The Crown alleges that each of them was attacked by Mark at around daybreak on a Sunday morning as they were jogging along the beach at Southspit. Each victim will testify that they saw a man whom they subsequently identified as Mark 'lurking' in the sand dunes near the Surf Life Saving Club, but did not apprehend any danger from him because he was wearing a hooded sweatshirt belonging to 'Southspit SLSC', and they assumed that he was a lifeguard. Each victim will further allege that as they ran back on the return 'leg' of their jog, Mark ran out of the dunes and raped them.

Advise on the following evidential issues that arise during the course of the trial.

(a) Mark's counsel, Greg, objects to all three charges being tried on the same indictment, and seeks 'separation' of the indictment counts, on the ground that 'My client will be unduly prejudiced by all three of these women telling the same story to the same jury.' Crown counsel Polly responds with the argument that 'Since there is a remarkable similarity between the allegations, in terms of time, place and modus operandi, the counts may be joined', because they 'form part of a series of offences of the same or similar character'. Argue *for and against* Greg's submission.

(b) Miss Y enters the witness box to give her evidence, and the first question she is asked by Crown counsel Polly is, 'On the morning you were raped, what was the weather like?' Defence counsel Greg leaps to his feet in protest and objects to the question. Is he correct?

(c) In cross-examination, defence counsel Greg asks Miss Y if she had any particular reason for noticing that her assailant was allegedly wearing a Southspit SLSC sweatshirt. She replies 'No, not really — I live away from the coast, and I'd never been to the Southspit beach before — I only remember the sweatshirt because of its distinctive logo of a surfer upside down in a barrel wave'. Defence counsel then seeks leave to cross-examine her to the effect that she has in the past been in a sexual relationship with at least three of the club committee members, and had been refused membership of the club because of her known promiscuity with surf lifesavers. Is he likely to be granted leave to pursue this line of questioning?

(d) Miss Z only came forward and made her complaint to the police after considerable publicity was given to the first two attacks by the local media, some two months after the date of the alleged attack on her. It is put to her in cross-examination by defence counsel Greg that she only made the allegation after legal advice to the effect that she could obtain Criminal Injuries Compensation for the attack on her, which she denies. When asked again, 'You're only doing this for the money, aren't you? You only complained of the rape two months after it allegedly happened', she replies, 'That's not true!' Greg then sits down without asking any further questions.

In re-examination, Crown counsel Polly asks her, 'You told my learned friend that it was not true that you first mentioned the attack on you two months after the event. Did you in fact tell anyone *before* that?' Defence counsel Greg objects to the question on the ground that it was not put to her during examination in chief, but the trial judge allows the question. Was this correct?

Miss Z's reply to the question is: 'I told my friend Ellie at work later that day, and she told me to call in the police, but I decided at that stage to let it go. It was only when I heard that other girls had suffered the same thing that I decided to come forward'. Crown counsel Polly seeks leave to call Ellie to testify to this conversation. Is she likely to succeed, and, if so, what will be its evidential effect?

(e) Towards the end of the Crown case, Crown counsel Polly seeks leave to call as an additional witness Dr Norah Bone, a partner in a local Sexual Health Clinic, to testify that, several days after the alleged attack on her, Miss Z consulted her in order to check that she had not contracted any sexually transmitted disease from the rape. Defence counsel Greg immediately objects, on the ground that 'It will add nothing to Miss Z's evidence, and it's of no obvious relevance to this case.' Is there any merit in this submission?

Assume that Dr Bone is allowed to give evidence, and is asked whether or not she examined a Miss Z on a certain date, and took various body samples from her. She replies, 'I see dozens of women every day, usually for the same thing. I can't be expected to remember every one of them months after the event. If you let me consult my records, I may be able to help you'. May she consult her records in the witness box, and, if she does, what evidential value will this have for the Crown's case?

Time allowed: 30 mins

Answer Plan

There are five questions to be answered in 30 minutes, and a degree in Higher Mathematics is not required in order to calculate that this allows six minutes per question. There is no indication that any question will attract higher marks than the others, and so your time should be equally divided between them. This does not allow a great deal of time for answering any one of them, but you may be able to avoid duplication of effort by utilising information supplied in answering one question when answering another. Also bear in mind that some matters require more detailed explanation than others.

You should also check carefully that nothing that 'comes out' in a later question affects the answer given to an earlier one.

Once again, the suggested answer that follows is based partly on Queensland legislation.

Answer

(a) ***This issue involves what is known as 'similar fact' evidence, which, in a criminal trial, is evidence that reveals that on some other occasion than the one on trial, the accused has committed an act, or acts, similar in nature to the one now alleged against him. It is obviously of considerable 'probative value' in the present case, but at the same time has the capacity to be unfairly prejudicial to the accused if used for the wrong reason***

6-15 That 'wrong' reason is to conclude, merely from the *fact* that the accused has offended on a previous occasion, that he is therefore more likely to be guilty on *this* occasion. This was described by Lord Hailsham in *Boardman v DPP* as 'forbidden reasoning', and over the years the courts have developed an alternative line of reasoning, under which, in a case such as this, there must be some 'striking similarity' between the previous behaviour and the behaviour now alleged before the evidence will be admitted. Under Australian common law, the test is that laid down by the High Court in *Pfennig*, namely that the similar fact evidence, taken together with all the other evidence in the case, leaves no hypothesis consistent with the accused's innocence.

This 'striking similarity', in the present case, appears to be that several complainants have come forward with the same apparently similar allegations against the accused — not only 'similar', but strikingly individualistic. In the present scenario we have the day of the week, the time of day, the clothing worn by the rapist, the location of the attacks, and the fact that each of the girls was raped only when she returned on the 'back leg' of her run. There are no *dis*similarities to offset against these, and the jury is likely to be very impressed with the fact that each of these victims tells precisely the same story, and identifies Mark as their assailant.

For that very reason, it is important to guard against 'collusion' — that is, a process whereby the girls have, consciously or unconsciously, been influenced by each other. However, under Queensland law, s 132A of the Evidence Act states that the possibility of collusion is merely a factor that the jury should take into account when deciding how much weight to attach to the evidence.

Section 567(1AA) of the Queensland Criminal Code states that the court, when assessing whether or not two or more 'counts' may be joined on the same indictment, on the basis that they '… are, or form part of, a series of offences of the same or similar character', may not have regard to the possibility that they may be 'the result of collusion or suggestion'.

The 'collusion' argument will most certainly not prevent the evidence being adduced, and defence counsel Greg can only argue that there is nothing particularly unique about the alleged behaviour of the offender; in short, that it is merely 'the stock in trade' of the average predatory rapist. This line of argument led to the High Court in *Phillips v R* (2006) 225 CLR 303 overturning a conviction in a Queensland sex offences case.

(b) ***Defence counsel Greg is perfectly correct, since this was a 'leading' question, which may be defined as one that either suggests the desired answer, or takes for granted something that has yet to be proved in evidence. These may not be asked of a witness 'in chief', and 'since this was the first question asked of Miss Y' the question clearly falls into the second category***

6-16 Even allowing for the fact that the weather may not be relevant, the order of questions might more properly have been (a) 'On the day in question, where were you and what were you doing?', (b) 'What was the weather like that day?', and (c) 'What, if anything, happened while you were jogging on the beach?'

(c) ***Section 4 of the* Criminal Law (Sexual Offences) Act 1978 *(Qld), which covers rape trials, imposes a general ban on questions put to a victim regarding their general sexual history. Such a question may not be put to a victim without judicial leave, and such leave will only be granted when (per subsection 3) it either has 'substantial relevance to the facts in issue', or it is 'proper matter for cross-examination as to credit'***

6-17 'Credit', in this context, is taken to mean 'credibility', and arguably Miss Y's assertion that she had never before been on Southspit beach can be proved to be a lie, given her previous history with the club and some of its members. The argument goes that, if she was lying about *that*, then she may be lying in other parts of her evidence. Additionally, it might be argued that she is trying to conceal the fact that she has a motive for 'getting back' at the club by fabricating a rape claim against someone she took to be one of its lifesavers; this constitutes 'bias' on her part, which on the authority of *Umanski* is an issue that may be pursued as an exception to the general ban on questions relating to 'collateral' issues, of which the 'credit' of a witness is one.

(d) ***There is a general rule that questions asked in re-examination must be restricted to issues that arose during cross-examination, and the corollary of that is that even though a question may not have been asked 'in chief', it may be asked if counsel for the other side raised it in 'cross'. This applies in particular to issues relating to the witness's credibility which could not have been asked in chief: R v Maiden and Petty (1988) 35 A Crim R 346. Greg raised the issue in cross-examination and Polly is entitled to deal with it, particularly since Greg did not allow the witness to give a full answer to his question***

6-18 Miss Z has been accused of a 'recent fabrication' of her evidence for financial reasons, and Crown counsel Polly is now entitled to rebut that allegation. Allegations of 'recent fabrication' are one of the exceptional situations at common law in which a witness can testify to having made a 'previous consistent statement', and when such evidence is led in rebuttal of a suggestion of recent fabrication, the effect of s 101(1)(b) of the Evidence Act 1977 (Qld) is that the evidence (in this case, the testimony of Ellie, who heard the complaint of Miss Z) is proof of its contents. In short, Ellie's evidence will be received as proof that Miss Z was raped.

(e) ***One may first of all question the relevance of Dr Bone's evidence, since we are not advised on the facts that Miss Z's consultation was said by her to have been following a rape. If not, then her consultation is equally consistent with her having engaged in consensual intercourse with someone, and not even Mark***

6-19 Assuming that Miss Z *did* complain to Dr Bone of having been raped, then Dr Bone's notes may be admissible as a 'fresh complaint' of rape by Miss Z (common law), or a 'preliminary complaint' of rape by her, permissible under s 4A of the Criminal Law (Sexual Offences) Act 1978 (Qld). In each case, it is not evidence that the rape actually occurred, but is admissible as evidence of Miss Z's consistency as a witness, which is another of the exceptional situations at common law in which a witness can testify to having made a 'previous consistent statement'.

So far as concerns Dr Bone 'refreshing' her memory from her consultation notes, the authority of *Gillespie v Steer* (1973) 6 SASR 200 is to the effect that when a witness such as a doctor or a police officer, who deals with many cases over a long period, has no actual memory of an individual case, but is prepared to testify to the accuracy of notes taken at the time, then those notes in effect become their 'memory'. So in this case, if

Dr Bone can confirm that she made her notes at the time of the consultation, and that she is sure that they are an accurate record of what was done and said, then she may consult them, and what is in them becomes her evidence of the truth of their contents.

Examiner's Comments

6-20 This is a comprehensive question, drawn from various sections of the previous chapters, and requiring a maximum number of words in a minimum period of time. Under this sort of pressure, students frequently omit answers to 'sub-questions' asked as part of a main question (eg, in part (d) of the above scenario, the question regarding whether or not Greg was correct in objecting to the question in re-examination not arising from cross-examination).

The examiner will be awarding marks for simple, economical but comprehensive answers to all the questions raised.

Keep in Mind

- As indicated above, a failure to answer every question, and every part of a question.
- Failing to 'spot the issue', and wasting time and words in attempting to 'fudge' the answer from first principles.
- Poor time management. You are more likely to get a higher mark for substantial answers to all questions (eg, $14 \times 5 = 70$) than for a well-answered question, three only partly-answered questions and a 'blank' (eg, $18 + (3 \times 9) + 0 = 45$).

Chapter 7

Hearsay

Key Issues

7-1 'Hearsay' evidence consists of a statement of fact offered to a court by a person who did not *themself* witness, or experience, what they are describing. For example, if A tells the court that he saw B hit C, that is A's 'original evidence' of what they saw. If, on the other hand, X attempts to tell the court that A told X that he saw B hit C, this is 'hearsay' evidence, since it is not something that X saw personally.

Some of the dangers of accepting hearsay evidence are obvious. For example, we are all aware of the inaccuracies that can creep into statements, however well-intentioned, that are passed from person to person. Secondly, the evidence of the person who actually witnessed the incident is not given on oath, and cannot be subjected to cross-examination. Nor can the 'demeanour' of the person giving the first-hand information be assessed.

For these, and other reasons, hearsay evidence is normally not admissible, in either civil or criminal cases, because it is *unreliable*. However, in many cases there was something in the circumstances in which the 'hearsay' statement was made which renders it more reliable than it may otherwise have been. Over the years, because of this additional reliability — and sometimes out of sheer necessity — the common law has come to recognised *exceptions to the hearsay rule*.

We therefore, at common law, have a '*hearsay rule*', and a growing list of *exceptions to the hearsay rule*. When it is acknowledged that almost every document, if offered as evidence of the truth of its contents, is 'hearsay' in nature, then the extent of both the rule itself, and the need for exceptions to it, can be appreciated. Documents (and their modern technical equivalents such as faxes, emails and text messages) are the standard currency of modern industry and commerce, and commercial litigation would grind to a halt almost overnight if an extensive range of documentary exceptions to the hearsay rule were not recognised by the courts. This recognition of documentary exceptions has, in the common law evidence jurisdictions, occurred almost exclusively through legislation, which varies from one jurisdiction to another. While reference is made in this chapter to the statutory exceptions in Queensland, you must ensure that you are familiar with your own, and can apply them when appropriate.

Before proceeding further, certain distinctions must be fully grasped. A statement is only hearsay when it is being offered *as evidence of the truth of its contents*. If, by contrast, the relevance of the statement is simply *the fact that it was made*, then this is not hearsay at all, and we call it *original evidence*. So, for example, the statement by Peter that 'I saw John beat his wife' must be given by Peter, and no-one else, if it is sought to prove that John did indeed beat his wife. But if John is suing Peter for defamation as the result of his assertion that John beat his wife, then it is *the fact that Peter said it* that one needs to prove, and the evidence of anyone who heard it said will suffice for that purpose. One of the leading cases to make this distinction, and one of the easiest to understand, is *Subramaniam v Public Prosecutor* [1956] 1 WLR 965.

Hearsay may take several forms other than an express statement. It may, for example, be *implied*, as for example when the emergency services receive a '000' call from an hysterical woman calling for police assistance, which is an implied statement by her that she feels herself to be in immediate danger (see *Ratten v R* [1972] AC 378). There can also be *hearsay by conduct*, a classic example of which is that of a person running away from a crime scene, the implied statement of fact being that they were responsible for the crime.

In this latter case, if the running away was witnessed by someone (A), then A may tell the court what they saw, and the guilty conscience of the person running away will be implied by the court using normal circumstantial logic. This process of reasoning has been expanded in cases in which, shortly before their death or other disappearance, A receives a telephone call from B while in the company of C. C can obviously only hear A's half of the conversation, but if A tells C who was on the other end of the line, or conducts their half of the conversation consistently with it being that person, then the court may receive C's evidence of what A said, or implied, about the identity of the caller, certainly as evidence that A *believed* the caller to be B, and possibly as evidence that it actually *was* B.

In *Walton v R* (1989) 166 CLR 283, the High Court extended the process even further, by admitting evidence of a person's expressed intention to meet with a certain person (in this case the accused) as evidence (by way of the 'presumption of continuance') that they later set out with that intention. The clear implication is that the person *did* meet the person they set out to meet, and if the maker of the statement was subsequently found murdered, and the person they set out to meet was the accused, the significance of that evidence is obvious. It must, however, be carefully distinguished from 'hearsay', which it is not (see also *R v Hytch* (2000) 114 A Crim R 573).

It is convenient at this point to list the major exceptions to the hearsay rule at common law. They are:

1. *Res gestae* statements (ie, statements made under the influence of the event they are describing, and which subsequently become

the events into which the court is enquiring): *R v Andrews* [1987] AC 281.

2. *Declarations by persons now deceased* that, when they were made, were against the 'pecuniary interests' of the maker, or were made in the course of a duty owed by the maker, or, in criminal homicide cases only, they were the 'dying declaration' of the maker as to their cause of death: *State of Western Australia v Montani* [2006] WASC 190.

3. *Statements made by a person regarding their health, fitness and mental state*, which are admissible as evidence of what they were experiencing at the time of the statement: *R v Perry (No 2)* (1981) 28 SASR 95.

4. *Statements made in previous proceedings* between the same parties: *Pallante v Stadiums Pty Ltd (No 2)* [1976] VR 363.

5. *Informal admissions.* This includes confessions by accused persons. Under the principle laid down by the High Court in *Edwards v R* (1993) 178 CLR 193, it can also include lies told by an accused.

As indicated above, there are also lengthy and detailed statutory provisions in each of the common law jurisdictions that allow the contents of documents to be admitted as exceptions to the hearsay rule when certain conditions are satisfied. They may be found in:

Evidence (Business Records) Interim Arrangements Act (NT) s 14;

Evidence Act 1977 (Qld), Pt 6 (ss 92–103);

Evidence Act 1929 (SA), Pts 5, 6, 6A (ss 46–59C);

Evidence Act 1906 (WA) ss 79C–79E.

Before tackling the questions below, please check that you are familiar with the following:

✓ the precise nature of hearsay evidence, and why it is generally inadmissible;

✓ the exceptions that exist to the hearsay rule at common law;

✓ the statutory provisions within your jurisdiction that permit the admission of documentary hearsay evidence.

Question 27

Paul, a medical student, is staggering home the worse for drink when he is mugged by Alfie, someone he recognises from his schooldays, and whom he last saw three years previously. A fierce struggle ensues for possession of Paul's mobile phone and wallet, during the course of which Alfie stabs Paul three times in the chest, grabs Paul's mobile phone and runs away.

The incident has been witnessed by Tracey, who knows Alfie by sight. She remembers Alfie from the days when she was a cheerleader for the school football team, in which Alfie was a star player, but she cannot recall ever seeing Paul before. She uses her mobile phone in order to contact the police and ambulance services, and she tells one of the police officers who arrives on the scene (Philip) that 'A guy who used to be in our school footy team — name of Alfie — knifed that guy (indicating Paul) in the chest and ran off with his mobile phone'. Phil records what Tracey says in his notebook, and communicates the information to his colleagues by radio.

While he is being loaded into the ambulance, Paul tells one of the paramedics (Maureen), 'You'll be lucky to get me to hospital in time — the grub got my left ventricle and it's pumping like mad. The guy who did it was Alfie Gordon — he lives above the bus station'.

Philip omitted to take Tracey's name and address, but still has his notebook entry of what she told him. Paul made a full recovery in due course, but now suffers from amnesia regarding how he finished up in hospital. However, as the result of what Paul told Maureen, Alfred Brian Gordon was arrested in his unit above the local bus station within an hour of the attack on Paul, and is now on trial for the attempted murder of Paul.

Is there any way in which the evidence of either Tracey or Paul may be used by the Crown?

Time allowed: 15 mins

Answer Plan

The question clearly asks for the admissibility of what appear to be the hearsay statements of two separate witnesses. It is therefore appropriate to begin with a general explanation of the nature of hearsay evidence, the hearsay rule and the existence of exceptions to it, and then to apply these principles to the proffered evidence of each 'witness' in turn.

(a) Nature of hearsay

Each of the crucial witnesses whose evidence the Crown is seeking to admit are, for different reasons, not available as witnesses to the events that they observed. Their evidence, if repeated by others, will therefore constitute 'hearsay'. It is therefore necessary, in each case, to identify some exception to the hearsay rule that would cover their evidence.

(b) Tracey's evidence

Tracey cannot be contacted because her name and address were not taken at the time. What she said to Philip cannot be covered under s 93 of the Evidence Act 1977 (Qld) as a statement supplied in the course of a 'trade or business' because police records are not classed as falling within either of these categories. Nor will it be covered by s 93B, because Tracey is neither dead nor unavailable for reasons of physical or mental illness. The best option is to attempt to classify it as part of the 'res gestae', but it is by no means certain that it qualifies.

(c) Paul's evidence

It is unclear whether or not the Queensland Ambulance Service would be classified as a 'trade or business', so as to permit Maureen to repeat what Paul said to her under s 93. However, given what appears to have been Paul's implied belief that he was likely to die, it could come within the 'dying declaration' exception to the hearsay rule. Alternatively, it may be argued to fall within the 'res gestae' of the case.

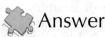 # Answer

(a) Hearsay evidence

7-2 Neither Tracey or Paul are now available to give direct evidence of their experiences, and if what each of them said at the time is to be narrated to the court by Phil and Maureen respectively, then it will constitute 'hearsay', which is, as a general rule, inadmissible under the 'hearsay rule' if it is sought to use the statement as evidence of the truth of its contents. However, there are many exceptions to that rule, both at common law and under statute, and in each case it may be possible to include the desired evidence under one of those exceptions.

(b) Tracey's evidence

7-3 The statement that Tracey gave to Philip was recorded in his notebook. However, it cannot be classified as 'information supplied' as part of the 'record of a trade or business' under the statutory exception to the hearsay rule supplied by s 93 of the Evidence Act because the Queensland Police are not considered to be a 'trade or business': *R v Eade* (1984) 14 A Crim R 186. Nor can Tracey's statement be brought within the provisions of s 93B of the Act, because the reason for her absence from the witness box is not one of death or serious mental or physical disability.

The best prospect for the Crown might be to have Tracey's evidence admitted under the common law 'res gestae' exception, which involves statements made at the time of the incident into which the court is now enquiring, which were so influenced by those events that there was neither the opportunity nor the desire to invent an untruth: *R v Andrews*. It may be argued that Tracey was still so traumatised by what she had seen that it was dominating her mind when she made her statement to Philip. It may be countered by any additional evidence that might cast doubt on the accuracy of what she was recalling (eg, the effect of shock, or her previous consumption of alcohol or drugs).

(c) Paul's evidence

7-4 Paul's statement regarding the identity of his attacker might also fall within the res gestae exception, since factually it is quite close to *Andrews*. However, we are told that he was under the influence of alcohol, and in *Andrews* this was identified as a possible ground for doubting the reliability of a res gestae utterance. Another alternative might be to have his statement admitted under s 93 of the Evidence Act, as information supplied as part of the records of a 'trade or business', if the Queensland Ambulance Service can be said to fall into this category.

But the strongest ground for admitting what Paul said to Maureen would be under the common law exception to the rule in the case of 'dying declarations'. This is limited to criminal homicide cases, and allows in statements made by a person who, at the time of making it, appeared to be in a state of 'settled, hopeless expectation of death': *R v Peel* (1860) 175 ER 941. It does not affect the operation of the exception if the person in question subsequently recovers, provided that at the time of the making of the statement they expected that they would die. This seems to fit the situation in which Paul found himself, given that he is a medical student, and that the condition that he described is frequently fatal unless treated almost immediately. Against the admission of this statement, it may again be argued that Paul was under the influence of alcohol, and that he had not seen Alfie for three years.

 ## Examiner's Comments

7-5 This is a straightforward question for students who have properly revised the hearsay rule and its exceptions. The examiner is looking for a crisp definition of 'hearsay', followed by a brief but accurate application of the exceptions to the rule that might apply in the factual scenarios created. It is also regarded as a 'better' answer if the student at least mentions other possible exceptions that might be thought to apply, and the reasons why they probably do not.

 ## Keep in Mind

- Attempting to answer the question if you are not confident regarding the exceptions to the hearsay rule, and the conditions that must be satisfied in respect of each of them. Even worse would be not even recognising that you are dealing with hearsay evidence.
- Diving straight into the answers to the specific applications without giving adequate background information regarding the rule and its exceptions.
- 'Tilting at windmills' regarding the exceptions that might apply. Analyse the facts you are given, and normally the likely exception will suggest itself (eg, Tracey is not dead or seriously ill, and Philip's notebook entry is not a 'trade or business' record. However, Tracey's statement was made shortly after the event it described, and might therefore qualify as a 'res gestae' statement).
- Wasting time by repeating the basic hearsay principles in answer to each part of the question. This is a common 'ploy' by students seeking to 'pad out' an inadequate answer, and does not impress the examiner. Deal with the issues common to both questions before you enter into a detailed answer to either of them.

Question 28

Sid is on trial for a burglary at the house then occupied by Phyllis, a pensioner for whom Sid did odd jobs around the house and garden. At the committal hearing, Phyllis testified that on the night in question, shortly after 1 am, she heard the sound of breaking glass from her kitchen, got out of bed and went into the kitchen, where she saw Sid in the process of climbing out through a broken kitchen window carrying her microwave. Phyllis had no difficulty in identifying Sid at the committal, but has since died, and will not be available as a witness at the trial. May the Crown use her evidence nevertheless?

Also in contention is the evidence of Bernard, a former employee of the government laboratory to which the police sent a sample of blood found under the window in Phyllis's kitchen, which Bernard 'matched' for DNA taken from Sid during the police investigation. Bernard subsequently retired, and was last heard of touring Canada in a camper van. He cannot be contacted, but the Crown still wish to use the DNA certificate that Bernard supplied. May they do so, and would their position be any easier if Bernard had died instead of retiring?

Time allowed: 20 mins

Answer Plan

The fact that 20 minutes has been allowed for this question should place the student on notice that it is not as straightforward as it may seem, and that a considerable degree of forethought may be required in answering it. Since the two witnesses who feature in the scenario are no longer available to testify at the trial, but the Crown wish to use their evidence, the 'answer' probably lies somewhere in the area of 'hearsay' evidence, and its many exceptions. The best approach to the answer is therefore a three-part one.

(a) The nature of hearsay evidence

The Crown is clearly seeking to use, as evidence of the truth of their contents, two items of evidence from 'witnesses' who will not be available in person at the trial. Since each item of evidence would therefore be 'hearsay' in nature, the Crown must find some exception to the hearsay rule under which to have it admitted.

(b) Phyllis's evidence

Although Phyllis is now dead, her evidence has already been given, on oath, in 'the same matter between the same parties'. The authority of *R v Thompson* [1982] 1 All E R 907 may be cited in support of the admission of the transcript of her previous testimony, under the common law exception to the hearsay rule relating to statements made in previous proceedings.

(c) Bernard's evidence

The most immediately obvious exception to the rule that might be held to apply to Bernard's evidence if he has simply retired is that supplied under s 93 of the Evidence Act 1977 (Qld), if it can be argued that the laboratory that employed Bernard was a 'trade or business' of which Bernard's report was a 'record'. Section 95A of the Act, which permits the use of a DNA certificate in evidence as proof of its contents, cannot be employed here, since Bernard cannot be called as a witness, as the section requires.

If Bernard is now dead, then s 93 may also be used, using a different 'ground' for the admission of his report. However, at common law it will also constitute a 'statement made by a person acting in the course of a duty' who has since died.

Answer

(a) The nature of hearsay evidence

7-6 Both items of evidence that the Crown is seeking to introduce constitute 'hearsay' if the makers of those statements are not called as witnesses, and it is sought to admit their statements, in their absence, as evidence of the truth of their contents. In order to be allowed to do so, the Crown must demonstrate that the challenged evidence in each case falls within one of the 'exceptions' to 'the hearsay rule'. In each case, they are likely to succeed.

(b) Phyllis's evidence

7-7 Fortunately for the Crown, Phyllis did not die without giving, on oath at the commital hearing, the evidence she would have given at the trial. Since the committal hearing and the trial are classified as 'proceedings between the same parties' (ie, the Crown and Sid), Phyllis's testimony falls not only within the common law exception to the hearsay rule that applies in such cases such as this, when the 'other party' has had an opportunity to cross-examine (*Pallante v Stadiums Pty Ltd* [1976] VR 363), but also under s 93(1)(b)(i) of the Evidence Act 1977 (Qld), because the transcript of the committal hearing is regarded in law as part of the 'records' of a 'trade or business', in respect of which Phyllis was the 'supplier of information'of which she may reasonably be supposed to have had personal knowledge.

In respect of the common law exception, there is a close factual analogy with *R v Thompson* [1982] 1 All E R 907, in which the elderly victim of a housebreaking and assault had given evidence identifying the offender at an aborted trial, and had died by the date of the new trial.

(c) Bernard's evidence

7-8 In the scenario in which Bernard is simply uncontactable, use may once again be made of the very versatile s 93. Provided that his DNA certificate can be classified as 'information supplied' that has become part of 'the records of a trade or business' which was compiled 'in the course of' that trade or business, then it is admissible under s 93(1)(b)(ii) or (iii). It cannot, however, be admitted under s 95A, which routinely allows in DNA certificates as evidence of their contents, because Bernard cannot be made available as a witness.

Even if Bernard is now dead, his certificate would still be admissible under s 93, but this time subsection (1)(b)(i). However, at common law it would *also* be admssible as the statement of a person now deceased who, at the time of its making, was under a 'duty' to make such a statement. This 'duty' may be one arising from a contract of employment, as Bernard's was.

However, even Bernard's death does not make his certificate admissible under s 95A.

Examiner's Comments

7-9 As with the previous question, the examiner is seeking a crisp but enlightening definition of 'hearsay', and an accurate identification of the possible exception(s) to the hearsay rule that might apply. Also, additional marks will be awarded for explanations of why certain other possible exceptions will not apply, in order to demonstrate that the student has thought the problem through.

Keep in Mind

- Failing to lay down the 'background' rules relating to 'hearsay', and simply jumping into the answers to each individual item.
- Not recognising the problem as one involving hearsay.
- Citing s 95A without appreciating that the analyst is required as a witness.
- Not considering possible alternatives. Simply because you have found one exception that works does not mean that there are no others that might, and you must mention them all.

Question 29

A 'class action' has been brought by a group of relatives of victims of a commuter train disaster in which 14 people died after a train, which was allegedly travelling too fast when it approached a curve, left the track and plunged down an embankment. Consider both the admissibility and the evidential significance of the following proposed items of evidence for the plaintiffs.

(a) The oral testimony of Paul, an ambulance officer who was in the process of 'stabilising' the badly injured guard (Joe), and had just administered a 'shot' of morphine to him when Joe said, 'I maybe should have applied the emergency brake, but I didn't think there was anything wrong, because I don't normally work this line'. Joe has since died, but Paul recorded what he remembered of the statement in his duty log at the end of the 12-hour operation to remove all the dead and injured from the wreck.

(b) The written log report of another ambulance officer, Jackie, who crawled into the driver's cab to administer what help she could to the comatose driver, Zoltan. She noted a half bottle of whisky in the top pocket of his uniform jacket, and the fact that he smelt strongly of whiskey. The bottle was smashed in the process of loosening Zoltan's clothing, and the remains of it were never found by either police or accident investigators. Jackie left the service a year later, and is believed to have emigrated to the UK, where all trace of her has been lost.

(c) The original statement of Kenneth, now aged 13, who was rescued largely uninjured from the front compartment of the wreck, and who immediately told PC Bill that he had seen the driver drinking from what looked to him like a whisky bottle when he (Kenneth) boarded the train at the last station before the crash, less than a kilometre from the crash scene. Bill recorded what Kenneth said in his notebook, and got Kenneth to sign it. Kenneth is prepared to give evidence, but due to post traumatic stress disorder (PTSD) is unable to recall anything between leaving home to catch the train and being discharged from hospital with minor injuries later the same day.

(d) The evidence of Margaret, an employee of the rail company (a government-owned commercial business) responsible for employee records, to the effect that two days after the crash, and the day before he died, Joe resigned from his job as a train driver. On medical grounds Joe was never allowed to be questioned about the accident before he died.

Time allowed: 40 mins

 Answer Plan

This is a longer question, with more time allowed for answers. All questions seem to relate to hearsay evidence, and exceptions to the hearsay rule seem to be available at both common law and under statute. The following plan suggests itself:

(a) General overview of the hearsay nature of the evidence

Inevitably, in 'disaster' cases such as this, the truth of what happened has to be constructed from bits and pieces that are still available, and will often be 'hearsay' in nature. Your answer should therefore begin with a general introduction regarding the problems associated with hearsay and the existence of many exceptions to the general exclusionary rule.

(b) Evidence from Paul's log

The 'statement' is essentially that of Joe, and it could at common law be a 'declaration against interest', or a 'declaration in the course of duty', but mention *The Henry Coxon* (1878) 3PD 156. Under statute, it might also qualify as part of the 'records of an undertaking', per s 92(1)(b) of the Evidence Act 1977.

(c) Evidence from Jackie's log

This cannot be admitted at common law under the 'declaration in the course of duty' exception because Jackie is not dead. However, it *can* come within the terms of s 92(1)(a) as a document created by a person who had personal knowledge of the facts within it.

(d) Kenneth's evidence

At common law, the only way Kenneth's evidence might be admitted would be as part of the 'res gestae'. Section 93A of the Evidence Act seems to be a possibility, but there will be problems about whether or not Kenneth is 'available as a witness', given his PTSD. If that fails, then it could come under s 92(1)(b), as part of the 'records' of the police, since they are classed as an 'undertaking' for s 92 purposes.

(e) Margaret's evidence

While the record of Joe's resignation might be admissible under s 93(1)(b), its only evidential significance would appear to be that, by resigning, Joe was making an 'implied admission by conduct' of his responsibility for the accident. However, this is capable of so many *other* interpretations as to be virtually worthless for that purpose.

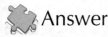 Answer

(a) The nature of the evidence

7-10 In cases of this type, the courts are required to reconstruct what happened from the recollections of those now dead, seriously traumatised, or simply repeating what someone else said. This makes it fertile ground for the use of 'hearsay' evidence, admitted under the various exceptions to the hearsay rule that exist both at common law and under statute.

(b) Evidence from Paul's log

7-11 The 'evidence' that comes from Paul's log is, in reality, evidence from Joe, to the effect that he failed to apply the brake. It is clearly 'hearsay', if offered as evidence of the *fact* that Joe did not apply the brake. But it may be allowed into evidence under the common law 'declaration against interest' exception to the hearsay rule, on the basis that Joe clearly exposed himself to discipline, and probably the loss of his job, by making the statement he did, and would hardly therefore have made it were it not true. This makes it more reliable than the average hearsay statement, and is admitted — partly out of sheer necessity — as one of the exceptional 'declarations by a deceased person'. The other conditions that have to be satisfied (namely that Joe had personal knowledge of what he was talking about, and realised that he was saying something against his own financial interests) appear to be satisfied.

Joe's statement might also qualify at common law under the exception to the hearsay rule known as a 'declaration in the course of duty', although it is not immediately obvious that Joe's duties would include talking about the cause of a train crash (unlike the mate of the vessel in *The Henry Coxon*, for whom making entries in the ship's log was all in a day's work). It might also, of course, be admissible at common law as an 'informal admission' (see (d) below) or as part of the 'res gestae'. It would be admissible in this latter category because it would seem that Joe made the statement under the psychological influence of what had just happened, and before he had time to invent any untruth.

Joe's statement would also be admissible in a civil case under the terms of s 92(1)(b) of the Evidence Act 1977, since it is now recorded in a 'document' (the duty log of the ambulance officer, Paul) which is part of the records of an 'undertaking', having been compiled from information supplied by someone who knew the facts (Joe), who is now deceased.

Under either common law or statute, the admission of the statement might, however, be challengeable on the ground of the length of time that lapsed between the incident and the entry in the log, the physical and mental state that Joe was in at the time when he made the statement, and the other calls that Paul had on his mind that day, which render it less likely that he could accurately recall Joe's precise words. Under the Evidence Act, this challenge might be brought under ss 94(1), 96, and 98. The weight to be attached to the statement in the circumstances can also be considered under s 102.

(c) Evidence from Jackie's log

7-12 The evidence that Jackie could have given, were she available, would have been crucial to the case. All that is left is her written log, which is 'hearsay' if it is offered simply as evidence of the facts that it records. Hence the importance of the log itself (which was of lesser importance in the previous instance, since the maker of the log entry — Paul — was available to give evidence, and the 'hearsay' in that instance did not consist of the log entry itself).

The closest common law exception to the hearsay rule to cover this item of evidence would have been that relating to a 'declaration made in the course of a duty'. The 'duty' was that of employment, and the log entry was made as part of the normal duties of an ambulance officer attending a victim. Jackie clearly had personal knowledge of the facts she was recording.

But a vital condition is missing for the admission of this document at common law — Jackie cannot be proved to be dead. The 'declaration in the course of a duty' exception *at common law* is one of those that only applies when the maker of the statement is dead, and it was to cover this sort of lacuna in the law that the Queensland Parliament enacted s 92(1)(a) of the Evidence Act, under which Jackie's statement would be admissible directly as a document created by a person who had personal knowledge of the facts, but who can no longer — with reasonable diligence — be located. This exception to the need to call her as a witness is found in s 92(2)(c).

Once again, there is a possible ground of challenge in the length of time that lapsed between the event and the entry in the log, and the accuracy of Jackie's powers of recall. All that was written above regarding ss 94, 96, 98 and 102 applies equally here, and indeed one could challenge the assumptions being drawn from the facts themselves. If the whisky bottle had already broken in the crash, this would account for the smell of liquor in the cab.

(d) Kenneth's evidence

7-13 There is only one possible common law exception to the hearsay rule to cover Kenneth's original statement, which he cannot now give as direct oral evidence because of his PTSD. This is the 'res gestae' exception, but it is unlikely that the amount of time that lapsed between the accident and Kenneth's statement would qualify as still within 'the agony of the moment' unless it may be argued that the trauma of the accident was so huge that it eliminated all possibility of original thought from Kenneth's head. Even then, he may have been in severe shock.

We therefore turn to the statutory provisions, and a possibility seems to emerge in the form of s 93A of the Evidence Act. Kenneth must have been under 16 when the accident occurred, and he therefore qualifies to have his statement admitted under s 93A, even though he is still alive, provided that certain other conditions are satisfied. Section 93A statements are normally associated with criminal cases, but the use of the phrase 'any proceeding' in the section renders such statements admissible also in civil cases such as this.

All but one of the conditions for the admission of a statement under s 93A are satisfied, since Kenneth was under 16 when he made the statement, had personal knowledge of its contents, made the statement soon after the events to which it related, and had it recorded in a 'document', namely the notebook of PC Bill.

The one condition that is *not* satisfied is that Kenneth is not 'available as a witness' in the sense meant by the wording of s 93A, which clearly implies that the witness actually *remembers* what was in the document, in order that they may be cross-examined. It is unlikely that the notebook entry will unlock Kenneth's memory, and therefore his statement may, arguably, not be adduced. There is, of course, the possibility of 'restoring' his memory, using the *Gillespie v Steer* argument. However, although there is conflicting authority in this area, logic suggests that there is no point in having a rule that regards a witness as having been 'called' when he or she was incapable of giving relevant evidence, and there is much one might wish to cross-examine Kenneth about regarding what he actually saw.

The plaintiff will therefore be likely to fall back, again, on s 92(1)(b) of the Evidence Act, which allows the admission of the statement on the grounds that it is part of the 'records' of an undertaking (the Queensland Police Service), and was compiled from information supplied by a person with personal knowledge of the facts who is not now able (by reason of 'mental condition') to give that evidence himself. The police service is regarded as an 'undertaking' for the purposes of s 92. It will of course be subject to the usual caveats of ss 94, 96, 98 and 102.

(e) Margaret's evidence

7-14 This appears to be an attempt to raise the possibility of an 'implied admission by conduct' in a civil case. The employee records are admissible evidence of the fact that Joe resigned when he did, perhaps under s 93(1)(b), but can they be used to imply that he felt in some way responsible for the accident?

Joe does not need to be dead before this exception applies, since it is based on the rationale that a person would not make even an informal admission (which is against interest) unless it were true. It is, to all intents and purposes, a species of circumstantial evidence, with the court making use of normal observed human behaviour, and assuming that Joe conforms to the norm.

It will be a matter for argument between counsel. The nearest case precedent we have is *Holloway v McFeeters* (1956) 94 CLR 470, in which the fact that a motorist failed to stop at the scene of an accident was taken as having impliedly admitted his liability for it. But the court must take careful note of any other possible explanation for the conduct. In this case, on a diet of morphine and still in shock, whatever belief Joe may have had in his liability for the accident may have been far from realistic.

In short, while the evidence might be technically admissible, its relevance is debatable.

Examiner's Comments

7-15 This is an exercise in writing comprehensively under time constraints and the pressure of examination conditions. In these circumstances, the temptation to 'cut corners' must be resisted, and the student must in particular guard against the urge to find a 'quick' answer to each section, and move on.

The examiner will be assessing not only the student's ability to 'pin the tail on the donkey', but also their capacity for taking on board alternative arguments, and subjecting their selected answer to detailed scrutiny. The successful answer will also demonstrate that the student has run a 'check list' of possible alternatives through their mind while seeking the answer.

Keep in Mind

- Selecting the first answer that comes into your head, without assessing *fully* whether your chosen exception to the hearsay rule ticks all the boxes.
- Failing to be honest regarding possible arguments *against* your chosen exception.
- Poor time management in answering the question, probably caused by blind panic when the sheer enormity of the question becomes increasingly obvious.

 Question 30

Amanda is suing the insurers of the other motorist in a road accident in which she was severely injured. Consider the admissibility of the following proposed items of evidence. In each case, identity the Queensland statutory provision that might be cited in order to justify its admission, and indicate what other sections of the same statute might affect either the admissibility of the item in question, or the weight to be attached to it.

(a) The report of Dr Proctor, a casualty surgeon employed in the A and E Department of the local hospital to which Amanda was taken following the accident. Amanda wishes to adduce Dr Proctor's report, which contains the assertion that she was close to death when first admitted. Dr Proctor is currently working in the USA, and counsel for the defendant (Alison) is objecting to his report being tendered in evidence without the possibility of his being cross-examined. At the same time, she wishes to call a witness (Fran) who worked as a casualty nurse in the same unit as Dr Proctor, and who will testify that he had a somewhat over-melodramatic approach to his work, and often exaggerated the extent of a casualty's injuries.

(b) The notebook entries of police constable Neil, who attended at the same road accident, and took statements from two eyewitnesses to the effect that 'the driver in the white Holden was to blame for the collision'. Unfortunately, Neil omitted to record any contact details for these witnesses, and he has since been invalided out of the force. A white Holden was the car being driven by Amanda at the time of the accident, and her counsel (Richard) objects to Neil's notebook entries being admitted: (a) because they are hearsay in the absence of Neil himself, (b) because they contain simply the 'opinions' of the motorists to whom he spoke, and (c) because the reason for Neil's retirement from the force on health grounds was his chronic alcoholism, including documented instances of his being drunk on duty.

Would your answer be any different if this were a criminal trial, and Amanda was charged with dangerous driving?

Time allowed: 20 mins

Answer Plan

Read the question carefully. There are two items of evidence, and each has to be assessed for its admissibility in *both* a civil *and* a criminal context. A certain amount of time and effort may be saved by dealing with each item *in each context*, before moving on.

(a) Dr Proctor's report

We are not told, but must assume, that the report is *written*. In the civil context, the statement will be admissible under s 92, either because Dr Proctor had personal knowledge of what he was recording, or as part of the records of an 'undertaking'; while in the criminal alternative, s 93 would cover the report, since hospital records are regarded as being those of a 'trade or business': *R v TJW* [1989] 1 Qd R 108. In both contexts, s 94 will cover the challenge to the report constituted by Fran's evidence.

(b) Neil's notebook entries

Once again, s 92 may be employed, bearing in mind that the evidence in question is that of *the witnesses who gave the information*, and not Neil, who simply recorded it. The police are regarded as an 'undertaking' for the purposes of s 92. Neil's alcoholism is a 'circumstance' from which inferences may be drawn regarding the accuracy of the record that Neil made, and can be dealt with under s 102.

The statements supplied by the witnesses may well be 'opinion' statements, which are inadmissible under s 92, unless the factual basis for the conclusion that the driver of the Holden was responsible for the accident is included within their statements.

In a criminal case, given that the police are not regarded as a 'trade or business' (*R v Eade* (1984) 14 A Crim R 186), Neil's notebook entries will not be regarded as admissible at all.

Answer

(a) Dr Proctor's report

7-16 It would seem that Dr Proctor's report (which one assumes is in written form) could be admitted as a document tendered in this, a civil case, under the provisions of, first of all, s 92(1)(a) of the Evidence Act 1977 (Qld) (since he had personal knowledge of what he was recording) and then either s 92(2)(b) (because he is out of the state and it is not 'reasonably practicable' to require his attendance at court), (d) (that he cannot reasonably be supposed to have any recollection of what is in the report) or even (f) (that undue delay or expense would be incurred in calling him as a witness) of the same Act. In each of these circumstances, the doctor himself need not be produced as a witness if the specified conditions are met. The prerequisite of s 92(1)(b) of the Act, that the document in question be part of a 'record' of an 'undertaking', also seems to be satisfied in the case of a hospital casualty surgeon's case notes.

Under subs (2)(b), the doctor need only be 'out of the state' in circumstances that make it 'not reasonably practicable' to secure his attendance. This may involve questions of the cost involved in bringing him back to Australia, or asking him to break some contractual agreement in the USA. However, these questions would then raise the possibility that he could be required to take part in a video-link with the court, from somewhere in the USA, which in the circumstances should not be difficult. Whether or not it *is* 'reasonably practicable' to secure his attendance is a matter for the trial judge, as also is the question of whether his evidence is sufficiently crucial to the case to order that he appear by video-link.

Subsection (d) allows Dr Proctor's report to be tendered in his absence from the witness box if, having regard to all the circumstances, he may not reasonably be supposed to have any recollection of the facts upon which it was based. There is an analogy argument here based on the decision in *Gillespie v Steer*, in which a similar doctor was allowed to 'refresh memory' for the same reason. If this can be established, then of course it weakens the argument that he should be available for cross-examination, when his memory is unlikely to be any better. This may be one of those occasions in which subs (3) of the Act is invoked, in order to receive an affidavit from the doctor to the effect that he has no memory of the events described in his report, but can vouch for its accuracy from the fact that he signed it.

The doctor's report would be equally admissible were the case a criminal one, since hospital records are regarded as being those of a 'trade or business': *R v TJW*. This being so, then s 93(1)(b)(ii) of the Evidence Act will allow the document into evidence as an exception to the hearsay rule because the doctor is out of the state, and it is not reasonably practicable to secure his attendance at court.

Whether the doctor's report is admitted under either s 92 or s 93, Fran's evidence will be admissible under s 94 of the Evidence Act, which states, in effect, that when, under either s 92 or s 93, a written statement is received as evidence of the truth of its contents in the absence of its maker, any evidence may be led which might have been led had that person been called as a witness, in order to challenge that person's credibility. The one condition precedent to that evidence being led is that the credibility evidence should not be of the 'collateral' variety, which could not have been pursued had the witness been called, and had they denied it. Given the tendency of our contemporary courts to allow the categories of permissible challenge to witness credibility to expand, this should not provide Alison with too much of a challenge.

There might, however, be a problem if Nurse Fran appears to be disagreeing with Dr Proctor's medical assessment, since protocol might suggest that he is the 'expert', and not her. However, experience also suggests that nurses are just as capable of assessing the extent of, and threat posed by, trauma injuries, and she will arguably be an 'expert through experience'.

(b) Neil's notebook entries

7-17 Once again, s 92 of the Evidence Act provides a valuable exception to the hearsay rule in the case of entries in a document (this time, Neil's notebook). What the witnesses told him is 'hearsay' if the contents of those notebook entries are employed as evidence of the truth of what was said, but, in terms of s 92(1)(b) of the Act, these were statements made by persons who may be presumed to have had personal knowledge of what was being recorded 'in the course of an undertaking'. The 'undertaking' in question is the Queensland Police Service, and the taking of witness statements occurred 'in the normal course' of that undertaking.

However, it will still be necessary for Alison to justify why the witnesses whose statements were recorded by Neil are not available, using one or more of the grounds specified in s 92(2), most likely (c), because they may no longer with reasonable diligence be identified. Even were Neil himself available, of course, this would not assist matters, since he is not the person who had the personal knowledge (the 'supplier of the information'), simply the maker of the record/statement.

The main issue with the *content* of those statements, at least as they are described in the question, is that they seem to take the form of 'opinion' evidence from the witnesses, whereas s 92(1) makes it clear that such statements must have been admissible had they been given in direct oral form, which 'opinion' evidence would not be. If, however, the statements give the factual bases for the conclusions drawn, then the facts may be adduced without the opinions.

The matter of Neil's alcoholism, and the reasons for his departure from the force, may be proved in terms of s 102 of the Act, which, in respect of any statement admitted under s 92, allows the court to have regard to any 'circumstance from which an inference can reasonably be drawn as to the accuracy or otherwise of the statement ...'. The alcoholism of the person recording it, and the known instances of his intoxication while on duty, may well fall into this category.

It would make the world of difference if the case were a criminal one, since s 93 of the Evidence Act, which deals with the admission of written statements in criminal cases, only covers such statements made in the records of a 'trade or business', which does not include the Queensland Police Service: *R v Eade*.

Examiner's Comments

7-18 This question not only called for a detailed application of those provisions of Pt 6 of the Evidence Act governing the admission of documentary hearsay statements, but also other provisions of Pt 6 that might be employed to resist their admission. The question also called for both processes to be followed in respect of the use of such statements in criminal cases. Students who failed to follow the instructions accompanying the question to the letter would have lost marks.

Keep in Mind

- Failing to follow the instructions.
- Poor time management. There were, effectively, four questions to be answered in 20 minutes, but as can be seen from the suggested answers given above, that time had to be allocated according to the complexity of each part. Careful advance reading of the *entire* question would indicate that the final question (ie, that of the admissibility of Neil's notebook entries) would be relatively short, allowing more time for the lengthier answer needed for the admissibility of the doctor's report.
- Failing to economise on time because of poor answer structure. Note how the suggested answer does not deal with the evidence of Fran until both aspects of the admissibility of the doctor's report have been dealt with, because it is common to both. Once again, this kind of saving can only come from a *thorough knowledge of the subject matter* and *careful prior reading of the entire question*.

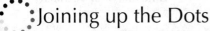 # Joining up the Dots

Refer to the section of the same name in Chapter 2 for the significance of this part of the chapter.

 # Question 31

Brian is on trial for the murder of Jim, a 72-year-old man who died in hospital from a stroke brought on by the stress of being mugged, the previous afternoon, at an ATM machine from which he had just withdrawn $400 in cash. Assume that the medical evidence linking the death to the mugging is unchallengeable. Consider the admissibility of the following items of evidence that the parties seek to tender at the murder trial.

(a) The oral evidence of PC Harry that when he attended the scene of the mugging, Jim was fully conscious and propped up against the bank wall, being attended to by ambulance officers. Jim told Harry that 'The bloke who attacked me had a very distinctive tattoo of a spider on his left hand. I'll easily be able to identify it again once I've been fixed up at the hospital'. Brian has such a tattoo, but his counsel objects to the use of this statement on the ground that 'The deceased knew my client, and a few days before the mugging he complained about my client riding his motorcycle past his house. He clearly had it in for my client'.

(b) The evidence of Detective Bruce, who had previous drug-related dealings with Brian, and brought him in for questioning as soon as he learned about the distinctive tattoo. Bruce will produce a videotaped record of interview in which, when first asked about the mugging, Brian claimed to have been on holiday in Cairns on the day in question. Following a break in questioning, the interview was resumed on the same tape, and Brian was informed that a telephone enquiry during the break had confirmed that Brian collected his prescription of methadone barely thirty minutes before the mugging, from a pharmacy he had never used before which was barely 200 metres from the ATM at which Jim was mugged. Brian replied, 'Bugger'. Brian's counsel is seeking to have the tape excluded from evidence because 'It is unduly prejudicial to my client, and his response has no evidential significance'.

(c) Unaware that the point is to be challenged, the Crown do not lead any evidence from the duty pharmacist who supplied the methadone. Brian elects not to give evidence, and his counsel then seeks leave to call Quentin, Brian's previous solicitor, who has in his possession a Statutory Declaration from Brian's brother Peter, to the effect that he was the person who collected Brian's methadone that day, using only Brian's non-photographic Medicare card as proof of identification. Peter is now in a mental hospital, severely retarded after a bad drug overdose. The Statutory Declaration pre-dates the overdose.

Time allowed: 40 mins

 Answer Plan

This is a criminal case, in which the admissibility of hearsay statements is restricted by statute, and is not as extensive as in civil cases. The following appear to be the issues:

(a) Jim's statement

Jim is now dead, but the statement he made related to his cause of death. However, it does not appear from the facts that he expected to die, so the 'dying declaration' exception at common law probably will not apply. Try s 93B of the Evidence Act 1977, which covers 'constructive murder' cases such as this.

(b) The interview tape

Brian has told what appears to have been a deliberate lie, conscious of the fact that his presence near the scene of the mugging could incriminate him. This lie may qualify as an implied admission of guilt, but the requirements of *Edwards v R* (1993) 178 CLR 193 need to be fulfilled.

(c) Peter's statutory declaration

Section 93B may be employed once again in order to accommodate Peter's statement, which is also an implied admission of guilt on his part to having committed a false pretence on the pharmacist. However, Brian's counsel omitted to mention this piece of evidence in cross-examination, and may fall foul of the rule in *Browne v Dunn* (see Chapter 5). By the same token, if the Crown seeks leave to re-open its case by leading the evidence of the pharmacist, it may be breaching the rule against the Crown 'splitting' its case: *R v Chin* (1985) 157 CLR 671.

Answer

This is a case of 'constructive murder'. It is therefore a criminal case, and we look to both the common law and the permissible exceptions to the hearsay rule for documents tendered in criminal cases for the answers.

(a) Jim's statement

7-19 Jim had no idea that he was going to die, and so the Crown cannot make use of the 'dying declaration' exception to the hearsay rule at common law, which requires a 'settled, hopeless expectation of death': *R v Peel*. Nor does it fit any of the other common law exceptions to the hearsay rule, except perhaps the 'res gestae' exception, given the extended definition of that exception supplied by the House of Lords in *Andrews*. But there is possible admissibility under s 93B of the Evidence Act 1977.

It is a case of homicide, Jim is obviously dead, and the statement he made was a 'representation' regarding an 'asserted fact' of which he had personal knowledge (ie, the description of his attacker). It was made shortly after the event to which it related, and is therefore potentially admissible under s 93B(2)(a), subject to the circumstances being proved that rendered it an unlikely fabrication.

However, it may be challenged for 'weight' on the ground that Jim had a motive for lying, and for that reason the trial judge may be expected to comply with any request by defence counsel under s 93C of the Act to warn the jury of the danger of accepting it, or giving it much weight. This will be because of Jim's potential — or alleged — bias. The trial judge might even be persuaded to exclude it altogether under s 98 'in the interests of justice', or to direct the jury in terms of s 102 to have regard to Jim's alleged bias when deciding how much weight to attach to his statement.

(b) The interview tape

7-20 We are dealing here with the evidential significance of lies as a potential implied admission of guilt, and the rule is that they are admissible provided that the trial judge gives the jury what has become known as an '*Edwards* direction' (*Edwards v R*).

This requires that the judge 'precisely identify' both the lie (that Brian was in Cairns on the day of the mugging) and the circumstances and events that are said to indicate that it constitutes an implied admission against his interest, namely that Brian appears to have been attempting to conceal the fact that he was only 200 metres away from the scene of the mugging 30 minutes beforehand, and that this was not a location from which he normally collected his methadone. This further implies that he knew where the mugging had taken place, and that his presence at the scene would therefore render him a suspect.

The judge must also formally instruct the jury that there may be other reasons than guilt of the mugging, for Brain's lie. Also, if the Crown are only using Brian's lie to cast doubts on his credibility as a witness, then the appropriate direction is a *Zoneff* direction.

(c) Peter's statutory declaration

7-21 The first question that must be asked is whether or not the admission of this late statement would infringe the rule in *Browne v Dunn*, which requires any party wishing to advance any factual assertion to give to the appropriate witnesses for the other side the opportunity to rebut that assertion.

It is arguable that it should have been put to Detective Bruce that the person who collected the methadone was not Brian; at least then the Crown would have realised, *before they closed their case*, that it might be a good idea to call the pharmacist to identify Brian, although a 'dock identification' is not the best form of identification. But at least it might have rebutted the suggestion that the pharmacist was in the habit of handing out methadone without photo-identification. The likely outcome of all this is that the Crown will be granted leave to re-open its case in order to allow the questions to be put to both Detective Bruce and the pharmacist.

There is also the counter-argument that to allow the Crown to call another witness, or re-call a previous one, after the close of its case, is allowing them to 'split their case' in the manner prohibited by the High Court in *Chin* (1985) 157 CLR 671 and *Soma* (2003) 212 CLR 299. This case may, however, be distinguished from *Soma*, in that whereas in *Soma* the re-opening of the Crown case was to the detriment of the accused, in this case it would not be, since it would allow him to recover from the breach of the rule in *Browne v Dunn* and lead evidence in his own defence regarding Peter's collection of the methadone instead of him.

The next question concerns the admissibility and evidential significance of the Statutory Declaration by Peter. At common law, it constitutes an informal admission by Peter that he was the one who collected the methadone. It *is* an admission, not of the murder, but of fraud against the pharmacist, and therefore it has some sort of status as an admission against 'penal interest'. However, that is not recognised under the common law exception to the hearsay rule (*obiter* in *Bannon v R* (1995) 185 CLR 1). But it may be a different story under statute.

Section 93 of the Evidence Act cannot be employed in this case, since it has no equivalent to s 92(1)(a) in civil cases, which allows in a 'first-hand hearsay' statement. But, since this is a murder trial, the defence may make use of s 93B of the Act. Peter made a 'representation' about an 'asserted fact' of which he had knowledge; he is now mentally incapable of testifying; and the statement was made against his interests at the time. For the purposes of s 93B, 'penal interest' *may be* recognised.

However, in the circumstances, it is subject to all the caveats and warnings against undue weight being attached to it as were referred to in (a) above, in relation to ss 93C, 98 and 102.

Examiner's Comments

7-22 This question not only tested the depth of the student's familiarity with all the exceptions to the hearsay rule, but it also contained the almost hidden 'trap' regarding the rule in *Browne v Dunn* and the *Chin* and *Soma* line of authority regarding the Crown 'splitting' its case. Students were also expected to identify, and deal with, the grounds upon which the admission of hearsay might be resisted, or lead to its reduced weight.

 ## Keep in Mind

- Failing to propery identify the appropriate exception to the hearsay rule, or to deal fully with the counter-arguments to admission.
- Failing to spot the issues of *Browne v Dunn* and *Chin* that had been worked into the question.
- Getting bogged down, deliberately or otherwise, in the side-issue of whether or not Jim really was biased against Brian. Students have been known to attempt to make their answer look longer by 'padding' it out with statements that begin with 'It may be that …'. Exam answers are assessed for their *content*, and not just their *length*.

Chapter 8

Opinion, Identification and Corroboration

Key Issues

8-1 The three seemingly separate issues dealt with in this chapter are in fact closely related, in that a consideration of each leads on to a consideration of the others.

Opinion evidence

8-2 In the same way that the desire of a court to hear only the factual evidence that can be given by each witness prevents a witness being allowed to give 'hearsay' evidence, a court is only interested in hearing from a witness the *facts* which that witness can relate, and not *the conclusions to be drawn from those facts*, since this is the ultimate function of the court. There is therefore a general rule at common law that excludes the 'opinion' evidence of any witness. To that rule there are two broad categories of exception:

1. *Opinion evidence of 'expert' witnesses.* If a person is an accredited 'expert' in some area (usually of science or technology) that is beyond the 'common knowledge' of the average judge or jury, then they may give the court the benefit of their *expert opinion*, in order that the court may more easily understand the facts upon which that opinion is based, and may more readily draw conclusions from those facts. However, the expert in question must be proved to be an expert, must be testifying within their area of expertise, and must not, when at all possible, appear to be deciding the 'ultimate issue' that the court is required to decide upon: *Makita (Australia) Pty Ltd v Sprowles* (2001) 52 NSWLR 705.

2. *Opinion evidence of non-expert witnesses.* In some cases, the only effective way in which a witness can convey what they experienced is to give evidence that is technically an opinion. This can often happen without the 'opinion' nature of the evidence being obvious, and the clearest example of that process occurs when a witness identifies an accused person as the one who committed the crime that the witness observed. A witness may also be 'qualified by experience' to give an opinion on a matter with which they are more familiar than most. An example would be a witness identifying the handwriting of a deceased relative: see also *Weal v Bottom* (1966) 40 ALJR 436.

Identification evidence

8-3 The process whereby a witness identifies something, or somebody, is fraught with hazard, given the inherent weakness of human recollection and the possibility of error. This hazard is most acute when the person being identified is an accused in a criminal case, not least because the witness may be convinced that their memory is accurate, and may therefore be all the more convincing.

Because of these potential hazards, the High Court, in *Domican v R* (1992) 66 ALJR 285, laid down a procedure for all trial judges to follow when directing juries on eyewitness identification of an accused. This led to the need for a '*Domican* direction' in all cases in which identification is a significant factor in the Crown's case against an accused. Additionally, in *Alexander v R* (1981) 145 CLR 395, the High Court considered the various forms that identification evidence may take, and ruled that the old-fashioned identity parade was still to be preferred, when feasible.

Corroboration

8-4 'Corroboration' is an item of evidence, independent of the evidence of the person whose testimony requires to be corroborated, which tends to *confirm* the evidence of that person. For example, in a criminal case it is evidence that tends to implicate the accused person in the commission of the crime: *R v Baskerville* [1916] 2 KB 658.

Most common law jurisdictions have now, by statute, repealed the need for corroboration in various situations in which it was previously required as a matter of *law* (see Evidence Act (NT) s 9C; Queensland Criminal Code s 632; Evidence Act 1906 (WA) ss 50, 106D), but in some cases corroboration may still be required as a matter of *practice*. In particular, convictions may be overturned on the ground of 'miscarriage of justice' if corroboration warnings are not given, as appropriate, in the following circumstances:

(a) in the course of a '*Domican* direction' (see above);

(b) as part of a '*McKinney* direction' in relation to an alleged 'verbal' confession (see Chapter 9);

(c) in cases in which one serving prisoner gives evidence that another serving prisoner confessed his guilt; see *Pollitt v R* (1992) 174 CLR 558;

(d) in cases in which a '*Longman* direction' is required. These are cases in which the defence has been prejudiced by some factor that prevented the accused from mounting an adequate defence. The most common of these cases in practice involve alleged sexual assaults committed many years ago, in which the passage of time has led to the defence being disadvantaged in rebutting specific allegations of fact.

Before tackling the questions below, please check that you are familiar with the following:

✓ the precise nature of 'opinion' evidence, and the reasons why it is not, as a general rule, admissible;

✓ the rules for the admissibility of (a) 'expert' opinion evidence, and (b) *some* 'lay' opinion evidence;

✓ the conditions laid down in *Domican v R* and *Alexander v R* for the admission of identification evidence;

✓ the circumstances in which corroboration of a witness's evidence is still sought.

 # Question 32

Carl is on trial for the 'home invasion' of the home now occupied by his former wife, Kim, and her new partner, Mitch, late one night. The Crown's case against Carl is that after standing on the front lawn of the house yelling abuse and demands for the door to be opened, Carl kicked in the front door to the house, armed with a hammer and with his face concealed by a balaclava, and, without another word, proceeded to smash a large quantity of fragile items in the lounge room of the house. At one point, Mitch attempted to grab hold of Carl, and in the process ripped off part of his shirt sleeve, which he was able to hand over to the police who were summoned as soon as Carl left, pulling off his balaclava once he got back behind the wheel of the car he had left parked at the side of the road outside the house.

Consider the admissibility of the following items of evidence that form part of the Crown's case against Carl.

(a) the evidence of Kim, who claims to have recognised Carl's voice as he yelled abuse from the garden;

(b) the evidence of Ethel, Kim's next door neighbour, who will assert that she looked out of her lounge room window when she heard all the commotion, and that she recognised Carl, when he removed his balaclava, as the person who called at Kim's house every other weekend in order to collect and return the children of the former marriage in accordance with the 'parenting agreement' reached at the time of the divorce;

(c) the evidence of Janice, a police scenes-of-crime officer who took possession of a shirt that police found in Carl's laundry basket, and who will testify that there was a piece missing from the shirt that matches exactly the piece retained by Mitch and handed to the police.

Time allowed: 15 mins

Answer Plan

The question clearly has to do with various means of identifying Carl as the person responsible for the home invasion. Identification evidence is notoriously unreliable, and when a particular identification is the main plank in the Crown's case against an accused, the trial judge may be required to issue a '*Domican* direction' to the jury, urging them to seek some corroborative evidence before relying upon it.

(a) Kim's evidence

Kim is arguably an 'expert by experience' in the sound of Carl's voice, and therefore well qualified to give her opinion that it was Carl who committed the invasion. Against this is the fact that the incident was one fraught with fear and other emotions which, by analogy with the facts of the *Domican* case itself, may make Kim's evidence less reliable. She may also 'have it in' for Carl.

(b) Ethel's evidence

Ethel's evidence is also subject to the same potential hazards as that of the witness in *Domican*, in that she only got a fleeting glimpse, in poor light, of a person whom she had only seen occasionally, this time through the windscreen of a car. There is also the possibility that her evidence has been 'tainted' by being told by Kim who the man was.

(c) Janice's evidence

Once Janice's credentials as an 'expert' have been established, she can advise the court of the 'match' between Carl's shirt and the piece retained by Mitch. The jury may then draw the circumstantial inference that it was Carl who was in the house. This may also, on the authority of *R v Clapson* [2004] QCA 488, be used as 'corroboration' of the identification evidence of both Ethel and Kim.

Answer

The Crown in this case is relying on three separate items of evidence that appear to identify Carl as the person responsible for the home invasion.

(a) Kim's evidence

8-5 Given that Carl is Kim's ex-husband, she may be classified as an 'expert by experience' of the sound of his voice, and that gives her identification of him as the offender greater reliability. This said, her evidence may be biased, and given the overpowering trauma of the situation it could be that she, albeitly innocently, imposed the voice of her ex husband on the true offender. The trial judge, in accordance with the High Court's strong ruling in *Domican*, may consider advising the jury to seek some corroborating evidence that the offender really was Carl before accepting Kim's evidence without question.

(b) Ethel's evidence

8-6 The circumstances under which Ethel claims to have been able to identify Carl were less than ideal, and in fact are very reminscent of those in *Domican* itself, being a fleeting glimpse of someone not known personally to the witness in conditions of semi-darkness. Ethel's only prior opportunity to observe Carl (upon which her 'opinion' comparisons have been made) was on occasions when he made brief visits to the house next door, when Ethel had neither the opportunity nor the motivation to study him carefully. Her sighting of the man responsible for the offence on the night in question was through a car windscreen some distance away in a no doubt darkened street. Ethel may seem confident when she gives her evidence, and she may genuinely believe that her identification is accurate, but these are precisely the circumstances in which a trial judge is required to give a *Domican* direction. This entails warning the jury of the dangers of identification evidence in general, and any aspects of the particular identification that give rise to concern, before urging them to seek corroborative evidence tending to confirm that identification before relying upon it.

Careful enquiry should also be made into the possibility that Ethel was told by Kim of who Kim suspected of being the intruder *before* she, Kim, gave her identification to the police. If there is any risk that this occurred, then Ethel's evidence should not be allowed to be used in corroboration of Kim's, and vice-versa, because it is not 'independent'.

(c) Janice's evidence

8-7 Before being allowed to give her evidence at all, Janice requires to be accredited as an 'expert' in forensic processes of the type she claims to have conducted on the shirt. Her evidence, if allowed in, then becomes 'expert opinion' evidence that will guide the jury when they come to compare Carl's shirt with the portion of it retained by Mitch.

If accepted by the jury, it is capable of constituting the very corroboration required by the identification evidence from Kim and Ethel, and the trial judge may direct them accordingly. This emerged in *Clapson*, in which a less-than-convincing eyewitness identification by an assault victim was allowed to be corroborated by evidence of a DNA 'match' between the DNA of the victim and blood found on the jeans worn by the accused during the assault.

Examiner's Comments

8-8 This is a straightforward question that should have easily been 'spotted' for what it was. The three components of the question may be simply answered on their own, and then combined at the end to demonstrate how 'expert' forensic evidence may be used as corroboration of identification.

Keep in Mind

- Not recognising that the first two questions involved the reliability of identification evidence, while the third focused on the use of 'expert' evidence.
- Failing to note how the evidence of Janice could be used as corroboration of the evidence of both Kim and Ethel, or the risk of allowing Kim's evidence to be corroborated by Ethel if there was any possibility of 'collusion' between them. It is these little 'refinements' that make the difference between a pass mark and a higher mark.
- Dwelling too long on the facts of the scenario *which should always be regarded as unchangeable*. Students will earn no extra marks — and will waste valuable time that could have been better employed — by advising the examiner how Kim may be determined to 'get back at' Carl, or even to amend the terms of his access to the children, by falsely accusing him. Likewise, the examiner does not wish to be advised that Ethel is a trouble-making busybody who should have been minding her own business. Nor does it need to be pointed out that the strength of the forensic evidence renders the identification evidence of Kim and Ethel almost superfluous.

 Question 33

In 1987, Alan Bradley and his older brother Adam were camping on a coastal island when they met up with a group of girls that included Simone Templeton. In the early hours of the morning, loud screams and protests were heard from the single tent that Simone was occupying, and as various campers rushed to her assistance she kept yelling 'I was almost raped by one of those guys I was talking to yesterday at the billabong!' The police were called, and Simone was transferred to the mainland, where she was attended by a police doctor, Eloise Harper. Simone told Eloise that she had been awoken by someone inside her sleeping bag who was attempting to remove her clothes, and that she struggled with the intruder, who eventually fled in the direction of the camper van that the Bradley brothers were occupying. In view of her allegations, various body samples and items of clothing were taken from Alan and Adam, but nothing more was heard of the matter for many years.

Adam Bradley was tragically killed in a car accident in 2005, but in 2010 Alan was informed that he was to be charged with the attempted rape of Simone Templeton in 1987. As the result of the introduction of DNA testing in the intervening years, police claim to have matched DNA extracted from a hair sample taken from Alan at the time of the assault with DNA from various items of evidence from inside the sleeping bag that Simone had been occupying. Alan's only recollection of the incident is that his brother Adam left their camper van that evening with the words 'One of those chicks has invited me over to her camp this evening, and with a bit of luck the excitement will be in tents'. As the shouting and screaming began a few minutes later, Adam returned, looking red in the face and flustered, with the words, 'Bitch! She thought that someone was coming, and started screaming rape!'.

Advise on the admissibility of the following items of evidence.

(a) The testimony of Eloise Harper, who has since retired from medical practice, but who has managed to obtain a copy of the medical notes she made at the time. She has only the vaguest recollection of examining Simone, but is prepared to base her evidence on the notes she took at the time, one of which was 'Patient trembling slightly and febrile. Demeanour consistent with sexual assault'.

(b) The testimony of Peter Parker, the laboratory technician who confirmed the DNA match between a sample labelled 'Extracted from sleeping bag at crime scene' and another labelled 'Hair sample from A Bradley'. Alan has offered to submit to a further DNA test to eliminate himself as the 'A Bradley' referred to in the report, but his counsel advises him that it is better to leave things as they are. Is she correct, and why?

(c) The evidence of Nicole Atkins, one of Simone's companions during the holiday, who will testify to Simone's distraught condition as she emerged from her tent, and her allegation that someone had attempted to rape her.

Prior to the trial judge's summing up to the jury, defence counsel reminds him, 'with respect', that 'There are clearly two warnings that your Honour must give them when they retire to consider their verdict'. To what is she referring?

Time allowed: 20 mins

Answer Plan

The two most obvious factors that leap out from this scenario are (a) the time lag since the alleged event, and (b) the fact that there were *two* men called 'A Bradley' from whom samples were taken. The first may well give rise to the need for a '*Longman* direction' (from *Longman v R* (1989) 64 ALJR 73), while the second rings a distant bell for those who are familiar with *R v Ryan* [2002] VSCA 176.

The need for a *Longman* warning is the first of the two warnings to which defence counsel is referring, while the second may well be the possible need for corroboration of Simone's claim of attempted rape. This is no longer required as a matter of law in Queensland (as the result of s 632 of its Criminal Code), but the jury must be warned against making too much of the evidence of either Eloise Harper or Nicole Atkins in support of the suggestion that what happened inside her tent was non-consensual.

These two themes require to be worked into the final answer, of which the following is a suggested outline.

(a) The need for a 'Longman' warning

Refer to *Longman* and other cases such as *Bromley v R* (1986) 161 CLR 315, *Tully v R* (2006) 231 ALR 712 and *Robinson v R* (1999) 197 CLR 162. It is not only the passage of time that can invoke a *Longman* warning, and there are other factors here that may be cited as well.

(b) The need for corroboration of Simone's allegations

No longer required by law, but may well be required in practice in a case such as this. Deal with the issue of 'self-corroboration', and cite *R v Meyer* [2007] VSCA 115. Dr Harper's evidence is subject to challenge on issue of 'expertise', and there is some doubt regarding whether the symptoms displayed by Simone were sufficiently 'independent' of her to constitute corroboration of her allegation.

(c) The evidence of Nicole Atkins

Of no evidential value once 'self-corroboration' by Simone is ruled out.

(d) The evidence of Eloise Harper

Her 'memory' may be reconstructed as per *Gillespie v Steer* (1973) 6 SASR 200, and she is a qualified 'expert' regarding matters of physical medicine. But Simone's 'demeanour' may be outside Eloise's area of expertise unless she can be proved to be 'expert by experience'.

(e) The evidence of Peter Parker

A classic example of an expert opinion being based on unsubstantiated facts. By analogy with *R v Ryan*, given that we do not know which 'A Bradley' the test sample was taken from, the expert evidence has no evidential value in proving Alan's guilt.

Answer

(a) The need for a 'Longman' warning

8-9 In *Longman*, it was held by the High Court that a jury should always be warned by a trial judge against convicting in a case in which a lengthy delay between the date of the alleged offence and the date of the trial has disadvantaged the accused's defence to the point at which there is a risk of a miscarriage of justice. In other cases such as *Bromley v R*, *Tully v R* and *Robinson v R*, the High Court has made it clear that it can be *any* factor that disadvantages the defence which can attract the need for a warning, and not just the passage of time. In this case, Alan has lost his only potential defence witness, Adam, who could have testified (a) that he was the one in the tent, and (b) that what occurred was consensual.

(b) The need for corroboration of Simone's allegations

8-10 While, as the result of s 632 of the Criminal Code (Qld), it is no longer required by *law* that the evidence of an alleged sexual offence victim be corroborated, it may well be required as a matter of *practice* in appropriate circumstances, such as those in *Robinson*. It is doubtful whether Simone's own apparently distressed condition will suffice as 'corroboration', since corroboration is normally something *independent* of the testimony of the person whose testimony requires to be corroborated, and 'self-corroboration' by a victim hardly falls within that category: *R v Meyer*. This is enough to negate any evidential value in the testimony of Nicole Atkins. So far as concerns the observations of Dr Harper, they are challengeable anyway, for the reasons which follow.

(c)   The evidence of Nicole Atkins

8-11   As indicated above, if all that Nicole's evidence consists of is the assertion that Simone was complaining of attempted rape, then it is of no evidential relevance, since Simone's 'self-corroboration' is not admissible.

(d)   The evidence of Eloise Harper

8-12   Although Eloise has no actual memory of her examination of Simone, her 'memory' may be reconstructed from her notes taken at the time, in accordance with the authority of *Gillespie v Steer*. However, while she was at the time well qualified, as a doctor of medicine, to describe any physical symptoms she may have noted, her reference to Simone's demeanour being consistent with that of a sexual assault victim may more properly belong in the field of psychiatry/psychology, in which we are not told she was qualified. The legal debate regarding the admissibility of her evidence on this point may focus on whether or not, as a police doctor who must have conducted many of these examinations in the past, she is 'qualified by experience'.

Even then, there is considerable doubt regarding the relevance of this aspect of Eloise's evidence, since its only value would have been in confirming Simone's apparent distress, which the defence will attempt to argue away as inadmissible 'self-corroboration' by Simone. However, there may be more of the necessary 'independence' in physical symptoms that are not easy to fake, and which may normally only be expected to be known by those who are medically qualified.

(e)   The evidence of Peter Parker

8-13   The evidence of Peter Parker suffers fatally from the most important failure of any 'expert' scientific evidence, namely that it cannot be linked factually to the Crown's case. There were two persons named 'A Bradley' staying in the camper van from whom samples were taken, and the label on the 'test' sample cannot now be proved to have been Alan's. We are not told that the 'reference' sample from the sleeping bag was retained, and so it may not be possible to compare it, now, with Alan's DNA. On the current state of the evidence, and by analogy with *R v Ryan*, a case with similar facts in which the DNA analyst had not been the person who took the original samples (which it is assumed Peter

Parker did not in the present case), the DNA 'match' has no relevance in the case, and cannot be used by the Crown, since it cannot be shown to have been Alan's.

Examiner's Comments

8-14   Apart from the obvious specific answers to the specific questions, the examiner will be looking to see if the student can match the parts to the whole, and show how the failure of each item of so-called evidence has the overall effect of depriving the Crown of any case. Also required will be reference to analogous or binding case-law.

Keep in Mind

- Failure to recognise that *Longman* warnings cover more than merely the passage of time.
- Poor answer structure. By setting up the need for corroboration at the outset, the question is more easily answered by reference to that need, and the natural structure of the answer suggests itself. Note how the evidence of Peter Parker was dealt with 'out of sequence' from the order in which the questions were posed, because the answers relating to the evidence of Nicole Atkins and Eloise Harper flowed more naturally from the *Longman* opening.

Question 34

> Christine is suing Border Line Coaches over the death of her husband, Rod, in a road accident at a remote location where two dirt roads met at an intersection. The 'impact' damage suggests that Rod was attempting to turn right onto the main road in his sedan car when it was hit by a fully laden coach travelling down the main road from his right. The bus driver, Cyril, remains so traumatised by the incident that he is unable, on medical advice, to give evidence.
>
> Consider the admissibility, and potential 'weight', of the following testimonies given at the trial.
>
> (a) The written report of David, a police accident investigator, who attended the scene of the impact and conducted all the standard tests. It is from him that the court learns that Rod was probably attempting to turn right when his car was hit by the bus. He is asked his opinion of who was to blame, and replies 'The impact damage was enormous. I reckon that the bus was travelling well over the 70 kilometres per hour speed limit when it hit the car, and that the car driver had no chance to avoid the impact'. Defence counsel leaps to his feet and demands that the question and answer be deleted from the court transcript. Is he correct, and what legal grounds might he have for making this request?

(b) The defendant calls Mike, a pharmacist, who testifies that 'Flu-Buys' is a patented medicine that can be bought over the counter, and is intended for use by hay fever sufferers. He is then asked, 'If a person had consumed two of these tablets on top of two glasses of wine over lunch, what would be their likely condition an hour later?', to which he replies, 'They would be very drowsy and lethargic. It warns you on the packet not to mix the tablets with alcohol. I reckon the driver in this case would have been too slow to react to the sight of an oncoming bus travelling at speed.' The trial judge asks defence counsel, 'Please explain to me why I should take any notice of this evidence'.

What might her concerns be?

Time allowed: 15 mins

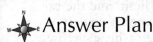 Answer Plan

(a) Conditions for the admissibility of 'expert' evidence

The detailed answers that are to follow will be based on the basic conditions of admissibility of all 'expert opinion', which are that (a) the expert must have the necessary expertise (*Makita v Sprowles* (2002) 52 NSWLR 705), (b) their evidence must be related to that area of expertise, and must not wander from it into areas in which they are not 'expert' (*R v Darrington and McGauley* [1980] VR 353, but see *R v Fazio* (1997) 69 SASR 54), (c) their opinion should not, if at all possible, be allowed to be given in such a way as to decide the 'ultimate' issue before the court (but see *Murphy v R* (1989) 167 CLR 94), and (d) the expert opinion should be based upon *proven fact* (*Farrell v R* (1998) 194 CLR 286).

The two items of evidence in this case seem to have each broken one or more of these rules.

(b) David's evidence

David's evidence may be objected to on the ground that it is deciding the 'ultimate' issue for the trial judge. It is also riddled with 'conjecture' regarding the speed of the bus and whether or not its approach should have been noted by Rod.

(c) Mike's evidence

There is, as yet, no evidence that Rod had either consumed the medicine or had two glasses of wine with his lunch. Mike has also 'overstepped the mark' by expressing an opinion on the liability for the accident.

 Answer

(a) Conditions for the admissibility of 'expert' evidence

8-15 Before the evidence of any so-called 'expert' witness will be decided as either admissible or relevant, certain conditions have to be met, and certain rules observed. The two items of evidence in this case have each transgressed more than one of these rules of admissibility.

(b) David's evidence

8-16 As an accredited crash expert, David may legitimately testify regarding matters that are within the recognised expertise that comes with this area (skid-mark length and direction, impact point etc.). On the whole, these consist of physical measurements and the conclusions that might be drawn from them, but David appears to have departed from that and ventured an opinion on the 'ultimate' issue of liability for the accident. While 'pre-impact speed' is a legitimate estimate from physical evidence (*McKay v Page and Sobloski* (1971) 2 SASR 117), it is stretching 'expertise' too far to go beyond 'the bus must have been travelling fast' to 'the bus was exceeding the speed limit, and the car driver would have had no chance'. This depends upon a variety of other factors well outside either David's knowledge or his expertise, and is no better than conjecture. An expert such as David should restrict himself to the facts he is able to give the court, and not the conclusions that may be drawn from them. Although a minority of the High Court in *Murphy v R* expressed the opinion that the rule against an expert testifying as to the 'ultimate issue' is no longer absolute, in this case it was not justified, and was potentially interfering with the course of justice.

(c) Mike's evidence

8-17 Mike, as a pharmacist, is qualified to give evidence regarding the side effect of proprietary medicines. He may even go on to explain that, if combined with alcohol, the medicine in question may cause drowsiness. *But we are not advised that there is any evidence yet before the court that Rod consumed either the 'Flu-Buys' or the wine.* Put more formally, there is no factual basis for the expert opinion that Mike has given, and this justifies the trial judge's question to counsel.

In *Farrell v R*, the High Court upheld the ruling of a trial judge that the evidence of a psychiatrist who gave a detailed explanation of the symptoms of various mental illnesses was of little assistance to the case when it was not then applied specifically to the witness whose evidence was under question. Similarly in this case, unless evidence is led that (a) Rod had taken the medicine, and (b) Rod had consumed two glasses of wine an hour earlier, Mike's evidence has no relevance to the case.

Even had those facts been proved in evidence, Mike was not entitled to go on and invite the trial judge to conclude that Rod would have been too drowsy to see the bus coming. The trial judge may ultimately conclude that, but this must be the *judge's* conclusion on the available facts, and not the opinion of an expert who is assuming unproven facts.

Examiner's Comments

8-18 This is a good example of a question in which the student was probably instinctively aware that there was something wrong with the evidence being offered, but may not have been able to articulate the reasons why. If you knew the subject area, the answers were relatively straightforward, and the examiner had not attempted to tangle the two items together.

Keep in Mind

- Giving only a generalised answer, unsupported by either legal principle or case law.
- Being tempted into the conclusion that 'It's the best evidence we're likely to get, so let's go with it'. It may have been the *only* evidence, but was it *safe* to rely on it?

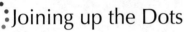

Joining up the Dots

Refer to the section of the same name in Chapter 2 for the significance of this part of the chapter.

Question 35

Julie is contesting the will of her late father, George, who died after falling down a flight of stairs at his home, where he normally lived alone, with regular visits from an 'Aged Care' nurse. There was no underlying health reason to account for his fall, which occurred during a visit from his son Barry, who was subsequently tried but acquitted of his father's murder.

The will that Julie is contesting was made five years before George's death, and in it George left everything to Barry, apparently under the belief that Julie had voted for 'The Greens' at the last election prior to the making of the will. Julie is contesting the will on the grounds: (a) that Barry murdered George; (b) that George was 'not in his right mind' when he made the will; and (c) that George had indicated an intention to revoke his will and leave everything to Julie.

Who bears the burdens of proof in all this, and what must they prove in order to discharge them?

At the hearing, Julie seeks leave to call, as a witness, George's solicitor, Graham, who is prepared to testify that George appeared to be irrational and obsessive regarding Julie's political loyalties when he gave the instructions regarding his will, which was the last will that Graham received any instructions for. May Graham give this evidence?

Julie has in her possession a handwritten note that arrived by post at Graham's office on the day after George's death, in which George appears to have written 'Changed my mind. Everything now goes to Julie', and nothing else. The note was undated, but Barry wishes to contest this item of evidence by testifying that the note is an crude attempt by Julie to forge George's handwriting, with which he — Barry — was very familiar. May he give this evidence?

Barry also proposes to ask his counsel to cross-examine George's 'Aged Care' nurse, Marie, to the effect that George had, in the few days prior to his death, begun to display signs of senile dementia. May he do so?

Time allowed: 30 mins

 ## Answer Plan

There are two separate groups of questions here: the first deals with burdens of proof, and the second with specific areas of identification and opinion evidence. They are best answered sequentially, in the order in which they have been asked.

(a) The burdens of proof

This is a civil case, and the burden of proof is on Julie to prove on 'the balance of probabilities' that George's original will had been revoked and replaced by one in her favour. Even though she is alleging that Barry murdered George, this is still the case, but *Briginshaw v Briginshaw* (1938) 60 CLR 336 applies. There is also a factual analogy with *Helton v Allen*, which adds that Barry's previous acquittal is of no evidential value either way.

The 'evidential burdens' in this case run with the legal burdens.

(b) Graham's evidence

There can be no question of 'legal professional privilege' applying, since Graham is simply being asked to recall matters that he himself observed: *National Crime Authority v S* (1991) 100 ALR 151. However, descriptions such as 'irrational' and 'obsessive' are *opinions*, and Graham may not be 'expert' enough to be allowed to express them.

(c) Barry's evidence

Barry may be regarded as an 'expert through experience' of his father's handwriting, but he obviously has much to gain by giving this evidence. But is he testifying about George's handwriting or Julie's? Cite *Duke v Duke* (1975) 12 SASR 106.

(d) Marie's evidence

Ordinarily, one would expect a medical expert to testify regarding senile dementia, but it might be arguable that, as a geriatric nurse, Marie has the necessary 'expertise through experience'.

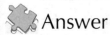 Answer

(a) The burdens of proof

8-19 Since Julie is alleging that the will was revoked by George's handwritten note, and replaced by a testamentary intention favourable to her, the burden of proof is on her, on the basis that 'He who asserts must prove'. If, at the end of the day, the judge is not satisfied that George had at least revoked his first will, in favour of Barry, then Julie must lose. The fact that Julie is accusing Barry of murdering George does not require an onus of proof any higher than 'a balance of probabilities', but, under the *Briginshaw* principle, Julie's evidence will need to be very persuasive in order to swing that balance her way. There is a factual analogy here with *Helton v Allen*, a Queensland case in which the High Court held that the burden of proof was still that on a balance of probabilities, and that the previous acquittal of the defendant had no evidential value for *either* party.

The 'evidential burdens' on the issues which go to prove that George had changed his mind rest with Julie, since she bears the legal burdens on those issues.

(b) Graham's evidence

8-20 Although Graham was George's solicitor, the information sought from him is not covered by 'legal professional privilege', since it does not relate to communications passing between the two of them, but simply Graham's observations of his client: *National Crime Authority v S* (1991) 100 ALR 151. However, given that what is being asked of Graham concerns matters of 'opinion' regarding George's mental state, then unless Graham may be said to be 'qualified by experience' regarding George's normal personality, it would seem that he must be disqualified from answering such questions unless he is also a psychologist or psychiatrist. Such questions are not the same as 'Did your client seem his usual cheery self?' or 'Did your client give the impression of being distracted by anything?'

(c) Barry's evidence

8-21 The question is ambiguous as to whether Barry is preparing to testify regarding George's handwriting or Julie's. However, in the circumstances he would seem to be 'qualified by experience' in respect of *both*. In *Duke v Duke*, it was confirmed that before this may occur, the witness must be very familiar with the handwriting in question, but this would not seem to be an obstacle in this case.

Barry will almost certainly be accused of 'bias' in his identification, since he has much to lose if George can be shown to have revoked the will in Barry's favour. Barry might therefore consider approaching Graham to give the same evidence, since his former client's handwriting is something he might be expected to be 'expert' in, and does not fall within the ambit of 'legal professional privilege'.

(d) Marie's evidence

8-22 At first glance, it would seem that Marie should not be asked these questions, because they are the 'expert' province of a geriatrician or a psychiatrist. However, if there is one other group of people who can be relied upon to be well acquainted with the symptoms of senile dementia, it is those who nurse the elderly, and Marie may therefore be considered to be 'qualified by experience' to comment on the suggestion that George was *exhibiting those symptoms*, which strictly speaking is not the same thing as testifying that he *was* suffering from it.

Examiner's Comments

8-23 This is a generous question, time-wise, provided that the student has prepared well for the exam, and does not spend too much valuable time 'spotting the issues'. Marks were there to be awarded for students who could identify and formulate counter-arguments, without getting bogged down in the 'What ifs?' This is meant to be an exam question, not a murder mystery.

The really 'switched on' students would have spotted the possibility of asking Graham to testify regarding George's handwriting.

Keep in Mind

- Being dissuaded from giving what you believe is the 'right' answer by the fact that so many of the answers seemed to focus on the same issue of 'expertise by experience'.
- Poor time management and answer structure.
- Failing to cite appropriate cases to support the legal statements made.

Chapter 9

Illegally Obtained Evidence

Key Issues

9-1 The courts have always looked askance at evidence that has been obtained by methods of which the law does not approve. Such 'illegally obtained evidence' is not automatically inadmissible. In each case the common law allows a trial judge a discretion as to whether or not to admit it. While the law is the same for both civil and criminal cases, it is primarily in criminal cases that a body of case law has developed, and a certain amount of statute enacted, to clarify the public policy approach to be taken to evidence obtained by tainted means.

In criminal cases, the common law precedents fall into two distinct groups.

1. The so-called 'Christie discretion'

9-2 In this group of cases, which derives its name from the English case of *R v Christie* [1914] AC 545, and was adopted into Australian law by the High Court in *R v Lee* (1950) 82 CLR 133, the concern of the courts is to prevent any unlawfully obtained evidence resulting in *unfairness to the accused*. Leading cases in this group are *Foster v R* (1993) 66 A Crim R 112 and *R v Davidson and Moyle; Ex parte Attorney-General (Qld)* [1996] 2 Qd R 505.

In another case in this group, *McKinney v R* (1991) 171 CLR 468, concern over the growing number of allegations by accused persons that they had been 'verballed' by police inventing fictitious confessions while they were in custody led to the High Court requiring that when such disputed confessions constitute a major element of the Crown's case against an accused, the jury should be directed to seek corroboration of the fact that such a confession was made.

In another development arising from concerns over alleged 'verbals', some jurisdictions have enacted legislation requiring police to record confessions, on pain of having them excluded from evidence if they are not: see Police Administration Act (NT) s 142; Police Powers and Responsibilities Act 2000 (Qld) ss 436–9; Summary Offences Act 1953 (SA) s 74D.

So far as concerns confessions obtained by means of covert recording, or 'pretext' conversations designed to secure an admission from a suspect, admissibility would seem to depend upon the extent to which the resulting admission or confession may be said to have been 'voluntary', reflecting the law's abhorrence of 'involuntary' confessions in breach of 'the right to silence' possessed by all criminal suspects and accused persons. This is more formally supported by the second group of cases, often referred to by reference to 'the *Ireland* discretion' that gave rise to this group.

The 'unfairness' discretion generally has found statutory form in Queensland, under the Evidence Act 1977 (Qld) s 130.

2. The so-called 'Ireland discretion'

9-3   This group of cases takes its title from the High Court ruling in *R v Ireland* (1970) 126 CLR 321, and is concerned *as a matter of public policy* to ensure that those who enforce the law obey it themselves. It penalises lapses in police and other official procedures designed to preserve the 'rights' of those under investigation, including 'the right to silence' (*R v Swaffield* 192 CLR 159; *Carr v State of Western Australia* [2006] WASCA 125) and the right to be dealt with in accordance to agreed statutory procedures: *Bunning v Cross* (1978) 141 CLR 54. The fact that the police have only obtained the evidence by themselves breaking the law can also play a significant role in the final decision to exclude that evidence: *Ridgeway v R* (1995) 185 CLR 19.

It is in this discretionary area that trial judges are often invited by defence counsel to disallow alleged confessions by accused persons because they were made 'involuntarily': *Cleland v R* (1982) 151 CLR 1. Historically, the law's antipathy to confessions obtained by 'threats or inducements' resulted in confessions thereby acquired being excluded even though they appeared to be reliable (in Queensland this exclusion is supported by legislation: see Criminal Law Amendment Act 1894 (Qld) s 10). However, in more recent years the emphasis seems to have reverted to a question of whether or not the confession is *reliable*: see *R v Long; Ex-parte Attorney-General (Qld)* (2003) 138 A Crim R 103; *R v Alice* [2006] VSCA 204.

One factor that at common law is regarded as significant in assessing whether or not a confession was made 'voluntarily' is whether or not the suspect was *cautioned* before making any statement to police. This caution is basically required to advise the suspect of their right to remain silent, and to advise them that anything which they say could later become an item of evidence at their trial. It is often found embedded in statutory provisions that prescribe the precise words that must be used when administering such a caution: see Police Powers and Responsibilities Act 2000 (Qld) s 431; Summary Offences Act 1953 (SA) s 79A; Police Administration Act (NT) s 140.

Before tackling the questions below, please check that you are familiar with the following:

✓ the discretion that trial judges may exercise with regard to the exclusion of illegally obtained evidence;

✓ the reasons why evidence may be held to have been 'illegally' obtained;

✓ the extent of an accused person's 'right to silence';

✓ the role played by the 'caution' in support of the right to silence;

✓ the meaning and extent of the terms 'threat or inducement' in the assessment of the voluntariness of any resulting confession.

 # Question 36

Max is on trial for the attempted rape of Janet, a fellow employee in the head office of a large national corporation, during an office party for all head office staff. Max's counsel is seeking to have excluded the terms of a conversation between Max and another colleague from the same firm, Dan, which came about in a somewhat unorthodox way.

Max was arrested in the early hours of the morning following the party, after a formal complaint was made to the police by Janet. Max was taken into custody and questioned, and his only response was: 'No idea who you're talking about. No further comment until I've seen a lawyer'. He was able to meet with the Legal Aid Duty Lawyer shortly before his appearance in court the following morning, and was then placed in a 'holding cell' in the courthouse awaiting his case being called. In the same cell was his work colleague Dan, who was charged with seriously assaulting a police officer on his way home from the same party, and in respect of whom the police were opposing bail.

According to Dan, when he asked Max why he was in custody, Max replied, 'You know Janet, that tasty little red-headed receptionist on the seventh floor? I thought she might be hot to trot after a few drinks, so I got her into the storage room, but she began screaming the place down when I tried it on, and here I am'. Dan traded this information to the police in return for their dropping their opposition to his bail, and the Crown intend to call Dan as a witness at the trial, in order to prove Max's initial lie about not knowing his alleged victim.

What line of argument may Max's counsel pursue, and is it likely to be successful?

Time allowed: 15 mins

Answer Plan

Dan's evidence could be damaging to Max's case, since his apparent lie about not knowing Janet could be used as an implied admission of guilt under the *Edwards* principle. The legal argument regarding its exclusion will focus upon whether or not it was 'voluntary', and/or whether it was unlawfully obtained by methods that should be discouraged as a breach of Max's 'right to silence'. Likely relevant authorities will be *R v Swaffield* 192 CLR 159 and *Carr v State of Western Australia* [2006] WASCA 125.

Swaffield has been distinguished in cases such as *R v Davidson and Moyle; Ex parte Attorney-General (Qld)* [1996] 2 Qd R 505 and *Tofilau v R* (2007) 231 CLR 396. It seems to make a difference if the person to whom the statement is made is regarded as an 'equal', and not a 'person in authority'.

Answer

9-4   One of the strongest principles of the common law of Evidence is the 'right to silence' possessed by a suspect or an accused in a criminal case. This right entitles them to choose whether or not to make any statement when questioned, and ordinarily the alleged confession of an accused will only be admissible in evidence when it proceeds from a free, unencumbered choice by them as to whether or not to speak: *Cleland v R.*

Closely aligned with this is the discretion given to trial judges to exclude confessions that have been obtained by means and processes that are not be encouraged (*R v Swaffield*), or that are likely to operate 'unfairly' against an accused: *Foster v R.*

The statement made by Max to Dan may be regarded as a 'confession', since, by contrast with the statement which Max initially gave to police about not knowing Janet, it may be regarded as an 'implied admission of guilt' by Max under the principle that emerged in *Edwards* regarding lies told by a suspect. Whether or not the evidence of Dan will be admitted therefore requires the circumstances in which Max made the statement to be assessed in the light of decided case law on the admissibility of confessions.

The facts of the instant case may be distinguished from those of *Swaffield* because although, in each case, the accused had already asserted his right to silence, in *Swaffield* it had been 'underhanded' behaviour by police that resulted in the confession that the High Court regarded as inadmissible because it came at 'too high a price', and should be rejected on the public policy ground of discouraging underhand police tactics. By contrast, in *R v Davidson and Moyle*, the Queensland Court of Appeal upheld the admission of a confession made by a suspect while he was serving another prison sentence, when that confession was made to a friend who was secretly tape-recording it for the police when he visited

Davidson in prison. Davidson had not previously claimed his right to silence, but the factor that seems to have been the most important was that Davidson had been speaking freely, without any pressure to do so, with a friend.

The 'absence of compulsion, threats and promises' was also the key factor in *Carr v State of Western Australia,* in which C, in the belief that he was not being recorded, made a confession of his guilt in a taunting manner to police officers who were escorting him to a cell, through an area of the police station in which audio-visual surveillance equipment was in operation. Even when the person to whom the suspect is speaking is an undercover police officer whom the suspect *believes* to be a friend, it is this 'volition' on the part of the suspect to speak that makes it admissible, as demonstrated by the High Court decision in the Victorian case of *Tofilau v R.*

Applying these principles and case authorities to the facts of the instant case, there is every reason to believe that any application to exclude Max's statement to Dan would be unsuccessful, since Max was speaking freely to a work colleague, and what he said was not the result of any threat or inducement to speak. However, under the principle that emerged in *Pollitt,* and by analogy with the suspicion with which 'jail-yard' confessions are regarded, the trial judge might be persuaded to warn the jury to seek some corroboration of Dan's evidence before accepting it. This may perhaps be no more than the fact that the cell custody records confirm that there was a period of time in which Max and Dan were confined together, during which Max could have made the statement alleged against him.

 ## Examiner's Comments

9-5 Not for the first time in this book, the comment may be made that 'You either knew the answer or you didn't'. If you did, then the question was straightforward enough, and the examiner would be looking for a clear, balanced exposition of the underlying law, and an intelligent application of it in respect of the growing trend towards considering whether or not the accused was speaking freely to an equal, or under pressure from the police. The reference to the possible need for a corroboration warning to the jury regarding the 'jail-yard' confession would be regarded as a bonus.

 ## Keep in Mind

- Not clearly expressing the underlying principles of law, and/or applying them to the facts.
- 'Waffling' through the answer without applying any law to it. Questions such as this have been known to draw forth paragraphs of moral outrage and academic indignation at the 'sneakiness' of modern police tactics, without recognising that (a) the police did

not arrange for the conversation to occur, and (b) even if they had, recent case law suggests that the resulting confession would still be admissible because it was given of the accused's free volition.

- Attempting to turn the question into one about 'confessions' in general, because this topic had been better revised than the one which the question entails. The examiner does not wish to be reminded that confessions are an exception to the hearsay rule. Even less do they require a moral monograph on the inadvisability of workplace liaisons.

Question 37

Kelly, a single parent, is charged with stealing various distinctive items of personal jewellery from women residents in the nursing home in which she was formerly employed as a domestic assistant. Various residents had complained of losing items, and, at the end of a particular shift, all the staff were searched. Kelly was found to be in possession of a gold charm bracelet belonging to one of the residents, and the police were called.

Kelly was briefly spoken to at her workplace by Detective Constable Brenda Murray before being transported to the local police station by car. During the car journey, Kelly told Brenda that she was a single parent, and that she had to collect her four-year-old daughter from the local child minding centre at 4 pm at the latest. 'Will I be released in time to do that?' she asked, and was told, 'Depends how soon you tell us what we need to hear.' This conversation was not recorded.

At the police station, Kelly took part in an electronically-recorded interview with Brenda, during the course of which Kelly became increasingly agitated as the time drew closer to 4 pm. At 10 minutes to 4, Kelly finally blurted out, 'Look, I know what you want to hear — I took all that stuff, and it's hidden in the stereo speakers in my lounge room. Here's my house keys — now can I go?'

Kelly was allowed to go, and police discovered over twenty items of stolen jewellery exactly where Kelly told them they would find them. At her trial, her counsel is seeking to have both Kelly's confession and the discovery of the stolen property excluded from evidence. Is she likely to be successful, and why?

Time allowed: 15 mins

 Answer Plan

There are essentially two questions here. The first concerns the admissibility of Kelly's confession, and the second — independent — question is the admissibility of the evidence relating to the finding of the stolen property.

(a) Kelly's confession

The police have been guilty of at least two breaches of the procedures required under common law when questioning a suspect, the second of which may be fatal to the admission of Kelly's confession. The first is the failure to record the conversation in the car (cite *McKinney v R* (1991) 171 CLR 468 and the Police Powers and Responsibilities Act 2000 (Qld) s 436), but since Kelly made no confession at that time, this is not likely to prove critical to the Crown's case. The second is the implied or 'adopted' inducement, which may be sufficient to have the confession ruled inadmissible.

(b) The discovery of the stolen property

Since Kelly handed over her house keys, the police did not need a search warrant in order to enter her house and find the stolen property. But since they only found the property as the result of a confession that was probably inadmissible, it constitutes 'the fruit of the poisoned tree'. The law states that although there may be no reference to the making of the confession, the Crown may 'lead' the fact that the property was found hidden in Kelly's house: see *R v N, GF* [2010] SASC 8.

 # Answer

There are two aspects of the police procedure in this case that have a bearing on whether or not the prosecution will be allowed, as a matter of law, to lead the evidence of both Kelly's confession and the finding of the stolen property where Kelly told the police they would find it. But the confession and the finding will be treated separately by the trial judge.

(a) Kelly's confession

9-6   The first breach by the police of the procedure that they are required to follow, where 'reasonably possible', was that they failed to record the conversation between Kelly and Brenda in the police car on the way to the police station. This is generally regarded at common law as the best procedure (*McKinney*), and under Queensland law is actually required by statute (*Police Powers and Responsibilities Act*, s 436). However, Kelly made no incriminating statement on the car journey, and if anything it is in the best interests of her defence for the jury to hear that she made police aware at that early stage of the fact that she was anxious to be released in order to collect her daughter from the child care centre. As a result, the defence are unlikely to object to evidence being led as to what was said in the car, and will probably cross-examine Brenda in order to bring it to the jury's attention.

This will establish that the police were aware of the psychological pressure on Kelly to be released, and took advantage of that in securing her confession at the police station by way of an 'adopted inducement' to confess. Under Queensland law (s 10 of the Criminal Law Amendment Act 1894 (Qld)), the existence of this inducement creates a 'rebuttable presumption' that the subsequent confession was thereby induced, which at common law is sufficient to give the trial judge a discretion to exclude it. On balance, it is not likely to be excluded, since the police did not instigate the inducement, although some might argue that they took cynical advantage of it, which is almost as bad.

(b) The discovery of the stolen property

9-7 Since Kelly handed over her house keys in an implied invitation to search her house, the police did not require a search warrant in order to enter and locate the stolen property where Kelly said they would. When evidence against an accused is discovered as the result of a confession that is by law inadmissible, that evidence is traditionally referred to as 'the fruit of the poisoned tree'. There is little case law on this point, but on balance it would seem that this evidence is independently admissible provided that no reference is made to the confession that led to its discovery (eg, the police witnesses may not even say 'As the result of something said by the accused, we searched her house and ...'). What *will* be admissible is evidence to the effect that 'We made a search of the accused's house, and we found ...'.

This independent admissibility of such evidence was confirmed fairly recently by the South Australian Supreme Court in *R v N, GF*.

Examiner's Comments

9-8 This was the sort of question that thoroughly tests the student's knowledge of the applicable law. It also catches out the 'sloppy' answer that does not deal with all the aspects of the question which call for mention.

Keep in Mind

- As already indicated, not pointing out that there are two separate aspects of the Crown evidence that might be open to challenge, but that they will be dealt with independently of each other.
- Overlooking the fact that it would have been better had Kelly's conversation with Brenda in the car been recorded, and failing to mention that in fact it will be *the defence* who will wish to use it, to establish the police's awareness of the pressure on Kelly to collect her daughter.
- Being unaware of the use to which 'the fruit of the poisoned tree' can be put, and its logical independence of any confession that may have revealed it.

Question 38

Police attend a domestic 'seige' situation following a telephone call from a man calling himself 'Brad', who claims to have shot dead his estranged wife's latest boyfriend, and to be holding his wife hostage in the former matrimonial home. Brad is obviously emotionally distraught, claims to have drunk almost an entire bottle of rum, and is threatening to shoot himself and his wife. The conversation with a police negotiator over the telephone, which in accordance with normal procedures is being recorded, continues for well over an hour, during which the negotiator can hear a female shouting for assistance, including the phrase 'Brad's drunk, he's crazy and he's going to kill me if you don't stop him! He's already shot Merv.'

While this conversation is going on, an armed police response team surrounds the house, and, using a loud hailer, demands that Brad give himself up. Eventually a shot is heard, and a man runs from the rear door of the house in an effort to evade police. He is brought to the ground by a police dog, and is 'tasered' in the small of the back by a police officer. Before passing out, he shouts, 'Just shoot me and get it over with — I shot Narelle, so you may as well shoot me'.

Assuming that Brad goes on trial charged with the double murder and pleads not guilty, may any of this evidence be used by the Crown?

Time allowed: 15 mins

Answer Plan

The facts should be vaguely familiar to Queensland students, since they are based on two recent cases from that jurisdiction that dealt with the circumstances in which confessions uttered in emotionally-fraught circumstances may still be admissible. The almost 'contemporaneous' description of the shooting of 'Merv' by the distraught female also revive memories of what happened in *R v Morrison* [2001] QCA 184.

The question may therefore best be tackled by reference to three areas of the law, which chronologically fall into two groups.

(a) The evidence of the telephone conversation and the first shooting

There are two potential items of evidence to prove that Brad shot Merv. The first is the hysterical evidence of the now-dead female, Brad's late wife Narelle. What she said about Brad having shot Merv is now 'hearsay', since she is dead, but what she said was close enough to what happened to qualify as part of the 'res gestae': cite *Ratten v R* [1972] AC 378 and *R v Morrison*.

Secondly, there is Brad's own confession, made over the telephone to the police. Assuming that there is no doubt that he was the maker of the call, then the analogy is with *R v Batchelor* [2003] QCA 246.

(b) The alleged second confession

Although Brad had been subjected to serious violence by the police immediately prior to confessing to having shot Narelle, it seems, on the authority of *R v Long; Ex-parte Attorney-General (Qld)* (2003) 138 A Crim R 103 that this is no bar to the admission of the resulting confession, provided that it may be regarded as 'reliable' in the circumstances. Distinguish between this and a 'dying declaration', which is restricted to statements made by *victims* regarding the cause of their death.

 Answer

The Crown are likely to wish to make use of three items of evidence arising from this scenario. The first two relate to the alleged murder of 'Merv', while the third involves Brad's alleged confession to the murder of Narelle.

(a) The evidence of the telephone conversation and the first shooting

9-9 The hysterical outburst from the woman whom the Crown will allege was Narelle is now 'hearsay' evidence, since Narelle is dead. However, it may be replayed to the jury by means of the tape-recorded telephone conversation under the exception to the hearsay rule that covers 'res gestae' statements, which are statements made under the dominating influence of the events to which they relate. There are strong analogies here to the facts in both *Ratten v R* and *R v Morrison*, in both of which similar uterances were admitted as evidence of the facts to which they related. In *Ratten* it was a call made to the police by an hysterical woman, pleading for their assistance, who was later found dead, which was used to prove that at the time of the making of the statement the caller felt herself threatened. In *Morrison* it was a murder that was heard as took place on the other end of a mobile telephone held by one of the victims, who had advised the other party that M had just entered the house, which was used as evidence of M's presence at the time of the murder.

Secondly, assuming that there is no dispute that the caller was Brad, the Crown may use the portion of the tape-recording in which Brad confessed to having murdered Merv, despite the fact that he was drunk and distraught, provided that the trial judge is persuaded that his confession was 'voluntary', in the sense that he made it of his own free will, and without 'threat or inducement' from the police. There is nothing in the facts to suggest otherwise, and the facts are closely analogous to those in *R v Batchelor*, in which it was held on appeal that the confession made over the telephone to a police negotiator was admissible because it appeared to be genuine, and in the circumstances it was not 'unfair' to the accused to admit it.

(b) The alleged second confession

9-10 While it might be thought that a confession of this sort (ie, Brad's confession to having shot Narelle), following as it does an act of serious violence by police, might be excluded as having been obtained by unacceptable means, this is not apparently the view currently taken by the law. This much emerged in the analogous case of *R v Long*, in which a fugitive on the run from police was tracked down, and shot twice in the chest before admitting his guilt of the crime for which he was being sought, apparently in the belief that he was dying. On appeal, it was held that not only was this confession 'reliable' in the circumstances (including L's belief in his impending death), but it was also not 'unfair' to admit that confession into evidence against him. No doubt in that case, as in this, it was significant that the violence was not inflicted in order to secure the confession.

This is, of course, not a common law 'dying declaration' exception to the hearsay rule, because this exception is restricted to statements made by *victims referring to the cause of their own impending death*.

Examiner's Comments

9-11 Once again, there is nothing challenging in this question to a student who has thoroughly revised the topic, and there is ample time allowed for a comprehensive but economical answer that refers to each of the legal principles that the facts of the scenario highlight.

Keep in Mind

- Failing to recognise the analogy with recent decided cases.
- Failing to deal with the scenario chronologically, which the facts suggest should be done.
- Opting for the 'obvious' answers that both confessions *should be* inadmissible because of the circumstances in which they were made, without reference to recent case law that suggests that 'reliability' has once again become a key factor.

Question 39

> Tony, aged 18, was a volunteer with a local charity called 'Hang the State Out to Dry', which was formed in order to assist recent flood victims rebuild their lives. Part of their activities involved collecting money in collection cans in local shopping malls, and Tony spent three weekends doing this until he fell under suspicion of having stolen from the charity when an empty collection tin was spotted in the boot of his car with its top prised off.

> Tony was asked to a meeting with the charity organisers, who had their Honorary Solicitor (Harry Markham) with them at the interview. Tony was asked to account for the empty can, and when his replies proved to be evasive, Harry Markham told him:
>
> 'Look, I represent kids like you all the time in court. The sentence is always less if people plead guilty as early as possible, so if you've got anything to tell us, tell us now, and then I can put in a good word with the magistrate.'
>
> Tony immediately admitted to stealing some $70 from the charity, but his new solicitor is seeking to have this confession deemed inadmissible. Is he likely to be successful?
>
> **Time allowed: 10 mins**

Answer Plan

Only one issue is raised by this scenario, and it is the possibility that Tony was 'induced' to confess by a person whom he believed was in 'a position of authority' over the case.

The issue will need to be argued both ways, and cited cases should include *McDermott v R* (1948) 76 CLR 501, *R v Kassulke* [2004] QCA 175 and *DPP v Toomalatai* (2006) 13 VR 319.

Answer

9-12 There is only one legal issue involved here, and it is that of whether or not Tony was 'induced' to confess by 'a person in authority' over the proceedings. In the leading case of *McDermott v R*, the Judicial Committee of the Privy Council emphasised that a confession cannot be regarded as 'voluntary' if it results from some 'hope of advantage' by confessing, which is 'held out' by 'a person in authority'. This covers not just police officers, but anyone who in the mind of the suspect could be in a position to 'make life easier' if they confess. In Queensland, this was recently extended, at least in theory, to a psychiatrist examining a patient whom the patient believed might be in a position to influence the bringing of charges: *R v Kassulke* [2004] QCA 175.

The first question is therefore whether Tony could be said to have 'reasonably believed' that Harry could influence what happened next if he 'made a clean breast of things'. In the circumstances this would not be an unreasonable belief on Tony's part, given his youth, but when one looks at what Harry actually *said*, the situation is not so clear. In classic 'inducement' cases, the inducement in question takes the form of dropping charges, allowing easy bail terms, reducing the charge(s) and so on. All that Harry said was that there was an advantage to be gained in terms of sentence if Tony entered an early guilty plea. This is nothing more than is pointed out to their clients by solicitors and counsel every day, and lies at the core of the controversy that surrounds so-called 'plea bargaining'. Had Harry said something along the lines of 'Be honest with us, and we'll see what we can do', that might have been different. As it was, the 'inducement' was not the prospect of charges being dropped in exchange for a confession, but a possible reduction in sentence by the ultimate sentencing court, over which Harry had no influence or control.

But it seems from cases like *Kassulke* that the approach of a trial judge will be from the standpoint of *what the accused actually believed*. In that case, there was no evidence given to the effect that K actually believed that the psychiatrist to whom he confessed could affect the outcome of proceedings, but the implication in the Court of Appeal judgments was that if there had been any evidence that K believed the psychiatrist to be someone in a position to affect the outcome of a criminal investigation, then this might have made a difference, and his confession might have been excluded. In *DPP v Toomalatai*, the Victorian Court of Appeal held that, because the 'independent person' who sat in on a police interview with the 16-year-old T was believed by T to be 'a person in authority', then in law he would be treated as such.

Tony is only 18, and he was no doubt in a highly nervous state when confronted, not only by the senior members of the charity, but also an experienced solicitor. It is conceivable that he did not reflect on what was actually being said, but responded instead to the apparently supportive *way* in which it was said. Even were he innocent, the facts looked ominous against him, and it is possible that Tony confessed to something he had not done because he was 'induced' to believe that it was in his best long-term interests to do so. If the court is convinced along these lines, Tony's confession *may* be excluded, primarily because there are grounds for doubting its reliability.

Examiner's Comments

9-13 In a question of this type, when there is only one 'issue' revealed by the facts, the examiner is testing the student's ability to argue *both* sides of a case, consider all relevant factors and reach a tentative conclusion regarding the likely outcome.

Keep in Mind

- The temptation with a question like this is to 'spot the issue', identify it and simply move on. As already indicated, the examiner is seeking to test the *depth* of the student's knowledge of the topic.
- Failure to argue *both sides* of the issue. While Harry, in this scenario, may not superficially *be* a 'person in authority', recent case-law suggests that the essential issue is whether or not the accused *reasonably thought that he was*. It is the effect on the accused that matters in such cases, because the 'inducement' principle is based in the desire to exclude *unreliable* confessions.

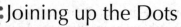

Joining up the Dots

Refer to the section of the same name in Chapter 2 for the significance of this part of the chapter.

Question 40

Bill and Ben are charged with an armed robbery in company on the 'Flowerpot Garden Centre'. The eyewitnesses to the robbery describe how two men — one considerably shorter than the other, and almost 'midget-sized' — held a shotgun to the head of Milly, the girl on the cash desk and forced her to open the till, making off with the contents, which included several 'Member Loyalty Discount Vouchers' that had been traded in during the day's business. Apart from Milly herself, the other two witnesses were Kerry, who was loading items onto a sales shelf in the centre of the sales area, and was able to observe events from behind, through a gap in the merchandise on the shelves, and Jim, one of the garden staff, who briefly saw the two men run to their car near the entrance to the garden centre, pulling off their disguise masks and throwing them on the ground.

Jim subsequently identified Bill and Ben from a photo-board, although he was incorrect in his memory of which of the two men was the 'midget'. Milly was too traumatised to identify anyone, while Kerry — who only saw events from behind — can recall only that one of the men was distinctly shorter than the other.

What difficulties might be encountered by the Crown in using this evidence?

Both Bill and Ben were immediately suspected by police, because they had previous convictions for armed robberies on garden centres and isolated refreshment kiosks in public parks. The first to be apprehended was Bill, the shorter of the two, who was grabbed by undercover officers as he left a local bar, and thrown into the back of a police 'drunk tank' containing three drunks who had been apprehended during a pub brawl down the road a few moments earlier, and who were continuing their hostilities in the back of the wagon. Bill, in fear of being seriously injured, hammered on the communicating panel to the driver's compartment and demanded to be let out of the wagon; the officer in charge of the wagon arranged to have Bill transferred to a separate vehicle only after he admitted that he had been one of the robbers of the Flowerpot Garden Centre.

Bill's counsel is seeking to have this so-called 'confession' excluded. On what grounds will he base this application?

Ben was brought into the same police station as Bill some 20 minutes after Bill had arrived, and the two men were placed in the same holding cell, in which covert surveillance equipment had been left running. In the conversation that followed, Ben told Bill that he intended to set up a false alibi for the day of the robbery. Ben duly 'fed' that alibi to his solicitor, and the Crown wishes to play to the trial jury the tape-recording of that conversation in the holding cell. May they do so?

During Ben's subsequent tape-recorded interview with police, he is told by Detective Chopper: 'You should do the smart thing like your pocket-sized friend Bill did. He coughed to the whole business, and he'll be getting a nice letter in a sealed envelope to the judge when it comes to his sentence'. Bill had in fact refused to take part in any interview with police. Ben immediately confesses to his part in the robbery. May this confession be used by the Crown at his trial?

During the trial itself, Bill is the first to give evidence on his own behalf, and claims that he was forced into carrying out the robbery because of his fear of Ben. In particular, he says, 'Ben's a mongrel, and on the last job he did, he left a bloke for dead. He's obviously a lot bigger than me, and I've got three kids'. May Ben's counsel now cross-examine Bill in respect of his three previous armed robbery convictions?

When Ben was arrested, police searched his house and found a bundle of Member Loyalty Discount Vouchers from the Flowerpot Garden Centre. Three of the original owners of these vouchers can testify that they had traded them in at the garden centre earlier on the day of the robbery. How might their testimony assist the Crown?

Time allowed: 40 mins

Answer Plan

There are several issues raised in this complex scenario, and some of them are connected. It is therefore *crucial* to an effective answer within the relatively short time limit to select a *critical path* through the issues in a logical order. One such order might be as follows:

(a) Bill's arrest and subsequent confession

It is arguable that Bill only confessed in order to get out of a situation of threatened violence. It may be disputed whether or not the police deliberately arranged things this way, but the 'bottom line' is that Bill's confession is less reliable because of the circumstances in which it was obtained; cite *R v Lee* (1950) 82 CLR 133 and Criminal Law Amendment Act 1894 (Qld) s 10, as well as *R v Ireland* (1970) 126 CLR 321. In the circumstances, his counsel may succeed in having it excluded from evidence.

(b) Ben's confession

One of the aspects of the police behavior in *Foster v R* (1993) 66 A Crim R 112 which led to F's confession being excluded was the fact that police had shown F (who was semi-literate) a piece of paper that they falsely claimed was his co-accused's confession. That was not the only bad behavior on their part, but the NSW Court of Appeal had no hesitation in rejecting the confession on *both* the 'unfairness' and 'public policy' grounds. Ben's counsel may use the analogy in order to seek the exclusion of Ben's confession.

(c) The covertly-recorded conversation between Bill and Ben

While public sentiment might regard this ruse as 'sneaky', there is plenty of case authority to suggest that the courts will admit recordings of conversations that contain confessions whenever they are satisfied that the confessor is talking 'freely', without any threat or inducement being applied; cite *R v Davidson and Moyle*; *Ex parte Attorney-General* [1996] 2 Qd R 505, *Carr v Western Australia* [2006] WASCA 125 and *R v Tofilau* (2003) 149 A Crim R 446.

(d) The identification evidence

The only witness who purports to be able to identify Bill and Ben as the robbers is Jim, and there is some doubt over the accuracy of his identification. This suggests the need for a '*Domican* direction' from the trial judge to the jury, warning them of the dangers of such evidence, and the need to seek some corroboration of it. This may come in the form of the vouchers found in Ben's possession, which by analogy with the DNA evidence in *R v Clapson* [2004] QCA 488 may be sufficient corroboration, since they appear to link Ben with the robbery that day. There is no such corroboration to assist in the identification of Bill, other than the somewhat tenuous one that he is much shorter than Ben.

(e) Bill's 'cut-throat' defence

Bill has 'given evidence against' Ben in terms of s 15(2)(d) of the Evidence Act 1977 (Qld). He has also 'cast imputations' on Ben's character in terms of s 15(2)(c), but the important subsection here is (2)(d), since under this one Ben's counsel does not require the 'leave' of the trial judge to cross-examine Bill in respect of his 'priors'. Such evidence goes not only against Bill *as a witness*, but also to his guilt, and the trial judge need not give the jury a 'propensity warning' to this effect; cite *Liu Mei Lin v R* (1989) 2 WLR 175 and Evidence Act 1929 (SA) s 18(1)(d)(iv).

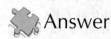 Answer

(a) Bill's arrest and subsequent confession

9-14   The circumstances in which Bill's confession was obtained were in direct violation of the basic principles laid down by the High Court in *R v Lee*, and to be found in statutory form for Queensland in s 10 of the Criminal Law Amendment Act 1894, namely that a confession will be presumed to have been obtained by 'threats' if it is preceded by actual or threatened violence, and will be inadmissible for that reason. It does not matter whether or not the police deliberately contrived to have Bill in effect locked up with a group of violent drunks by whom he felt threatened, because the logic behind the exclusion is that confessions obtained by such means are less likely to be reliable, and that it would be 'unfair' to admit them against the accused. To that may be added the sentiment exemplified by the High Court ruling in *R v Ireland* that confessions obtained by such means come at 'too high a price'.

Bill's counsel should experience little difficulty in having this confession excluded on either or both of these grounds.

(b) Ben's confession

9-15 The same concerns of 'unfairness' and the encouragement of unprincipled police practices may also result in the exclusion of Ben's confession, obtained as it was by the 'ruse' of pretending that Bill had confessed. This was one of the aspects of police behaviour in *Foster v R* that persuaded the NSW Court of Criminal Appeal to reject the confession in that case on *both* the 'unfairness' and 'public policy' grounds. Although there was more to the bad police behaviour in *Foster* than that displayed by Detective Chopper in the instant case, there is sufficient analogy for Ben's counsel to proceed with some confidence in his attempt to have Ben's confession excluded.

(c) The covertly-recorded conversation between Bill and Ben

9-16 While most non-lawyers would condemn this sort of 'underhanded' behaviour by police, the courts are required to uphold a law that takes a more lenient view of any evidence that appears to proceed 'voluntarily' from the mouth of a suspect. As the recent leading authorities of *R v Davidson and Moyle* and *R v Tofilau* demonstrate, 'voluntariness' is everything in cases such as this. Bill and Ben were talking as equals, and there is no reason to believe that what Ben said was the result of any 'threat or inducement' by either Bill or the police. It is therefore the more likely to be *reliable*, and, by analogy with *Carr v Western Australia*, the fact that Ben was being recorded within a police station without his knowledge will not serve to qualify his resulting statement as having been obtained at 'too high a price'.

(d) The identification evidence

9-17 While the evidence of Milly and Kerry will be useful to the Crown in describing what happened, the only eyewitness evidence which tends to identify Bill and Ben as the robbers is that of Jim, which took place in far from ideal circumstances. The analogy here is with *Domican*, in which the High Court laid down, in a similar case of alleged identification in difficult circumstances, that whenever identification is a 'significant' element of the Crown's case, the jury should be 'directed' by the trial judge of the dangers of identification evidence generally, and the particularly concerning factors of the instant case, before being directed to seek some form of corroboration of that identification. In *R v Clapson* it took the form of a DNA link between the accused and the victim, and in the present case the fact that Ben was found to be in possession of the Loyalty Vouchers tends to confirm that he was present as one of the robbers.

It is not, strictly speaking, any evidence in corroboration of the identification of Bill, however, and the mere fact that Bill is shorter than Ben is not likely to carry the Crown much further; the only evidence that would do that would be evidence that confirms Bill as the person in the company of the man (Ben) who *has* been identified as one of the robbers. Bill may in fact do that for the Crown in the next piece of evidence that has to be considered.

(e) Bill's 'cut-throat' defence

9-18 Whenever one accused seeks to save his own skin by placing some or all of the blame for a crime on a co-accused, this is referred to as a 'cut-throat' defence, and this is what Bill is attempting to do by pleading 'duress' or 'coercion', in effect admitting that both he and Ben were the ones who committed the robbery, but that he only did so out of fear of Ben. But those who employ cut-throat defences have to pay a heavy penalty.

Bill has opened the door to the disclosure of his own previous convictions for armed robbery. In terms of s 15(2)(d) of the Evidence Act 1977 in Queensland (and s 181)(d)(iv) of the Evidence Act 1929 in South Australia) he has 'given evidence' against his co-accused, Ben. Ben's counsel may now, *without the need to seek any judicial leave*, cross-examine Bill regarding his own previous convictions.

Whereas in other subsections of s 15, the evidence of Bill's 'priors' would be admissible only on the issue of his credibility as a witness, and the trial judge would be required to give to the jury a 'propensity' warning to the effect that they must not reason from the fact that Bill has done this sort of thing before that he is therefore more likely to have done it this time, the position is different under s 15(2)(d), in respect of which it seems that the evidence is admissible on proof of Bill's *guilt*: *Lie Mei Lin v R*. In evidential terms Bill has done himself a considerable disservice.

Examiner's Comments

9-19 This is a complex problem, in which the examiner will be assessing the student's ability to knit seamlessly together various different elements of the course syllabus that they have been studying.

Keep in Mind

- Panicking at the first sight of the variety and complexity of the issues that arise for consideration.
- Being 'psyched' into the belief that you must begin answering the question immediately in order to meet the time deadline, instead of spending a moment or two planning the 'order of play' of your answers. For example, a moment's reflection suggests that the evidence relating to the Loyalty Vouchers may supply the necessary corroboration of the eyewitness identification that will almost certainly be called for under the *Domican* direction.
- Failing to cite authorities for your submissions of law.

Chapter 10

The Final Hurdle

Key Issues

10-1 If you have successfully completed the first nine chapters of this book, you are probably half-ready for the final exam. Only 'half-ready', because you have yet to take on the challenge of a series of questions drawn from *the entire syllabus all at once*. This chapter is designed to prepare you for that challenge.

The following are a few examination 'tips' for you to follow. Just because everyone else has already given you all of these does not entitle you to ignore them.

1. Read the examination instructions *carefully*.
2. If time permits, *read the entire question thoroughly* before attempting to answer any part of it.
3. *Make a note* of places in which one question may be linked with another.
4. Let your brain *'ring bells'* if any question reminds you of a case you have studied, or a statutory provision with which you are familiar.
5. Always *answer every part of every question*, as per the examination instructions.
6. Allocate such time to each question as the exam paper indicates, either by a time allocation or a mark allocation.

In the questions that follow, specific reference has been made in places to Queensland legislation. Students from other jurisdictions should cite their own, where appropriate. Queensland case law may be cited regardless of where you are from, since it is a constituent part of Australian common law.

 ## Question 41

On Friday 27 June, at 9 am, a City Council employee discovered the body of 17-year-old Samantha Davies in the sand dunes at Brodies Point. She had been strangled, but there was no sign of sexual interference, and no DNA evidence. However, next to her body was a dead seagull with a length of red ribbon tied around its beak. A post-mortem examination revealed that Samantha had been two months pregnant. Time of death was certified as having been between 8.30 pm and 10.30 pm the previous evening (26 June), and 'cause of death' was given as manual strangulation.

Almost a year later, David Fletcher was convicted of Samantha's murder. He seeks your advice on the prospects for a successful appeal against conviction on the following grounds.

(a) The trial judge allowed in the testimony of Michelle Dixon, Samantha's best friend, in whom she confided all her secrets. Michelle told the court that Samantha had recently told her about a brief affair that she had conducted earlier in the year with Fletcher, a married man aged 30 who was a junior coach at her netball club, a relationship that she had been trying unsuccessfully to end. Samantha had also told her that she was pregnant to another man, Phil, whom she had been dating for the previous few months, and whom she wanted to marry.

On the afternoon of 26 June, she and Samantha had been out shopping when Samantha received a call on her mobile phone. Michelle heard Samantha say, 'Oh, hello David', and she (Michelle) formed the impression from the tone of Samantha's voice that she was not pleased to receive the call. She then heard Samantha say, 'Okay, I suppose so. Eight o'clock, but I can't stay long'.

After the call, Samantha said to Michelle, 'That was Fletch' (her name for Fletcher). She added, 'He wants me to meet him this evening at Brodies Point. I'm really going to have to tell him about Phil and the baby, and then perhaps he'll get the message. He scares me sometimes, though. Will you come with me?' Michelle declined, and that was the last time she saw Samantha alive.

(Allow 10 minutes)

(b) The trial judge also ruled as admissible the evidence of Maree Goodwin, a former girlfriend of Fletcher's, who had read a newspaper account of the bizarre circumstances in which Samantha's body had been found, and had immediately called the police.

In her evidence, she related how, when she had tried to end her four-month relationship with Fletcher, some seven years previously, she had been subjected to a campaign of terror in which dead pigeons with red ribbon tied around their beaks would appear in the most unlikely places, including her letterbox, her garden shed and even her office desk at work. Her brother and two of his rugby football team mates had visited Fletcher at home and threatened to break his legs if he left Maree any more dead pigeons. Fletcher said nothing in reply, but there were no more incidents involving dead pigeons.

(Allow 10 minutes)

(c) Also admitted after lengthy and unsuccessful legal argument by Fletcher's defence counsel was the written evidence of Brian Walters, who shortly before 9.30 pm on 26 June had been walking his dog along the beach adjacent to Brodies Point. He had heard a man and woman arguing, during the course of which the woman was heard to say, 'Phil's better at it than you anyway — being a sports coach doesn't mean you're any good in bed, Fletch'. He had then heard what he described as 'a gurgling noise', but had been unable to hear or observe anything further because his dog (a black Labrador) became involved in a fight with another dog (a Silky Terrier).

At the request of the police, Brian dictated, and subsequently signed, a sworn statement in relation to what he had heard. He had also been cross-examined by defence counsel at the committal hearing, but had made no change to his testimony. Brian was subsequently killed in a car crash, and at the trial the judge allowed Brian's sworn statement into evidence, despite protests by defence counsel that he would have wished to cross-examine Brian regarding a suggestion that his evidence was false, and was the result of the fact that his daughter's junior netball team had been beaten in the state finals by a team coached by David Fletcher. The trial judge offered defence counsel the opportunity to call other evidence to this effect, but he declined. The trial judge also refused to admit the transcript of Brian's testimony at committal, in which he also denied having invented his evidence, on the ground that 'It adds nothing to what is in the written statement'.

(Allow 12 minutes)

(d) Further evidence for the Crown came from Nancy Carter, the owner of a Silky Terrier dog that she had been exercising near the sand dunes at Brodies Point on the evening of 26 June ('sometime before 10', according to her evidence) when it became involved in a fight with a black Labrador that resulted in her dog being badly bitten on the neck. She had been so concerned about these injuries that she had telephoned her husband on her mobile phone, and asked him to collect both her and the dog in order that they might take the dog to the vet. While waiting for her husband to arrive, she sat on a bench near the entrance to the sand dunes, and saw a man running out of the sand dunes carrying what appeared to be a length of ribbon, which he stuffed hastily into his pocket when he became aware of Mrs Carter watching him.

When she reported what she had seen, in response to a request for assistance from the police, Nancy was invited to attend the local police station at her earliest convenience, in order to give a statement. While she was waiting in the front foyer for someone to come downstairs to meet her, she saw Fletcher through a window that looked out over the police station car-park, where he was getting out of an unmarked police car in which he had been brought in for questioning. Nancy immediately walked up to the enquiry desk in the foyer, pointed to Fletcher through the window, and said to the officer behind the desk, (PC Server): 'I don't know what he's doing here, but he's the man I saw at Brodies Point the night that girl was murdered'.

Nancy was allowed to repeat all this to the jury, and PC Server then gave evidence that Fletcher was the man pointed out by Nancy.

(Allow 15 minutes)

(e) A search of Fletcher's garbage bin by police scenes-of-crime officers two days after the murder yielded a length of red ribbon. Forensic tests confirmed that (a) the ribbon bore Fletcher's fingerprints, and (b) the cut end matched exactly one of the ends of the ribbon tied around the beak of the seagull left next to Samantha's body.

Fletcher chose not to give, or lead, any evidence. The summing-up to the trial jury by Poppin J contained the following passage:

> 'Only the accused could have told you how his fingerprints came to be on the remains of the ribbon which, it is not contested, was associated with the bizarre death of this unfortunate girl. He could have entered the witness box and told you how this came about, but he chose not to do so. He is entitled in law to take that course, but the Crown says that his fingerprints were on the ribbon because he was the person who tied it to the seagull's beak. In the absence of any alternative explanation from the prisoner, you may find that easier to believe than you might otherwise have done'.

(*Allow 12 minutes*)
Total time for examination question: 60 minutes

Answer Plan/tips towards recognising the 'issues'

(a) Michelle's evidence

These facts should ring the bell labeled '*Walton*'. They involve the giving of evidence regarding something said by a person who has since died regarding their intention to meet with the person now accused of killing them.

Begin by explaining that Michelle's evidence is strictly 'hearsay', and only admissible because the case authorities now permit the 'original' evidence of what Samantha actually *said* to be admitted as evidence of *what she went on to do*. Cite *Walton* and *Hytch*.

Also included within Michelle's testimony is the fact that Samantha was apprehensive of Fletcher's likely reaction when she ended their relationship, or at least told him of her pregnancy to another man. Cite *Matthews*.

(b) Maree's evidence

The behavior described is bizarre, and appears to have been connected with Fletcher on a prior occasion in circumstances from which one might conclude that it was him on *this* occasion. This suggests 'similar fact evidence', and the test in *Pfennig*.

There is a need to argue *both* sides of whether or not the behaviour is the same, given that there appear to be marginal differences. There is also an issue of whether or not the previous behaviour really *was* Fletcher's. Cite *HML*.

(c) Brian's evidence

Brian's evidence is of considerable 'circumstantial' value to the Crown, because it gives us an *implied* name for a person talking to a girl who may be *inferred* to have been Samantha, who referred to a man named 'Phil' and insulted the manhood of the person she was talking to. She called that person 'Fletch', which was her name for the accused (cite *Morrison* here), and shortly after the insult there was a 'gurgling' noise, which inferentially was the girl being strangled.

The main problem for the Crown is that Brian is now dead, so that the whole of his evidence is 'hearsay' if and when it is given to the court in the form of his sworn statement. The Crown must therefore justify its admission under one of the exceptions to the hearsay rule, of which the common law exception relating to evidence given in earlier proceedings on the same matter between the same parties (cite *Pallante v Stadiums Pty Ltd* and *Thompson*) and the statutory exception under s 93B suggest themselves (cite *Lester*).

Deal with the counter-arguments 'on the run'. Cite s 102(b) of the Act.

Note that Brian's evidence is given additional reliability by way of the corroboration from Nancy in the item that follows.

(d) Nancy's evidence

Nancy's evidence is also of circumstantial benefit to the Crown, since, apart from confirming the presence at the scene of a man who may be inferred to have been Brian, it links the man who, also by inference, may be taken to have been the one who strangled the girl with a positive identification of Fletcher. Not only that, but this same man appears to have been behaving 'guiltily' immediately after the 'gurgling' noise, which inferentially was the sound of Samantha being strangled.

The defence will obviously wish to challenge Nancy's identification, and it may do so:

(a) using the *Domican* argument that the trial judge should have warned the jury to look for corroboration before relying upon it (but cite *Clapson* for the possible corroborative effect of (i) the naming of the man as 'Fletch', and (ii) the finding of the ribbon in Fletcher's garbage bin);

(b) arguing that a formal identification parade would have been better than what transpired; cite *Alexander*, s 617 of the *PPRA* and *Burchielli*.

Note also that Nancy's evidence regarding Fletcher's alleged behavior was 'opinion', but that in the circumstances she was probably competent to give it; cite *Fryer v Gathercole*.

(e) The evidence of the ribbon

The ribbon is 'real' evidence, and in the circumstances Fletcher had a 'tactical burden' to overcome by explaining how the 'cut end' finished up in his dustbin. He did not, and this should bring to memory the *Weissensteiner* case. But it might be argued that Fletcher may not have been able to give any explanation, so cite *Peel*.

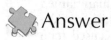 ## Answer

(a) Michelle's evidence

10-2 In strict law, evidence given by Michelle relating to what she was told by Samantha would be classed as 'hearsay', if offered as evidence of the *truth* of what Samantha said. Logically, it can only be offered as 'original evidence' of the fact that Samantha actually *said* it (*Subramaniam*). However, a series of superior court decisions have rendered such evidence admissible in order to suggest what the maker of that statement may have gone on to do.

Thus, in *Walton* it was held by the High Court that a statement by a person receiving a telephone call from a person they identified, either expressly or impliedly, and with whom they made an appointment to meet at a later time, could be received as original evidence of (a) the maker of the statement's belief regarding the identity of the person they had been speaking to, and (b) their intention, at the time of the making of the statement, of meeting with them at the designated time and place. The common law 'presumption of continuance' is then employed in order to infer that the maker of the statement subsequently acted in accordance with that intention, and at least set off to keep that appointment.

In *Hytch*, a minority of the Queensland Court of Appeal took this a stage further and admitted a statement by a girl who was subsequently assumed to have been murdered (her body has never been found) to a friend that she intended to meet with a boyfriend (Hytch) who was seeking to terminate their relationship, and that she intended to tell him (falsely) that she was pregnant in order to extort money from him, as evidence, not only that she kept that appointment, but also of the accused's motive for killing her.

In *Matthews*, the South Australian Court of Appeal admitted evidence of a statement by an estranged wife who had agreed to meet her husband as proof of the facts (a) that she was to meet him, and (b) that she was frightened of him and apprehensive of the meeting. It may therefore be argued in this case that Michelle's own observation of Samantha's lack of enthusiasm during her phone conversation with 'Fletch' is direct original evidence that she is competent to give because of her acquired 'expertise' in respect of Samantha's personality and moods.

Michelle's testimony was therefore admissible evidence that:

(i) Samantha intended to meet with the accused (known to her as 'Fletch') at Brodies Point at 8 pm on the night she died;

(ii) Samantha was not happy about having to meet with him, but intended to tell him about her pregnancy and her new affair;

(iii) Samantha was apprehensive of his likely reaction.

It would therefore seem that there are no grounds for appeal here.

(b) Maree's evidence

10-3 The similarity between the bizarre behaviour allegedly demonstrated by Fletcher on a prior occasion, and the behaviour of someone who may have been associated with Samantha's death, bring this item of evidence from Maree into the 'similar fact evidence' category. Basically, the issue is whether or not, despite its undoubtedly *prejudicial* nature, this evidence should be admitted because its *probative value* in shedding light on how Samantha may have met her death cannot in all logic and justice be ignored.

The test under Australian common law is now that laid down by the High Court in *Pfennig*, namely whether, when one adds together *all* the evidence (including the similar fact evidence), 'there is no reasonable view of the evidence consistent with the innocence of the accused'. If that is the case, then the similar fact evidence in effect adds 'the final nail to the coffin', and may be admitted.

There are two possible lines of argument in this case regarding whether or not Maree's evidence *should have been* admitted. The first relates to how 'similar' the two described behaviours are. It may be argued that a dead pigeon is not a dead seagull, but against that it may be argued that they are both birds, and that a seagull might be much easier to acquire on a beach than a pigeon. It may also be argued that whereas in Samantha's case the dead bird was part of a murder ritual, in Maree's case it was only part of a sadistic program of 'stalking'; against that it may be argued (a) that Maree may regard herself as fortunate that it never became fatal in her case, and (b) that both cases demonstrate Fletcher's bad reaction to rejection by a woman.

It also has to be assumed that whoever carried out the murder (Fletcher, on the Crown's 'theory of the case') attended the meeting with Samantha pre-armed with a length of red ribbon; either that, or it was a chance encounter by her with someone completely at random, who just happened to have a length of red ribbon handy, and had a penchant for killing birds. The inherent unlikelihood of this latter possibility is what makes this type of similar fact evidence admissible.

But the strongest argument *against* the admissibility of this evidence comes from the recent High Court ruling in *HML*, in which it was re-confirmed that before similar fact evidence may be employed, it must be proved 'beyond reasonable doubt' to have been behaviour *by the accused*. There is the 'coincidence' that the behaviour complained of by Maree ceased immediately after Fletcher was 'warned off' by her brother and his friends, but is that sufficient to prove beyond reasonable doubt that he was the one leaving the pigeons? Against this, once again, is the argument that if *was* purely coincidence, then Fletcher has been the very unlucky victim of the most unlikely series of events.

However, it would seem that there is a possible ground for appeal here.

(c) Brian's evidence

10-4   Brian's statement was of considerable value to the Crown's 'theory of the case', consisting as it did of the following potential pieces of 'concomitant' evidence:

(i)   That at around the time that Samantha died, a man named 'Fletch' was arguing with a woman in the sand dunes, and was being taunted with the information that someone called 'Phil' was better 'in bed' than he was. The use of the name 'Fletch' will be admissible for the same reason that the witness overhearing a fatal incident in *Morrison* was able to recount hearing the name 'Blocky', by which the accused in that case was known. In this case, however, it is only *implied* that the woman was speaking to 'Fletch'.

(ii)   This was followed by a 'gurgling noise' consistent with the girl being strangled.

Because Brian had since died, it was important to justify the admission of the evidence that he had left behind him (and which without his presence in the witness box would be 'hearsay') by way of one of the exceptions to the hearsay rule. There are at least two that might be appropriate:

1.   At common law, sworn evidence given in previous proceedings between the same parties, relating to substantially the same issues, is admissible in transcript form if the witness subsequently dies, provided that the party against whom it will now operate had the opportunity to cross-examine the witness at the time of that testimony: *Pallante v Stadiums Pty Ltd*. The most likely application of that principle in criminal cases arises, as here, between a committal hearing and the trial following that committal, and its validity in that context was confirmed in the English case of *Thompson*, while s 111 of the Justices Act confirms the admissibility of the committal transcript for that purpose. The trial judge was therefore incorrect in refusing to admit the full transcript of the committal hearing (which, in accordance with the rule in *Walker v Walker*, goes into evidence 'warts and all'), although Fletcher will have incurred no forensic disadvantage, given that at the committal hearing Brian denied, on oath, any bias on his part. There is therefore likely to be no ground of appeal on this point.

2.   Under s 93B of the Evidence Act 1977, a statement made in connection with certain 'prescribed' criminal proceedings (of which homicide is one) by a person now dead who had personal knowledge of what they were stating, is admissible provided that one of several conditions is satisfied. One of these is that the statement was made in circumstances making it highly probable that it is 'reliable'. Arguably, this is true of a sworn statement, and it certainly *is* true

of evidence given on oath and subject to cross-examination. In *Lester*, the Queensland Court of Appeal went a step further and ruled that even if a witness might be thought to have been initially biased in the statement that they gave, it is given added reliability if it is subsequently testified to without amendment at a committal hearing, which is precisely what happened in this case.

Defence counsel was certainly entitled to call rebutting evidence tending to show Brian's alleged bias, and this is confirmed in the case of any statement admitted under s 93B by s 102(b) of the same Act, which states that in estimating the 'weight' to be given to such a statement (ie, how persuasive it is), regard must be had to 'any incentive to conceal or misrepresent the facts' which the maker may have had. Had there been any evidence of bias, then the trial judge would have been required, on request from defence counsel, to warn the jury of it, but defence counsel in this case made the forensic decision not to lead any such evidence, and any possible ground of appeal is thereby blocked.

Whatever doubt may remain regarding the reliability of Brian's evidence that he was where he says he was (as opposed to doubts regarding his possible bias) are allayed by the fact that the next witness, Nancy, confirms the presence at the scene of a man with a black Labrador, who may be inferred to be Brian, but who should, at the committal hearing, have been asked by the Crown if he remembered his dog being involved in an incident with another dog, just to 'tie up the loose ends'.

(d) Nancy's evidence

10-5 Nancy's evidence fits the Crown's theory of the case perfectly, since it:

1. confirms the presence of Brian Walters, with his black Labrador, at or near the crime scene at the time he claimed to have been there;
2. places someone identified by Nancy as Fletcher in the dunes immediately after Brian heard what he did, displaying two 'circumstantial' indications of a guilty conscience, namely (i) the running away, and (ii) the attempt to hide the ribbon, which may or may not be the same ribbon as that featured in this scenario. The timing of her sighting is also consistent with the known time of death.

The challenge in this scenario is to the validity of Nancy's identification, as Fletcher, of the man whose actions she described. This challenge has two aspects:

(a) The circumstances in which she came to see 'Fletcher' were not ideal. It was dark (this fact may be 'judicially noted' from the time of day), and she was emotionally stressed due to the injuries to her dog. Her glimpse of the man was also a fleeting one, and was merely one of 'resemblance' rather than 'recognition', since Nancy did not know Fletcher prior to this incident. This is reminiscent of the far-from-perfect identification evidence in the leading High Court case of *Domican*, in which the court laid down the rule for the future that whenever eyewitness identification forms a 'significant' part of the Crown's case, the jury should be given a warning (which became known as a '*Domican* direction') about the hazards of identification evidence generally, and any particular points of concern in the instant case. They should also be warned that identification witnesses can present as very convincing, because they are certain that they are correct in their identification, whereas in fact human observation is a very frail commodity. Subsequent courts were instructed to assume that the identification evidence was the *only* Crown evidence, and warned that a failure to give a *Domican* direction would normally result in a guaranteed acquittal on appeal, unless the rest of the Crown case was overpowering without it.

However, the strict rigour of this requirement was diluted somewhat by the subsequent Queensland Court of Appeal decision in *Clapson*, in which it was held that *other* circumstantial evidence implicating the accused as the offender could in effect make up for any perceived defect in identification. In this case, one might point to the strong circumstantial case that exists already from Brian's evidence regarding 'Fletch', and the finding of ribbon in Fletcher's garbage bin.

(b) In *Alexander*, the High Court suggested that the only valid form of identification procedure is the identification parade, although s 617 of the Police Powers and Responsibilities Act 2000 allows alternatives such as a photo-board or a video tape, given that an accused in Queensland cannot be forced to take part in an identification parade. In this case, none of these procedures was followed, and a possible defence challenge might be mounted on that basis. However, against that is the argument that (i) Nancy made the identification without any prompting (unlike the witness in *Burchielli*, who was asked if the person in the back of a *marked* police car was the offender), and (ii) to ask her to take part in a photo-board line up after that would have been meaningless, since the memory of Fletcher's face would 'substitute' itself, whether or not he actually *was* the person seen in the dunes.

A final point of note is that it may be argued that in stating that the man she saw 'stuffed the piece of ribbon hastily into his pocket' when he became aware of Nancy watching him, Nancy was giving 'opinion' evidence, but it was an opinion she was entitled to express, as the only effective way she could relate what she had perceived (cf. *Fryer v Gathercole*).

(e) The evidence of the ribbon

10-6 The finding of what might be termed 'the other end' of the ribbon used to tie around the seagull's beak is an important piece of 'real' evidence supporting the Crown's theory of the case, because the ribbon associated with the death can be linked with the accused (a) by the forensic evidence regarding the cut, and (b) by the presence of his fingerprints on the 'left-over' end. The seagull itself is clearly also a piece of 'real' evidence linked to the death itself.

It may be assumed that, from the defence perspective, there is no challenge to either (a) the forensic evidence itself, or (b) the legality of the searching of the accused's dustbin, since neither has been raised as a point for appeal. Instead, we are asked to advise on the comments made by the trial judge to the jury regarding Fletcher's failure to testify. As an accused, Fletcher was, in terms of s 8(1) of the Evidence Act 1977, competent but not compellable to testify, and since he chose not to, the resulting question is what, if any, evidential significance may be attached to that choice. This is known to Evidence lawyers as failing to discharge the 'tactical burden' that is placed upon him by 'the theory of the case' (ie, the suggested interpretation of the known facts) for the Crown.

The governing law in this area is still primarily that laid down by the High Court in the 1995 case of *Weissensteiner*, in which it was held that a trial judge must always make it clear to a jury that an accused has a legal 'right to silence', and that no implied admission of guilt may be construed from the fact that they exercise that right. Equally, the accused's failure to testify may not be used so as to make up for any gaps in the Crown's proof of the 'elements' of the charge on the indictment.

This said, it was held by the High Court to be permissible for the trial judge to advise the jury that it may be easier for them to accept the hypothesis consistent with *guilt* offered by the Crown, when no alternative hypothesis has been offered by the defence. To this extent, the words of the trial judge in this case probably cannot be faulted, except in so far as (a) the words 'alternative explanation' might imply that the burden of proof has somehow 'shifted' to the accused, and (b) they suggest that Fletcher *could have* given an explanation of how his fingerprints came to be on the remains of the ribbon.

In *Peel*, the Queensland Court of Appeal held that it had been incorrect for the trial judge to give a *Weissensteiner* direction in a case in which P's fingerprints (and only his) had been located on an empty Diet Coke bottle that had only been used to make a fire bomb. For one thing, P had been asked for this explanation some 11 months after the event, and, secondly, it was 'judicially noted' that such bottles often become used as household containers for other liquids, and pass from hand to hand in such a way that it can soon become impossible to recall how one came into contact with any particular bottle. This case may perhaps be distinguished from *Peel* on the bases that (a) the time delay was much shorter (two days after the murder), (b) a length of red ribbon is more distinctive, and less common, than a soft drink container, and (c) the item was in Fletcher's dustbin.

If Fletcher had at least testified that he had no memory of having handled such a ribbon, that would have been something. As it was, his failure to even go into the witness box and say *something* meant that the jury could not, in the words of the High Court in *Weissensteiner*, 'be required to shut their eyes to the consequences' of his silence on the matter.

Once again, there would seem to be no ground for appeal here.

Examiner's Comments

10-7 This was a real-life examination question endured by my students two years ago. On the whole, it was well answered, although some students ducked out of answering at least one of the questions, while others gave me the usual 'running out of time' indication, in the form of a 'gloomy face' symbol.

There was nothing in this question beyond the capabilities of students who had taken the course, and revised thoroughly before the exam. There were also opportunities for the better students to point out the links between the various items of evidence in the overall 'Crown theory of the case'.

Keep in Mind

- Not reading the *entire question* before beginning to write.
- Not indicating when one item of evidence can impact on another.
- Poor time management.
- Failure to correctly identify the topic suggested by the question.

Question 42

> Michelle is suing Hot As Pty Ltd for damages arising from injuries that she sustained when a solar panel that had been installed by Hot As on the roof of her house became detached and blew off during a storm in January. Michelle had been in the garden, attempting to collect washing from the line, when the storm first broke, and the panel tore loose from its roof mountings and landed on her head, causing her serious facial injuries.
>
> The panel had been installed by Hot As as part of a Commonwealth Government program that rapidly became discredited when it was revealed that many 'cowboy' companies had entered the solar panel installation industry, attracted by the high government subsidies payable to householders. Michelle claims that Hot As was one of these, and that the panel had not been installed in such a way as to withstand normal storm-force winds of the type regularly experienced in her locality around Christmas time. Advise on the following evidential issues that arise in connection with the case.
>
> (a) The Quality Assurance Manager of Hot As, Brendan Bodger, inspected the installation after it was finished, and was heard on his mobile telephone telling someone on the other end of the call that, 'These panels wouldn't survive a sparrow's cough on a cold morning'.

Michelle's counsel, Martha, is looking forward to cross-examining Bodger, and is enraged when counsel for Hot As (Kevin) announces that he will not be calling Bodger as a witness. What evidential inferences may be drawn from this decision by Hot As?

(Allow 5 minutes)

(b) Hot As wish to lead evidence that during the storm in which Michelle was injured, the wind did not exceed 90 kilometres per hour, even during the strongest gusts. What form is their evidence likely to take?

(Allow 5 minutes)

(c) The actual installation was carried out by a building sub-contractor, 'Stackem and Run', whose site manager, Martin, submitted a 'clearance certificate' from his firm in which he stated that the solar panels would withstand a wind force of at least 100 kilometres per hour. Hot As wish to use Martin's evidence regarding the wind resistance of the installed panels. Unfortunately Martin died last year. Is there any way in which his evidence might still be admitted?

(Allow 10 minutes)

(d) Michelle has secured the services of Hugo, a structural engineer, who is prepared to testify that the metal used in the retaining bolts which were holding the solar panels in place was severely corroded, due to constant rain during an especially wet few months prior to the accident. Is the calling of his evidence likely to meet with any resistance by counsel for Hot As, and why/why not?

(Allow 5 minutes)

(e) Assume that Michelle succeeds in her action, and receives $220,000 in damages. Hot As then seek to sue Stackem and Run for a contribution towards the damages they have been ordered to pay Michelle, on the ground that the true cause of her injuries was negligence on the part of Stackem in not ensuring that suitable corrosion-proofed retaining bolts were used during the installation. What argument may Stackem use in order to resist this claim?

(Allow 5 minutes)

Total time for examination question: 30 minutes

Answer Plan/tips towards recognising the 'issues'

(a) The failure to call Bodger

Whenever a party in a civil action fails to testify, or to call a witness who might be thought to be essential to their case, the 'rule in *Jones v Dunkel*' applies. Apply it to the facts here, adding a reference to *West v GIO*.

(b)   The evidence of the weather on the day in question

This evidence should be a matter of public record, which the judge may simply 'judicially note'. However, unless the weather on that day was so 'notorious' as to be beyond dispute, the judge will need to note the matter 'after enquiry'.

Note the relevance of the 'presumption of the accuracy of scientific instruments'.

(c)   The evidence of Martin

Since Martin is now dead, his clearance certificate, if offered as evidence of the truth of its contents, will be classed as 'hearsay', and may only be admitted by way of an exception to the hearsay rule.

Sections 92(1)(a) and (b) of the Evidence Act are obvious possibilities, but can be challenged on the ground that Martin was expressing an 'opinion' that he would not have been allowed to express had he been giving the evidence 'live' from the witness box. The counter-argument is that he was 'expert by experience', citing *Weal v Bottom*.

A third possibility is the common law exception for a 'statement made in the course of a duty'. Cite *The Henry Coxon*.

(d)   The evidence of Hugo

Clearly, Hugo is an 'expert' structural engineer, but does this extend to the corrosive effect of water on metal? Cite *R v Darrington and McGauley* and *Weal v Bottom* (again).

Another ground of challenge may be that the court does not require 'expert' guidance on something within 'common knowledge', or that may be 'judicially noted'.

(e)   Proposed new action

Whenever you are told that a party to a previous action is seeking to raise a new one, whether against the original other party or not, the central 'issue' is almost certainly 'cause of action' estoppel. If the matter is one which *could* have been raised in the previous action, then you are dealing with '*Anshun* estoppel'.

 # Answer

(a)   The failure to call Bodger

10-8   The so-called 'rule in *Jones v Dunkel*' states that, if a party to a civil action fails to testify, then the court may find it easier to accept the theory of the case advanced by the other party. Put another way, where an inference is open on the facts to be drawn from the evidence led by the other party, then the failure of the party to testify makes it easier to accept that inference, although that failure cannot be employed so as to make up for any deficiency in the other party's case.

In *West v GIO*, this was extended so as to apply to any material witness who might have been called, in circumstances in which the failure to call that witness is not satisfactorily explained. In this case, given that Brendan is the Quality Assurance Manager for Hot As, one would expect him to be called, particularly since it is likely that counsel for Michelle will already have led evidence of Brendan's telephone statement, as evidence of his state of mind when he made the assertion.

The failure to call him may well justify the conclusion that Michelle's assertion that the installation was faulty is the correct one to draw, although what Brendan was overheard expressing was simply his opinion. However, given his 'expertise through experience', this opinion would be admissible: *Weal v Bottom.*

(b) The evidence of the weather on the day in question

10-9 While matters such as the recorded weather on a given day are not something that can ordinarily be disputed — and may therefore be 'judicially noted' — this cannot be done in a situation such as the one posed in this case without 'enquiry' being made by the trial judge.

The obvious place to make that enquiry would be with the Bureau of Meteorology, who may be called upon to send a witness who can 'speak to' the recorded wind speeds at the nearest recording point to Michelle's house. If the nearest point is not near enough, then there will probably be no other way of securing this evidence. If, on the other hand, it proves possible to give this evidence, it will be difficult to rebut. The court will make use of the common law 'presumption of the accuracy of scientific instruments' when receiving the evidence from the wind speed recorders.

(c) The evidence of Martin

10-10 The person who might have testified to the issue of the clearance certificate, Martin, is now dead, with the result that the document that he would have produced (the certificate itself) has become a piece of 'documentary hearsay' if it is hoped to use it in order to prove that the installation passed the quality assurance processes of Stackem.

There are three exceptions to the hearsay rule under which this document might be admitted, and the first two are found in the same statutory provision, namely s 92 of the Evidence Act 1977. Under s 92(1)(a), the certificate would be admissible as a statement by Martin in respect of something of which he had personal knowledge, while under s 92(1)(b) it would be part of the records of an 'undertaking' (Hot As) based on information supplied by a person (Martin) who may be supposed to have had personal knowledge of the matters in it. In both cases, the requirement to call Martin as a witness is waived under s 92(2)(a) because he is now dead.

However, both subsections are subject to the pre-condition that 'direct oral evidence' of that fact would have been admissible had Martin been alive to give it, and this raises the difficulty that it may be argued that what Martin put in the clearance certificate was simply his *opinion* that the panels would withstand 100 kilometre per hour winds. Against this it may be argued that it was an opinion based on experience, and that, on the authority of *Weal v Bottom*, Martin would have been qualified to give that evidence orally from the witness box.

Clearly, counsel for Michelle will protest that she would have wished to cross-examine Martin on many matters relating to his certificate, not the least of which being his alleged expertise, and the trial judge may be invited to reject the certificate under s 98 of the Act 'in the interests of justice', or give it less weight in the circumstances, as is permitted under s 102(b) of the Act when it can be alleged that the maker of the statement 'had any incentive to conceal or misrepresent the facts'. Given that it is being alleged that the entire installation was defective, the signing of allegedly misleading clearance certificates might well fall into that category.

There is a common law exception to the hearsay rule that might authorise the admission of the clearance certificate without many of these complications. This arises when a person now deceased previously made a statement in the course of a 'duty' to make it.

It was held in *The Henry Coxon* that this duty extended to one imposed by terms of employment, but two conditions imposed by the common law may prevent this exception being employed. The first is that the person making the statement must have had personal knowledge of what they were saying (which Martin may not have had), and the second is that he or she must not have had any motive for placing their actions in a good light. A false clearance certificate would clearly be self-serving in the overall context of a defective installation.

(d) The evidence of Hugo

10-11 Hugo is a structural engineer, and his evidence is therefore arguably that of an 'expert' who, by law, may give an 'opinion' on matters within his expertise, as an exception to the general rule that witness evidence must be confined to facts. His evidence is clearly crucial to Michelle's case, and counsel for Hot As will probably seek to argue either (a) that a structural engineer is not expert in the effects of water on metal, which is the province of a metallurgist (*R v Darrington and McGauley* is authority for the submission that an expert must not be allowed to wander outside their area of expertise), or (b) that the corrosion of metal due to the effects of water is a matter well within 'common knowledge' (so that expert opinion evidence is not required on it), or might even be 'judicially noted' as being 'notorious', and not requiring evidence to prove it.

However, the effect of metal corrosion on structural integrity *is* a matter within the expertise of a structural engineer, and Hugo may well have acquired vast experience in this area such as to justify the reception of his evidence under the authority of *Weal v Bottom*.

(e) *Proposed new action*

10-12 In the leading High Court case of *Port of Melbourne Authority v Anshun*, it was held that 'cause of action' estoppel applies so as to prevent a party bringing to court, as a new cause of action, a matter which might effectively have been litigated in previous proceedings, whether between the same parties or not. In that case, the intended parties had both been joint defendants to a previous action in which their liability to the plaintiff had been apportioned between them, and the intention in the new action was to have that apportionment varied on the basis of a contractual arrangement between them, which might clearly have been raised as an issue in the previous action.

Equally, it might be argued here that Hot As could (and should) have joined Stackem as Second Defendants in the original action against them by Michelle. The issue of the overall liability (if any) for the injury to Michelle was clearly on the agenda in the previous case, and, if Hot As were seeking to place the blame on the installers, then *that* was the occasion to do so, and not in a new action.

This new action is therefore likely to be 'estopped'.

Examiner's Comments

10-13 As you may already have deduced, the Law of Evidence is far more complex in its application to criminal cases than it is in civil actions. This means that there is a limited range of topics that the examiner can choose from, and this question just about covered the lot.

Keep in Mind

- Not 'spotting the issues'. Given what was written above regarding the relative shortage of them in civil actions, the examiner is likely to be particularly unforgiving in this regard.

The Exam Question from Hell

Question 43

> Two players from the 'Western Wombats' NRL team, Robbie and Bennie, are jointly on trial in respect of offences they are alleged to have committed on the night of Saturday 12 / Sunday 13 March, on the campus of Lakeview University, where their team was being accommodated in the Conference Centre, following their pre-season 'warm-up' game against the 'Lakeview Larrikins'.
>
> Both men are charged with having jointly broken into a student residential block known affectionately to the students as 'Colditz'. It is the Crown's contention that Bennie (who is by far the smaller of the two accused)

stood on Robbie's shoulders in order to gain entry to the block via the sliding veranda door to unit C14 (occupied at the time by student Lucy Livingstone), which was partly open. It is further alleged that Bennie then hauled Robbie onto the balcony by means of a rope that they had stolen from outside the Campus Security Office. Both men deny this offence.

Bennie is further charged that, once inside 'Colditz', he forced entry to several student units and stole various items, including cash, a laptop computer and personal identification documents. Robbie, on the other hand, is further charged that once inside unit C14, he entered a bedroom in which Lucy Livingstone was sleeping, and raped her while concealing his identity by means of a pillowcase worn over his head. These charges are denied by both men.

The following evidential issues arise during the course of their joint trial. Answer all of them.

(a)   At 8.30 am on 13 March, the Wombats team members were carrying their luggage from the Conference Centre to the team bus when Zac, the nine-year-old son of the Centre Manager, and an avid NRL fan, offered to carry Bennie's team bag. Bennie happily agreed, and when they got to the team bus, Bennie jokingly handed Zac a 'tip' in the form of a bank note. Zac handed it to his mother, who had already heard of the break-ins to the student units, and who noticed that the note was in Malaysian currency. Since she was already aware that one of the student victims was Malaysian, she handed the note to the police.

Counsel for Bennie objects to the admission of Zac's evidence on two grounds, upon *each* of which you are required to comment:

(i)   because of Zac's age, and the fact that he attends a special school for children with 'Attention Deficit Disorder';

(ii)   because Zac identified Bennie from a 'Wombats' team photograph from the previous season, in which Bennie was sporting a beard. He no longer has the beard, but Zac made no comment on the change in Bennie's appearance when he identified him.

(Allow 15 minutes)

(b)   The police first attended at 'Colditz' at 9.30 am on 13 March, when summoned by Campus Security. They interviewed most of the students in residence that day, but not Lucy Livingstone, who only contacted the police with her rape allegation on Tuesday 15 March. When asked why she had not reported the offence earlier, she replied: 'I was due at my parents' place for Sunday lunch, and I had an assignment to finish for the next day while I was there. I knew you guys would keep me most of the day, and I had other things to do'.

What effect, if any, is Lucy's explanation likely to have on (a) the admissibility, and (b) the weight to be attached to her evidence at the trial? Would it make any difference if she had told the campus nurse of the rape on the Monday morning, when requesting an AIDS test?

(Allow 10 minutes)

(c)   At the trial, Lucy testifies that she awoke in the early hours of Sunday morning to find the rape in progress, and she recounts that the rapist was wearing a football sock over his head, and that he began mockingly chanting the 'Wombat Warcry' when he realised that she was awake.

May the Crown adduce evidence that, three years previously, Robbie was charged with the rape of a young female cheerleader for the 'Montville Mongrels', with whom he was then a player, and that the evidence against him was that he attacked the girl as she left the playing field after the game, and raped her while wearing a team sock as a facial disguise and singing the team song 'Yeah yeah, we're the Mongrels'?

Would your answer be any different whether Robbie had been convicted of this offence, or whether the charge had been dropped by the DPP on the grounds that there was insufficient evidence of identification?

(Allow 10 minutes)

(d)   When first interviewed by police, Robbie denied all knowledge of any rape, and further denied ever having met Lucy Livingston. He initially refused to supply a DNA sample, but one was obtained from him under a court order. Forensic evidence led in chief for the Crown at trial is to the effect that Robbie's DNA has been identified on Lucy's bed linen.

Cross-examination of Lucy at the trial by counsel for Robbie is confined to the issue of her identification of the rapist. Specifically, Lucy is asked no question regarding 'consent'. In his evidence in chief in his own defence, Robbie admits that he had intercourse with Lucy, but claims that it was consensual.

Crown counsel objects to this line of questioning. Is she correct, and what options are open to the trial judge?

May the Crown now adduce, for the first time, Robbie's record of interview tape, in which he denied ever meeting Lucy?

(Allow 15 minutes)

(e)   Once the police became aware of the presence of the Wombats on campus on the night of the offences, they stopped the team bus on its way home, and searched all the players. You may assume that these searches were lawfully conducted. Bennie was found to be in possession of several hundred dollars in Canadian currency, and since the police were aware that one of the student victims was Canadian, Bennie was asked to account for his possession of the notes. His explanation was that he had purchased them immediately before the game the previous day from a foreign exchange booth in Lakeview Plaza, because he was planning a trip to Canada the following week. He was unable to produce any documentation relating to this alleged transaction, and no reference was made to it during his evidence at the trial.

Crown counsel makes two submissions, on *each* of which you are required to comment:

(i) that since only Bennie could explain where the Canadian currency had come from, but had remained silent on the issue at trial, the judge should give the jury 'a certain direction'; and

(ii) that the Crown should be allowed to adduce in evidence the business records of the only foreign exchange dealer in Lakeview Plaza, in order to show that no transaction took place that day involving Canadian dollars. Would your answer be any different if these records had been generated by the dealer's computer?

(Allow 15 minutes)

(f) During the search of the team bus, a laptop computer (later identified as belonging to a student at Colditz) was located in the luggage of another Wombats player, Norman. Norman initially advised police that he had bought it from Bennie the previous day for $5, after Bennie told him that he had received it as a present but didn't even know how to turn it on. It is nearly new, and is valued at over $1,500.

At trial, Norman first of all refuses to answer any questions relating to his possession of the laptop, because 'It wouldn't look good for me'. The trial judge insists that he answer the questions. Is she correct?

Norman then insists that he acquired the laptop from a pawnshop in nearby Coaltown the previous day, although he is unable to name the pawnshop. What options are now open to Crown counsel?

(Allow 15 minutes)

(g) Once police became aware that the rope discovered below the balcony to C14 had originally been in a pile of crowd control equipment carelessly left outside the office of Campus Security, they monitored a CCTV security video that had been surveilling the area at the relevant time. Robbie can clearly be seen in a portion of the video, removing the rope from the pile and walking away towards 'Colditz'. When first questioned about the rope, Robbie denied any knowledge of it, and further denied being anywhere near the Security office that night. When shown the video, he hesitated briefly, then explained that he had 'borrowed' the rope in order to secure his over-full suitcase. When located on the team bus, his suitcase had no rope around it, and was only moderately full.

Crown counsel requests that the trial judge give the jury 'a certain direction' regarding this dismal performance by Robbie. To what is she referring?

(Allow 10 minutes)

(h) During cross-examination by Crown counsel, Bennie is asked to account for the presence in his luggage of a Hong Kong drivers' licence and a bank card, both in the name of one of the student victims from Colditz. He denies that it was in his luggage when the team left the university, and is asked, 'So you're asking the court to believe that the police must have planted it on you, is that it?' Bennie replies, 'That's possible. All I'm saying is that I'd never seen it before they claimed to have found it in my sports bag'.

Crown counsel then asks for a voir dire, during which she seeks leave of the trial judge to adduce in evidence a previous conviction that Bennie has for a fraud committed 10 years previously. Is such a request justified, and, if granted, what would be the evidential significance of Bennie's 'previous'?

(Allow 10 minutes)

Total time for examination question: 100 minutes

Answer Plan/tips towards recognising the 'issues'

(a) Zac's evidence

The question is in two parts, and should be clearly answered in that way.

(i) Since Zac is a 'child', s 9 of the Evidence Act 1977 applies, and the relevant questions will be whether or not he can give an 'intelligible' account of events, and whether or not this may be on oath. Cite s 632 for the fact that corroboration is not required by law, but that (i) it will be required anyway under *Domican*, which follows in the second part of the answer, and (ii) there is probably quite a bit of corroborating evidence to link Bennie with the crimes anyway. The Attention Deficit Disorder is not likely to be an issue; cite *Hill* (1851) 169 ER 495 and s 9C, s 632 and *R v M*.

(ii) The second issue is clearly that of the reliability of Zac's identification. Cite the cases of *Domican*, *Alexander* and *Burchielli*. Should an ID parade have been held? Cite Police Powers and Responsibilities Act s 275. N.B. the difficulty regarding the beard.

(b) Lucy's lack of 'fresh complaint'

Lucy is testifying to rape, but appears to have made no complaint about it immediately afterwards. This suggests that the court will consider the credibility of her testimony regarding the rape in the light of the 'fresh complaint' requirements at common law. Cite *R v M*, and argue 'for and against'. Note that fresh complaint goes only to complainant *credibility*.

If she had complained to the campus nurse, this would not only have constituted the desired 'fresh complaint', but it would also qualify as a 'preliminary complaint' under s 4A of the Criminal Law (Sexual Offences) Act 1978. Explain what these are, and note that it is *not* evidence that the rape actually occurred.

(c) Possible Crown use of 'similar fact evidence'

The bizarre behavior described suggests that the Crown will attempt to cite it as 'similar fact evidence' tending to prove Robbie's guilt on this occasion. Cite *Makin, DPP v P*, and *Boardman v DPP*, but add the caveat that it must be shown to have been Robbie's 'modus operandi' on the previous occasion (cite *HML*).

This leads naturally on to the caveat in this question — if it cannot be proved beyond reasonable doubt that Robbie did it last time by reference to any conviction, then the only hope for the Crown is to use 'coincidence reasoning' per *Smith*.

(d)   Robbie's late 'consent' defence

Deal with the two linked issues individually.

(i)   Lucy has not been cross-examined on what will become Robbie's defence of 'consent'. This is a breach of *Browne v Dunn*. Deal with likely judicial responses, and cite *R v Foley* [2000] 1 Qd R 290.

(ii)   The Crown may not 'split its case' so as to deal with this unexpected turn of events; cite *Soma*.

(e)   Bennie's silence

Two questions are asked, so answer them separately, even though they are connected.

(i)   Bennie is competent as a witness in his own defence (Evidence Act 1977 s 8), but he is not compellable because of his 'right to silence'. But that silence can be a trap when the accused fails to discharge a 'tactical burden' placed upon him, and the trial judge may be entitled to give the jury a *Weissensteiner* direction. But cite *Ryan*, because Bennie *did* give the police an explanation of sorts.

(ii)   The Crown is seeking to admit, as evidence of its contents, a document. This is 'hearsay' evidence, and an exception to the hearsay rule must be found. Section 93 of the Evidence Act applies in criminal cases, and the trading records of the foreign exchange dealer would qualify. If it is a computerised document, then apply s 95 of the Act.

(f)   Norman's failure to cooperate

Once again, two separate but related questions are asked, and it is clearer if they are answered separately.

(i)   It seems from what he said that Norman is apprehensive of exposing himself to prosecution for 'receiving' the laptop. Explain the common law privilege against self-incrimination, and s 10(1) of the Evidence Act; cite *R v Boyes* (1861) 121 ER 730. But in reality, Norman is being asked to say nothing that he has not already said to police, so query the privilege's application in his case.

(ii)   Norman's performance strongly suggests that he may be 'hostile' at common law, and 'adverse' under s 17 of the Evidence Act. Explain the effect of s 18 and s 101(1)(a), and the fact that Norman may then be cross-examined 'generally' by Crown counsel.

(g) Robbie's lie

A demonstrable lie told by an accused can be used to demonstrate two things: firstly, that the accused may not be a reliable witness (*Zoneff*), and secondly that his lie may be indicative of his 'guilty knowledge' arising from his commission of the crime: *Edwards*. Go through the process that the trial judge must follow in giving an '*Edwards* direction'.

(h) Bennie's alleged accusation against the police

Bennie is giving evidence in his own defence, and is therefore protected by the 'shield' of s 15(2) of the Evidence Act 1977. Explain how subsection (c) may be invoked if Bennie casts 'imputations' on the character of a police witness. Deal also with the possible exception in relation to a legitimate defence (cite *Phillips* as an example of a gratuitous attack on a witness's character), and the decision in *R v York* [2001] QCA 408 that disapproved of tactics such as this by Crown counsel.

If admitted, Bennie's 'previous' for fraud is technically only admissible in respect of his *credibility as a witness*, and the trial judge should issue a 'propensity' warning.

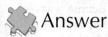 Answer

(a) Zac's evidence

10-14 This question requires to be answered in two parts.

(i) Section 9(1) of the Evidence Act 1977 establishes a rebuttable presumption that anyone, even a 'child' (defined as a person under 16, per s 3 of the Act) is a competent witness. Objections to competence (ie, attempts to rebut the presumption) are dealt with under s 9A, subsection (2) that contains the only ground upon which a witness may be deemed incompetent, namely that they cannot give an 'intelligible account' of events that they have experienced. These rules apply whether or not the proposed evidence is to be given on oath.

Section 9C allows the trial judge to seek 'expert' opinion on whether or not the witness should be allowed to testify, and in particular whether or not they can give an 'intelligible' account of events. Given that there is also a suggestion that Zac's ADD disability may affect his competence as a witness, it is more than likely that such expert testimony will be sought in this case.

Another question will be whether or not Zac may give 'sworn' evidence (ie, evidence on oath), which under s 9B(2) requires that he satisfy the trial judge that he understands that the giving of evidence is a serious matter, and that if allowed to testify on oath, he will have an obligation to tell the truth that is 'over and above the ordinary duty to tell the truth'. If he cannot satisfy this test, then he may still testify 'unsworn', but the trial judge must at least explain to him the duty of speaking the truth.

Given the current case law in Queensland, it would seem that Zac would most likely give his evidence unsworn, but even so, the judge must not suggest to the jury that his evidence carries any less weight as a result: *Robinson*. However, given that a '*Domican* direction' is likely to be given as the result of what follows in (ii) below, it is also likely that the judge will give the jury a warning to at least *look* for corroboration of Zac's evidence, even though this is no longer required as the result of s 632 of the Queensland Criminal Code (it was held in *R v M* that a failure to give such a warning could make the verdict 'unsafe and unsatisfactory'). There is, in any case, a good deal of corroboration from the rest of the evidence that Bennie was in possession of foreign currency the day after the break-ins.

The issue of Zac's ADD is also raised as an objection to his testifying, but the rule at common law is that it can only affect the weight of his evidence if his affliction has the capacity to directly influence what he says in evidence: *Hill*. It may be a matter for expert testimony, but, on the face of it, it is hard to see how his ADD (which is a behavioural disorder) could affect his memory or his perception of events as they were occurring.

(ii) There may be a perception that Zac's identification of Bennie was less than satisfactory because it was by photo-board rather than by identification parade, which was the preferred method laid down by the High Court in *Alexander*, in which they added that photo-boards should only be used as a second-best alternative to such a parade. Section 275 of the Police Powers and Responsibilities Act 2000 allows Queensland police to use this method if the accused has declined an identification parade, but we are not even told if Bennie was offered one.

The team photograph may be regarded as a sort of photo-board, but, if not, the evidence may meet the same objection as in *Burchielli*, to the effect that simply showing a witness a photograph of the accused is not a valid form of identification. There is also the point that everyone in the photograph was a player in the same team. Against this is the argument that, since Zac is such a fan, it would be easy for him to identify Bennie.

The biggest source of challenge to Zac's identification of Bennie is the fact that Zac made no reference to the beard. This has echoes of *Domican*, in which a witness amended her identification to refer to a false wig and moustache that the offender may have been wearing only *after* this became known to police. Arising from this case was the insistence by the High Court that trial judges, in cases in which a challenged identification is a crucial element of the Crown's case, should issue what has become known as a '*Domican* direction' to the jury, warning them against being lulled into accepting a false identification by the confident demeanour of the eyewitness, and pointing out to them the factors in the instant case that make the identification questionable, and the need to seek corroboration.

Such corroboration may take many forms and, as indicated in (i) above, there is plenty of additional evidence linking Bennie with the break-ins anyway.

(b) Lucy's lack of 'fresh complaint'

10-15 Common law has always required, as a matter of practice, that the victim of any sexual offence make a 'fresh complaint'; that is, a complaint as soon as 'reasonably practicable' after the event. The rule operates as an exception to the usual ban on the adducing of 'previous consistent statements' by a witness, and while the absence of such a complaint is not fatal to the Crown's case, its presence serves to boost the credibility of the victim as a witness. It is not, however, evidence that the offence actually occurred, which is a difficult distinction for many juries to make.

Recently, and particularly in connection with young victims, the courts have become more realistic in their expectations of when, and to whom, such statements ought to be made, and factors such as shame, fear and shock have been recognised as likely to lead to a delay in complaining: see *R v M*. Lucy is a young(?) lady living away from home, and she had credible reasons for wishing to go to lunch with her parents instead of being delayed by a rape investigation. One might, however, have expected her to complain to her parents, unless there are credible reasons why not. Lucy certainly comes across as a typical student with deadline pressures, but is the reason she gives for the delay a credible one in all the circumstances? Cross-examination might be along the lines that she is a 'drama queen' who felt left out of all the action, or someone with the main eye on criminal injuries compensation.

If she had told the campus nurse the following day, then this would have been not only a 'fresh complaint' to bolster her witness credibility at common law, but also a 'preliminary complaint' under s 4A of the Criminal Law (Sexual Offences) Act 1978. A 'preliminary complaint' is simply one made prior to the formal complaint to the police, and there is no 'reasonable time' imposed as to when it should be made. A 'preliminary complaint' is no more evidence of the fact that the rape actually occurred that a 'fresh complaint', and, like it, is only evidence of Lucy's *credibility as a witness*. However, and confusingly, it is admissible whether Lucy gives evidence or not; if she does, then, as indicated above, it is also a 'fresh complaint'.

(c) Possible Crown use of 'similar fact evidence'

10-16 This is an attempted use by the Crown of 'similar fact evidence', in which it will seek to support its 'theory of the case' that Robbie committed the rape by revealing to the jury the fact that he committed another one in identical circumstances in the past.

In *DPP v P*, the principle was said to be that evidence of previous 'misdeeds' by an accused may not be revealed to a jury unless their 'probative' value exceeds their 'prejudicial' tendency. The test to be employed in striking this balance was laid down by the Privy Council in *Makin v AGNSW* as being one in which the facts of the previous case bore a 'strong nexus of similarity' with those of the present case. In other cases such as *DPP v Boardman*, senior courts have continued to warn against the 'forbidden reasoning' that, if a person has committed a certain offence in the past, he is more likely than others to have committed it in the present case.

The current test under Australian common law is still that of the High Court in *Pfennig*, namely that the similar fact evidence may be admitted if, and only if, when added to the facts of the new offence, it leaves no 'reasonable hypothesis' of innocence. Applying this test, it is highly predictable that Robbie's 'previous' will be admitted, since the starkly individual methodology of each rape, and its bizarre execution, seem to come from the same sick mind. This form of ritualistic sadism for sexual gratification is a 'modus operandi' (what psychologists call 'signature behaviour') that cannot be ignored, *provided that the previous incident may be proved to have been Robbie's handiwork.*

If Robbie was found guilty of it previously, then there can be little argument. But if the charge was dropped by the DPP, and was therefore never tested in court, then at the very least the Crown will need to lead evidence proving beyond reasonable doubt that Robbie was the perpetrator of the first rape: *HML*. The previous case then becomes the subject of 'coincidence reasoning' to the effect that it would be stretching coincidence too far to accept that two women, years and kilometres apart, are describing the actions of two different men on two occasions when the accused had the opportunity to be the offender: see *Smith*.

(d) Robbie's late 'consent' defence

10-17 There are two separate, but linked, issues here. The first concerns the failure to cross-examine Lucy regarding possible consent, while the second is whether or not the Crown may be allowed to 'split its case' in order to meet Robbie's unanticipated defence of 'consent'.

(i) The so-called 'rule in *Browne v Dunn*' requires Party A — before they make any assertion of fact adverse to Party B — to give Party B the opportunity to comment on it. This has resolved itself into a rule in criminal cases that, before any particular line of defence may be run by an accused, he must put it to those witnesses for the Crown whom it affects. In the present case, therefore, Robbie should not be asserting that the intercourse was consensual without allowing Lucy the opportunity to comment on that allegation. The underlying principle is one of 'fairness', and if it is breached the trial judge has several options.

The best might be to allow Lucy to be recalled, in order that she may comment. A second option is to allow the defence to continue, but for the trial judge to point out to the jury during her summary that the defence of consent was never 'tested' on the person best placed to dispute it. The third — and most drastic — would be to prohibit the defence from alleging consent, but, as the case of *Foley* suggests, the most likely outcome of such a choice would be a finding of 'mistrial' on appeal.

(ii) It was confirmed by the High Court in *Soma* that the Crown may not 'split its case' by raising, in its cross-examination of an accused, matters that were not led 'in chief'. It is a sort of mirror-image of the *Browne v Dunn* rule, and is based on the 'fairness' principle that, by the close of the Crown case, the accused must be made aware of *all* the allegations against them, since this can affect their options (eg, whether or not to go into the witness box). Since the Crown in the present case did not 'lead' the interview tape, they cannot now rely on it as ammunition against Robbie, galling though this may be. The net effect of this rule is that the Crown has one arm tied behind its back whenever an accused gives evidence in chief that they can refute, but had not anticipated.

(e) *Bennie's silence*

10-18 There are two distinct issues involved here, although they are logically connected.

(i) By virtue of s 8(1) of the Evidence Act 1977, Bennie is a competent but not compellable witness for 'the defence', which includes himself. He is not compellable because of the overriding 'right of silence' that every accused possesses at common law. However, this may become a trap when, by exercising his right to silence, Bennie fails to discharge a 'tactical burden' placed upon him by the Crown's case.

There is clear evidence that Bennie was in possession of Canadian dollars, and everyone looks to him to explain where he got them, other than by breaking into a unit at the university. The 'certain direction' to which Crown counsel refers is something called a '*Weissensteiner* direction', from the High Court decision in the Queensland case of *Weissensteiner*. This direction is to the effect that if there are facts that the accused could have disclosed to account for some state of affairs which the Crown maintains was a criminal action by the accused, and he fails to give those facts, or *any* explanation, then it is easier to accept the Crown's theory of the case (that Bennie obtained them by means of a break-in) than it might otherwise be. In this case, Bennie has the dollars, and the Crown's theory is that he stole them from Colditz. If in fact he got them from somewhere else, then he has a 'tactical burden' to explain where, otherwise the jury will be more entitled to conclude that he did indeed steal them.

However, a limitation on the *Weissensteiner* direction emerged in *Ryan*, in which it was held that it cannot be given when the accused *has* previously given an explanation, even if that may not have come out in his evidence. Here, we are told that he advised the police of where he got the dollars, and that is enough (as in *Ryan* itself) to eliminate the possibility of a *Weissensteiner* direction. Another limitation on the use of such a direction is that it may not be used in order to plug gaps in the Crown's case, but there is no risk of that here.

(ii) All documents are, by their very nature, 'hearsay', if they are offered as evidence of the information that they contain. To accommodate the many occasions in practice upon which it is necessary to adduce such evidence, many statutory exceptions to the hearsay rule have emerged over the years. One of these is under s 93 of the Evidence Act 1977, which is the appropriate one for the Crown in the present case.

When a document is part of the records of a 'trade or business' (which the currency exchange would be), and it is no longer possible to produce the person who supplied the information that formed the basis of that record (as here, because no-one can be expected to remember all the transactions performed by various assistants during the course of a day), then it may be admitted as evidence of its contents under s 93(1)(b)(iv).

If the transaction record is computerised, then in terms of s 95 of the Act it may still be admitted, provided that the conditions laid down under subsection (2) can be satisfied. They are:

1. that the document was produced during a period when the computer was regularly used to store or generate such information;
2. that information of the type involved in this case was regularly supplied to the computer during that period;
3. that the computer was working properly during that period, at least so far as concerned that purpose;
4. that the record that is being adduced is derived from information supplied to the computer in the ordinary course of those activities.

Assuming that the record in question is some sort of 'daily transactions summary' for that day, there is every likelihood that the statement will meet these conditions, and will be admissible under s 95.

(f) Norman's failure to cooperate

10-19 Once again, there are two questions that require separate, but related, answers.

(i) Section 10(1) of the Evidence Act 1977 confirms the continuation of the old common law privilege against 'self-incrimination', which was defined in *R v Boyes* as being any question, the truthful answer to which would put the witness in 'real and appreciable danger' of being convicted of a crime. It was created to avoid the spectacle of a man being forced to condemn himself out of his own mouth, but by virtue of s 10(2) does not apply to an accused person in his own trial. Since Norman is not the one on trial, this exception does not apply to him.

It will be Norman's argument that, by answering the question, he will expose himself to prosecution for 'receiving' the laptop. But has he not already exposed himself to this, by giving the statement to the police in the first place? And what could be more likely to have him prosecuted for receiving than the fact that he was in possession of the laptop in the first place, making use of the common law presumption that arises from the possession of recently-stolen property?

No adverse inference may be drawn from the fact that Norman claims the privilege: *R v King*. However, he was *not* allowed to claim it, and the trial judge's decision was correct, for the reasons given above.

(ii) There are two options open to Crown counsel. The first is to call the police officer to whom Norman made the statement, and leave the jury to sort it out between the conflicting stories. The second is to apply to the trial judge under s 17 of the Evidence Act for a 'voir dire' to establish whether or not Norman is an 'adverse' witness (formerly described as 'hostile' under common law). An 'adverse' witness is one who is 'not desirous of telling the truth in the furtherance of justice' (*R v Haydon and Slattery*), and, in making this decision, the trial judge may take into account the sort of factors identified in *R v Mullins*, which include the fact that he has made a previous inconsistent statement. In this case, in addition, the trial judge will be aware that Norman is skirting around the truth in order to save himself from a receiving charge.

Norman will be asked whether or not he has made a previous inconsistent statement. If he admits that fact, the jury is recalled and the same question is put to him, and he agrees to what he originally told the police. If he denies it, then per s 18 of the Act, he may be cross-examined on it in front of the jury, and if he continues to deny having made it, then a police witness may be called to prove that he did. Since the trial judge has already adjudged that Norman cannot claim the privilege against answering the question, this will be allowed. The statement itself then becomes evidence of its contents per s 101(1)(a) of the Act.

Once deemed 'hostile', Norman may also be cross-examined generally by Crown counsel, as an exception to the general rule that counsel may not 'impeach' their own witness.

(g) Robbie's lie

10-20 This question raises the issue of the evidential significance of provable lies told by an accused as an 'implied admission of guilt'. The theory is that by lying about some fact that he knows is material to his guilt in the case, the accused has by implication demonstrated his consciousness of the relevance of that fact towards the proof of his guilt, and must therefore have been the perpetrator.

If the lie relates only to something that is non-material to the case, then it is simply evidence that the accused is a liar, and detracts from his credibility as a witness: *Zoneff*. However, when it relates to some fact 'material' to the case, it may go beyond that, and may be used by the jury as evidence of guilt.

Before that may happen, however, the trial judge must give what is called an '*Edwards* direction' (from the High Court decision in the case of *Edwards v R*) which is the direction to which Crown counsel is alluding. This requires the trial judge to:

1. draw the jury's attention to the precise lie on which the Crown relies;
2. indicate how the accused must have known that the truth would implicate him in the crime;
3. advise the jury that there can be many reasons why someone utters a lie (eg, fear or panic), which are not necessarily indicative of guilt.

(h) Bennie's alleged accusation against the police

10-21 Section 15(2) of the Evidence Act 1977 provides, to every accused who chooses to testify in their own defence, a 'shield' against questions designed to reveal previous misdeeds by them in the past. It also prescribes a list of circumstances in which this shield will be lost, one of which arises under s 15(2)(c) when the accused has attacked the character of a Crown witness, which arguably Bennie has done by impliedly accusing a police officer of 'planting' evidence on him. Even then, the leave of the trial judge is required before the exception may be invoked, which is why Crown counsel is seeking leave in this case.

It emerged in cases exemplified by *R v Phillips* that s 15(2)(c) may only be invoked where the attack on the Crown witness is gratuitous, in the sense that it is not essential to the proper development of the accused's defence. Arguably, that is not the case here, since Bennie is simply trying to explain that he did not put the items in his luggage. When it is suggested to him that he is alleging that the police 'planted' the items, he has no option but to concede that this is one possibility. It would seem that Crown counsel is trying to corner him into making this accusation in order to invoke s 15(2)(c), which was disapproved of as a practice in *R v York*.

Assuming that the trial judge allows the evidence in, it will go only to Bennie's *credibility as a witness*. Since it is a 'previous' for fraud, this will be damaging enough, but given that Bennie is charged with other property/dishonesty offences in this case, the trial judge must ensure (by giving what is called a 'propensity warning') that the jury do not also use it as evidence of Bennie's guilt on *this* occasion.

Examiner's Comments

10-22 If you managed to handle this question reasonably well, then you have probably made good use of the previous chapters. It was a fairly comprehensive review of the leading evidential issues in criminal cases, and it is unlikely that any future examination question will be quite so exacting, although this cannot be guaranteed.

Keep in Mind

- Blind panic at the start of the question, and mental exhaustion towards the end, can lead to minor points being overlooked. Several of the scenarios posed more than one question, and several of them contained possible lines of argument arising from the facts that were not alluded to by the examiner. This is intended to sort out the 'adequate' candidates from the 'very good' ones, and, if you wish to be classified among the latter, then you need your wits about you throughout the *entire* question.
- As always, failure to spot the 'issues'. It is always a good policy to state what the issue is at the start of your answer, in case either you forget or the examiner cannot deduce from the river of confusion that follows that you had actually spotted the point.
- Once again, the perennial difficulty of time management. In the question supplied, a suggested time limit was provided in respect of each section. If the examiner gives a mark indication instead, a few quick calculations are required. For example, if the *total marks* for a 60 minute examination are 60, then a 10 mark section should take up no more than *10 minutes of the overall time.*
- Failure to relate one section of the question to another. This question involved a single trial scenario, and obviously each part of it would interact with the remainder, so that, for example, when dealing with the need for corroboration of Zac's evidence in part (a), reference could be made to Bennie's possession of the Canadian currency in part (e) and the laptop in part (f).

Index

References are to paragraphs